Reading Dylan Thomas

Reading Dylan Thomas

Edited by Edward Allen

EDINBURGH
University Press

Edinburgh University Press is one of the leading university presses in the UK. We publish academic books and journals in our selected subject areas across the humanities and social sciences, combining cutting-edge scholarship with high editorial and production values to produce academic works of lasting importance. For more information visit our website: edinburghuniversitypress.com

Edinburgh University Press Ltd
The Tun – Holyrood Road, 12(2f) Jackson's Entry, Edinburgh EH8 8PJ

First published in hardback by Edinburgh University Press 2019

Typeset in 10.5/13 Adobe Sabon by
Servis Filmsetting Ltd, Stockport, Cheshire and
printed and bound by CPI Group (UK) Ltd,
Croydon, CR0 4YY

A CIP record for this book is available from the British Library

ISBN 978 1 4744 1155 4 (hardback)
ISBN 978 1 4744 7317 0 (paperback)
ISBN 978 1 4744 1156 1 (webready PDF)
ISBN 978 1 4744 1157 8 (epub)

Contents

Acknowledgements

Reading Dylan Thomas began life as a conversation in 2012, when a group of commissioning editors and academics convened in Cardiff Broadcasting House to talk about the forthcoming Thomas anniversary. Thanks to the AHRC and BBC, a number of us were encouraged to continue the conversation, which we did at several events in 2014, in Swansea, Pittsburgh and Cambridge; the last of these played host to a conference whose proceedings loosely form the basis of this book.

In the first instance, then, we are grateful to the Faculty of English, Cambridge, for various kinds of administrative and financial support, and to Christ's College and Murray Edwards College for funding some of the artwork and copyrighted material contained in the following pages. The team at Edinburgh University Press, and the book's early reviewers, have been helpful, patient and meticulous; we're particularly indebted to James Dale, Jackie Jones, Adela Rauchova and Ersev Ersoy. Thanks, too, are due to a series of individuals who have responded swiftly and cheerfully to a variety of queries and requests, large or small: Steve Arnold, Jenny Bavidge, Rosemary Clark, David Higham, Sarah Howe, Yvonne Morris of the Wilfred Owen Association, Esther Osorio Whewell, Jen Pollard, Christopher Wait, and Rick Watson at the Harry Ransom Center.

There are a few people, closer to home, without whom the volume would not look or feel quite the same. Fiona Green has proved, as always, the trustiest of confidantes; India Lewis is responsible for the cover art; and Kristen Treen has scrutinised just about every word and punctuation mark going. John Goodby and Leo Mellor have been with me every step of the way – Cardiff, Swansea, Pittsburgh and Cambridge – and I thank them for their good humour and energy.

Lastly, I wish to express my gratitude to Alyson and Barry Allen, and to Semele Assinder, for their unstinting support in all things.

We would like to thank the following estates, institutions and related staff for permission to use copyright material: the Trustees for the Copyrights of Dylan Thomas, for extracts from *The Collected Poems of Dylan Thomas* and *Poet in the Making*, by permission of Weidenfeld & Nicolson, J. M. Dent, David Higham Associates and New Directions Publishing Corporation; the Manuscripts Section of the Library at the Harry Ransom Humanities Research Center, University of Texas at Austin; the BBC Written Archives Centre, Caversham; the National Museum and Gallery of Wales, and the Ceri Richards Estate; and Pentti Sammallahti and The Photographers' Gallery, London.

Notes on Contributors

Edward Allen is a Lecturer in the Faculty of English, University of Cambridge, and a Fellow of Christ's College. His research centres for the most part on modernist literature, transatlantic exchange and sound media.

Deborah Bowman is a Fellow and College Lecturer at Gonville and Caius College, University of Cambridge. She is currently writing about scale in modernist literature and the visual arts, and editing William Empson's *Seven Types of Ambiguity*.

Philip Coleman lectures in the School of English and is a Fellow of Trinity College Dublin, Ireland. His most recent books are *John Berryman: Centenary Essays* (co-edited with Peter Campion, 2017) and *George Saunders: Critical Essays* (co-edited with Steve Gronert Ellerhoff, 2017). With Calista McRae, he is editing a selection of John Berryman's literary correspondence for Harvard University Press.

John Goodby is a poet, translator and broadcaster, and Professor in English Literature at Swansea University. His critical publications include *Irish Poetry since 1950: From Stillness into History* (2000) and *The Poetry of Dylan Thomas: Under the Spelling Wall* (2013). He is currently working on a biography of the poet and an edition of his recently discovered fifth notebook.

James Keery teaches English at Fred Longworth High School in Tyldesley. A collection of poems, *That Stranger, The Blues* (1996), and an edition of Burns Singer's *Collected Poems* (2001) have been published by Carcanet Press. Recent writing has focused on the battlefield poetry of Kingsley Amis and the Apocalyptic 1950s.

Leo Mellor is the Roma Gill Fellow in English at Murray Edwards College, University of Cambridge. His first monograph was *Reading the Ruins: Bombsites, Modernism and British Culture* (2011), and he recently co-edited a special issue of *Critical Quarterly* on 'the long 1930s'.

Rod Mengham is Reader in Modern English Literature at the University of Cambridge and Curator of Works of Art at Jesus College. He has published monographs on Dickens, Emily Brontë and Henry Green. He is also the author of several poetry publications, most recently *Chance of a Storm* (Carcanet, 2015), and of translations, most recently *Speedometry* [poems by Andrzej Sosnowski] (2014).

Peter Robinson has published volumes of poetry, fiction, aphorisms, translations and literary criticism. As well as Professor of English and American Literature at the University of Reading, he is poetry editor for Two Rivers Press.

Vincent Sherry is the Howard Nemerov Professor in the Humanities and Professor of English at Washington University in St Louis. His books include *Ezra Pound, Wyndham Lewis, and Radical Modernism* (1993) and *The Great War and the Language of Modernism* (2003). His *Modernism and the Reinvention of Decadence* was published in 2015. He is currently writing *The European War of 1914–1918: A Literary History*, which is under contract to Princeton University Press.

Zoë Skoulding is a poet whose collections include *Remains of a Future City* (2008) and *Teint: For the Bièvre* (2016). Her monograph *Contemporary Women's Poetry and Urban Space: Experimental Cities* was published in 2013, and she was editor of the international quarterly *Poetry Wales* from 2008 to 2014. She is Reader in the School of English Literature at Bangor University.

Tom Walker is Ussher Assistant Professor in Irish Writing at Trinity College Dublin, Ireland. He has published research on several aspects of Irish writing and modern poetry, including *Louis MacNeice and the Irish Poetry of his Time* (2015).

John Wilkinson is Professor in the Department of English at the University of Chicago, where he chairs Creative Writing and Poetics. His selected poems, *Schedule of Unrest*, was published in 2014 by Salt, and a new collection, *Ghost Nets*, appeared in 2016 from Omnidawn.

Abbreviations

CL   *The Collected Letters*, ed. Paul Ferris, 2nd edn (London: Dent, 2000).

CP14 *The Collected Poems of Dylan Thomas: The New Centenary Edition*, ed. John Goodby (London: Weidenfeld & Nicolson, 2014).

CS   *Collected Stories*, ed. Walford Davies, intro. Leslie Norris (London: Weidenfeld & Nicolson, 2014).

EPW   *Early Prose Writings*, ed. Walford Davies (London: Dent, 1971).

LVW   *Letters to Vernon Watkins*, intro. Vernon Watkins (London: Dent/Faber, 1957).

NP   *The Notebook Poems: 1930–34*, ed. Ralph Maud (London: Dent, 1989).

QEOM *Quite Early One Morning*, ed. Aneirin Talfan Davies (London: Dent, 1954).

TB   *The Broadcasts*, ed. Ralph Maud (London: Dent, 1991).

TCSP *Dylan Thomas: The Complete Screen Plays*, ed. John Ackerman (New York: Applause Books, 1995).

UMW   *Under Milk Wood*, ed. Walford Davies and Ralph Maud, intro. Walford Davies (London: Dent, 1995).

Introduction: Beyond Milk Wood

Edward Allen

In May 2014, just over sixty years since its first appearance on British airwaves, *Under Milk Wood* was treated to a makeover. A good deal had happened in those intervening decades to alter production norms at the British Broadcasting Corporation (BBC), to say nothing of listening figures or changing tastes. In January 1954, following its author's untimely death the previous November, *Under Milk Wood* had been positioned in the radio schedule in such a way as to pique the curiosity of the highbrow listener: nestled between a programme about the Spanish art song (or *canción*) and a musical setting of Eugene O'Neill's early monologue *Before Breakfast*, Dylan Thomas's last work had aired on the Third Programme at 7.25pm, with Richard Burton in the role of First Voice.[1] On 5 May 2014, by contrast, the play appears to have courted a different sort of company in the listings – prefaced, on the one hand, by local news, weather and sports reports, and followed, on the other, by the latest bust-up in *EastEnders*.[2] What Thomas would have made of either schedule is anyone's guess, though it's nice to imagine that he'd have approved in 2014 of the BBC's effort to set his 'play for voices' in some kind of dialogue with the ongoing theatrics of Albert Square. In the saltiness of its bartering, in its performance and perforation of social contracts, in the echoic disquiet of its players ('Oh, what'll the neighbours say'), *Under Milk Wood* is no less driven than latter-day soap operas tend to be by the rhythms of gossip and quasi-gospel truth, or by the semblance of returning storylines that are part and parcel of a fiction set in and around a busy thoroughfare.[3] It has been noticed before – but is worth repeating – that *Under Milk Wood* not only helped in 1954 to stimulate some interest in an emerging brand of regional melodrama, but also seems to have paved the way for one of Britain's best-loved serials by staking out that well-known regal territory. 'Listen', we're urged in Thomas's opening monologue, 'it is night moving in the streets, the processional salt slow musical wind in Coronation Street ...'[4]

That prompt to 'listen' becomes something of a mannerism in *Under Milk Wood*, whose opening voices appear out of nowhere – for that is the way of radio talk – and whose dense, obfuscating medium is therefore wont to seem as 'starless and bible-black' as the very night in question.[5] By any measure, the play represents a high-water mark in acousmatic art, in the sense that it sets out to frustrate the listener who would ascribe origins to its many drifting voices: some of them are too slippery to be named, and merely bubble up in the form of numbered types – First Neighbour, Second Neighbour, Second Drinker, Third Woman, Fourth Drowned – while others remain just below the surface, like Captain Cat, '*the retired blind seacaptain*', who finds in the dead of night a chorus of lost sailors lapping at his 'earhole'.[6] This is soap opera at its most surreal, yet the curiosity of tracing the play's affinities, of assuming the long view of melodrama, and indeed of recognising the ways it has lately risen or sunk (depending on how you look at it) in the prime-time schedule – to do any one of these things is also to apprehend the play's precarious historicity, and the extent to which its author may yet have things to tell us about the murky backwater we're coming to know as late modernism. That, in essence, is the guiding thought of the present volume.

For as much as *Under Milk Wood* might be thought to have warmed the public up for all the flimsy sets and flattened subjects of post-war serials, it should be clear to us now that Thomas and his play bear a complex relation to the English pageant experiments of yesteryear, and particularly to the local colourists who intervened so importantly, in Jed Esty's account, in 'the cultural transition between empire and welfare state'.[7] Just as T. S. Eliot, E. M. Forster and Virginia Woolf had found ways in the 1930s to touch up the fading qualities of pageantry – 'its function as a modern folk ritual, its technical demand for collective or choral voices, and its tight unity of place coupled with an almost magical dilation of historical time' – Thomas too makes a case in *Under Milk Wood* for stepping back in time, seduced by the shapes of local prayer and sea shanty, and alive to all the 'curious customs' one might discover upon washing up in a 'small, decaying watering-place'.[8] That would serve nicely for a description of so many local-colour experiments in the dying days of British modernism, particularly a novel like Woolf's *Between the Acts* (1941), which commences with some county council gossip and the subject of a cesspool.[9] And of course it's easy to see (or hear) where Thomas is coming from when you consider the ways in which Woolf manages the texture of her last novel – a novel of disembodied voices – whose festivities are punctuated by lowing cows, snatches of half-remembered lyrics, and the effusions of a conflicted chorus: 'To the valediction of the gramophone hid in the bushes the audience departed. *Dispersed*, it wailed, *Dispersed are we.*'[10]

For a variety of reasons, *Between the Acts* and *Under Milk Wood* have been considered late works, yet Thomas's may seem especially late, may even seem *belated*, because it surfaced at a time when the technologies that had done so much to influence the mechanics of interwar writing had begun to give way under the pressure of a new medium. Indeed, Thomas's advocates were quick in the late 1950s to give those who were shelling out on the licence fee what they thought they wanted – not more of the same, but an *Under Milk Wood* that would appeal to an audience on whom television had begun to work its magic. What this meant in practice – whether by accident or design, it's hard to say – was a move to erode and marginalise the radio text, first by consigning repeats of the original production to the twilight hours, and then by trimming the recording itself from 94 minutes to a little over 60, ostensibly because an abridged version was deemed easier to schedule and more attractive to export.[11] Meanwhile, the likes of Douglas Cleverdon and Henry Sherek set about remediating the play, both as a theatre piece – in keeping with the mode of Thomas's early readings – and in a series of televisual outings, which included the first full-blown production in May 1957.[12] Numerous critics inclined to elegy in the wake of this first screening, bemoaning from their desks and armchairs the sorry sight of a masterpiece that had lost its way. Still, where some were bound to see the flaws and creases ('backcloths, wobbling trees, and two-wall interiors' did little to impress *The Times*), others could see a glimmer of hope in the play's transposition into black and white.[13] 'Altogether it was a most encouraging demonstration of several TV propositions which I favour in my optimistic moments', Maurice Richardson crowed in *The Observer*, before going on to clarify in parentheses the content of these insurgent propositions: '(That nothing is too difficult for television. That you can't keep a good script down. That you can't go wrong with the Welsh)'.[14]

As it transpires, Richardson's optimism in 1957 was well founded, if somewhat misguided on the essential details. Over half a century later, we find ourselves with a production of *Under Milk Wood* that serves both to corroborate and complicate the drift of those propositions. For the beauty of Pip Broughton's 2014 version consists, not in its strict fidelity to the first script, nor in any blinkered sense that its rightness resides exclusively in its Welshness, but in its effort to realise the full imaginative possibilities of a play for voices.[15] Yes, there are still all the indices one would expect of a local-colour sketch – the call of seabirds, the response of rolling surf – yet the televisual medium also allows for a seagull's soaring view of the Carmarthen coastline by way of a prelude, and from that perspective, it becomes much harder to isolate the likely inspiration for the fictional town of Llareggub. To pinpoint Laugharne in this regard would be to miss the point somehow, for this is a production that seeks from the very outset to recuperate Thomas's itinerant wonderings, and so to loosen the sense of attachment that comes with the territory of fetishising an author's stomping ground: rather than settling, with the seagull, for the coign of a chimney pot in South Wales, the roving camera-eye proceeds to jump from one location to another – Laugharne to Los Angeles, New York to London – which has the effect of revealing the sheer latitude of the poet's globetrotting in the early 1950s, and of gauging the reach and quality of his influence, then and now.

Under Milk Wood remains an ensemble piece, then, but the members of this particular ensemble are scattered across the western hemisphere, little fazed by the sorts of devices that facilitate their scattered interactions: studio microphone, mixing desk, mobile phone and the ubiquitous laptop – each of these has a part to play in an *Under Milk Wood* whose remediation will make perfect sense to anyone who has ever thought of Thomas as an early pioneer of the global village.[16] In rendering such devices so visibly instrumental, Broughton's production does not so much spoil or quash the acousmatic trickery of Thomas's play as multiply the difficulties one may experience in the course of determining whose voice is whose, and who is hearing whom. Sound engineers and floor managers come and go in the production's introductory sequence as cast members ready themselves for performance, and the impression that one has slipped behind the scenes is magnified to some degree in Michael Sheen's opening monologue, which not only fades in and out with scenes of 'cobblestreets' and the 'fishingboat-bobbing sea', but is intercut too with shots of other, less salubrious watering holes, in which attendant chorus members wait to have their say. Perched at the bars of Thomas's favourite pubs, the White Horse Tavern and Brown's Hotel, Matthew Rhys and Aimee-Ffion Edwards pore over their computer screens, rapt by Sheen's instruction to 'hear and see', and perhaps newly sensitive to the come-ons of the monologue – 'Come closer now' – which at once make a show, and a mockery, of the kind of virtual intimacy Thomas so often simulates in his writing. Thomas never knew the joy of a reliable hotspot, but in this case the construction of a chatroom does help to accentuate the structural tussle in *Under Milk Wood* between its apparently seamless polyphony and the spectacle of remote connection ('From where you are, you can hear their dreams'). To some minds, in the end, it may be that watching someone watching someone amounts to little more than a clever recursive operation, an illusion conjured up for the new-media generation. But Broughton's production does make you think. For even as you watch Rhys and Edwards whiling away a happy hour in the White Horse Tavern and Brown's Hotel, you might find yourself wondering at the addictive nature of communication, and the curious fact that a laptop, and not a bottle, has taken pride of place in the poet's vision. If nothing else, this *Under Milk Wood* finally shows that there's more to Dylan Thomas than the drink.

*   *   *   *

From ear-rinser to eye-opener, the evolution of *Under Milk Wood* is an instructive one in the field of modernist studies, and it sets the scene for the action of this book, which seeks to gauge how far we've come since the mid-1950s, the first wave of Thomas mania. Following the poet's rise to the queasy heights of bohemian legend, those years witnessed a remarkable surge in print and vinyl culture: taken together, *Under Milk Wood* and the *Collected Poems: 1934–1952* served to transform the fortunes of the Thomas estate, while the market for spoken word recordings – particularly in North America – showed no sign of dwindling.[17] In gaining this momentum, the Thomas 'industry' proved nigh on impervious to dissenters in these early eulogistic years. In late 1954, for instance, Robert Graves sought in vain to debunk the growing myth, not by rinsing Thomas as others would in more abstemious times – on the contrary, Graves was swift to suggest that 'the common report that most of Thomas's poems came out of the beer barrel cannot be accepted' – but rather by claiming that the Welshman had regularly written under the influence of a cocktail, no less potent, of 'virtuosity' and 'nonsense': 'Dylan Thomas was drunk with melody, and what the words were he cared not.'[18] Such a criticism must now sound to us like sour grapes, all the more so when you consider, as we've seen, the ways in which Thomas's audience was to swell and diversify in the late 1950s. Within a matter of weeks of *Under Milk Wood*'s first full screening in 1957, the Prime Minister Harold Macmillan was telling his party that the public had 'never had it so good', and the same may well be true of Thomas's readers, most of whom had come to value Thomas precisely because he'd never shied, in Macmillan's phrase, from 'new thoughts, ideas and invention'.[19]

But was it all too good to be true? That was Macmillan's question in 1957, and he was right to worry about the shelf life of post-war prosperity. The Conservative government struggled increasingly in the early 1960s to make ends meet, and to disguise the fact of Britain's defensive posturing in the wake of decolonisation and shifting nuclear capability. 'Defensive', at any rate, was the word that sprung to Raymond

Williams's mind in 1961, which seemed to him the proper moment to wonder whether Britain's largely improvised response to 'the democratic revolution' abroad had in fact begun to distort the complexion and complexity of domestic politics:

> Britain seems [...] a country with a fairly obvious future: industrially advanced, securely democratic, and with a steadily rising general level of education and culture.
>   There is substantial truth in this reading. It is not only the general consensus, but most attempts to challenge it seem unreasonable; even powerful local criticisms do not fundamentally disturb the sense of steady and general advance. Yet in deeper ways, that have perhaps not yet been articulated, this idea of a good society naturally unfolding itself may be exceptionally misleading.[20]

One reason for this inarticulacy, it seemed to Williams, had to do with 'the common habit of supposing our society to be governed by single patterns, arrived at by averaging the overall trends in familiar categories of economic activity, political behavior and cultural development'.[21] In seeking to break that habit, Williams's advice throughout *The Long Revolution* was not only to materialise 'different forms of analysis, which would enable us to recognise the important contradictions within each of the patterns described', but also to identify *alternative* patterns to the predominant orthodoxies of political economy and English national culture. So as well as noting, for instance, 'that the ordinary optimism about Britain's economic future can be reasonably seen as simple complacency' – how right he proved to be – Williams sought in an earlier chapter of the book to undertake his own audit of the years 1870–1950, and to suggest that 'an unusual proportion of the important imaginative literature of these years was written by people outside the majority English pattern':

> This had been true to some extent of the Victorian novel, but in these later years the relative importance of writers from abroad or from minority groups, as well as of women, is marked. Hardy, James, Shaw, Synge, Yeats, Eliot, Conrad, Lawrence, O'Casey, Joyce, Thomas compose a short list of some significance, not in the fact that, with the exception of the Irish, any particular minority is noticeable, but that the difficult questions are raised about the majority pattern, the normal English mode, which certainly seems, in this period, relatively uncreative.[22]

Thomas looks a bit of an afterthought in that oddly ordered list, but his inclusion in Williams's pattern of 'minority' voices was no accident in 1961. On the contrary, Thomas had been at the forefront of Williams's thinking for a while, and the appearance of *Under Milk Wood* had done its bit to strengthen Williams's resolve to end *The Long Revolution* by 'offering an account of the essential language – the created and creative meanings – which our inherited reality teaches and through which new reality forms and is negotiated'.[23] Here, indeed, was a play with important things to say about literacy and 'new means of communication', a play whose relation to 'the normal English mode' was nothing if not creative.[24] In its resistance to the ethic and principles of naturalist theatre, *Under Milk Wood* seemed to Williams a recherché, but unusually rich, demonstration of the Expressionist method, and a reason to feel optimistic about the way British writing was going, not towards 'representation', but with a view to articulating 'a pattern of experience'.[25]

It is now plain to see that Williams was ahead of his time, and that his attempt to populate a cultural revolution with the likes of Dylan Thomas was bound to divide opinion if, as Williams implied, such a figure was to play even a ghostly cameo in the drama of social change. Where he and others had come to see *Under Milk Wood* as a welcome elaboration on the poet's early praxis – as a bid to 'express all the varied life that was actually his experience' – the 1960s witnessed a souring of mood among critics who could detect no such depth or plurality in Thomas's work.[26] Just as Williams was making the case for a minority pattern in 1961, George Steiner was likening Thomas's charisma to 'the flair of a showman', whose 'largely unqualified audience' had been well and truly taken in by 'a froth of Swinburnean rhetoric'.[27] Steiner didn't doubt for a moment that Thomas had tried to 'make language new', only that he'd 'diminished' the medium in doing so 'to barrenness and obscurity', a charge that was by no means peculiar to the drift of 1960s criticism.[28] As numerous critics have since recognised, there was nothing especially new or creative about the anti-Thomas offensive in these years; rather, as the cult of the poet's celebrity continued to blossom further afield, particularly in North America – with the publication of monographs, a stream of life writing, and the completion of editions, glossaries and guides – others sought to put him in his place once and for all by echoing the objections of the Movement, whose loosely organised band of editors, poets and critics had done their best in the mid-1950s to dismiss Thomas and his alleged nonsense.[29] Kingsley Amis, Robert Conquest, Donald Davie, D. J. Enright – any attempt to map the genealogy of Thomas's detractors must be considered partial as well as provisional, even now; yet there's no doubting the force or influence of these complainants, whose over-starched belief in a plainer style encouraged anthologists well beyond their circle to take a similarly dim view of Thomas's intellection. Although very differently configured to Enright's *Poets of the 1950s* (1955) or Conquest's *New Lines* (1956), Al

Alvarez's *The New Poetry* (1962) did little to correct the prevailing view that Thomas had led readers a merry dance. 'His followers [. . .] used his work as an excuse to kiss *all* meaning good-bye', Alvarez concluded, with a subtle smack of the lips. 'All that mattered was that the verse should sound impressive.'[30]

All kinds of things come out in the wash when you begin to reflect on the ways Thomas has been neglected over the years. In the case of his early detractors, Thomas's poetry seems to have stimulated a gag reflex quite as strong and involuntary as the workings of the poet's own 'larger than normal libido', yet it should be clear to us now that the impulse was ideological, and not only (or merely) the result of a squeamish kind of affect display.[31] To his credit, Alvarez was at least prepared in 1962 to acknowledge that Thomas had once 'had something rather original to say', but concessions of this sort were to become ever more rare and over-qualified in the following decades.[32] In one way, of course, Thomas was always bound to fall foul of academy reshuffling – a favourite on school syllabi, thanks to a handful of pastoral lyrics, yet something of a lost soul in the riven landscape of anglophone poetics. But in another – and here's the real curiosity of his disappearing act in the 1970s and 1980s – Thomas seems to have given high theory the slip at precisely the moment of his work's greatest potential. It's a curiosity that has begun to puzzle critics. For who could mistake the Welshman's muddied and mutable relation to identity politics? Isn't his an ideal body of work on which to spell out the limits of *différance*? And why, John Goodby wonders, when it comes to characterising this most slippery of poets 'is the default position one of presumed pathology, rather than, say, calculated subaltern role playing and textual *jouissance*?'[33]

One answer has to do with the fact that Dylan Thomas has simply proved too much of a shape-shifter for anyone, or for any one critical school, to account for his singularity. His singularity, rather, consists in his multiplicity, a quality often remarked but seldom harnessed in any meaningful way by those who would like to see his walk-on part bumped up to a starring role in the narrative of twentieth-century literature. '[I]t confounds standard distinctions and haunts the histories in which it is un- or misrepresented', Goodby observes of Thomas's work: 'A gnawing sense of this is what makes Thomas a constant absent presence.'[34] Goodby has done more than anyone to right this state of affairs, by providing an expanded and newly annotated edition of *The Collected Poems* (2014), and by articulating the importance of materials that have only just come to light, including the poet's fifth notebook.[35] It remains to be seen what critics will make of this astonishing discovery, and indeed it is too early to say whether those same critics will heed

Goodby's parting suggestion in *The Poetry of Dylan Thomas* (2013) that his subject has yet to come into his own: 'At some point, the dialogue will have to turn to Thomas, who holds the answers to so many of the questions which need answering.'[36]

In the meantime, and in the spirit of elaborating on Goodby's work, the aim of *Reading Dylan Thomas* is to explore the many dimensions of Thomas's writing, from the earliest lyrics and short stories to his late-modernist assignments in audio and visual culture. Here you will find excursions into the science of reading – whose psychological and somatic effects Thomas found ways to nurture – as well as chapters on reading as a performance art, from modes of recitation and improvisation to the sort of studied and beholden habits of reception we may be able to detect in Thomas's admirers. Taking their cue, in part, from the imaginative designs of Broughton's *Under Milk Wood*, the contributors to this volume have remained open to the thought that 'reading' has come to mean many different things, and that to sit in silence with a book propped open is unlikely to tell you all there is to know about the quality or scope of Thomas's ambitions. Thomas would certainly have had something to say about the ways the word has been contested in recent times – from 'symptomatic' to 'surface' reading, and from 'close' to 'distant' modes of attention – though it's worth remembering that, for him too, the word had hidden depths:[37]

> Each genuine poet has his own standards, his own codes of appreciation, his own aura. Reading a poet for the first time, one cannot be acquainted with him, & therefore, judging him by preconceived standards – however elastic those standards may be – one cannot fully appreciate him. One should take first an empty brain and a full heart to every poem one reads: an impossible task.[38]

Even as he purports to favour an 'unbiased mind', Thomas gestures in this early letter to a more workaday mode of textual encounter, and so begins to imagine the approach of a reader for whom the tension of knowing things and not knowing things is crucial to what might happen next. 'The only possible way lies in the reading & re-reading', he goes on to suggest, before adding that reading 'aloud' has always seemed to him the best way of unwinding in the company of a poem: 'I often think that baths were built especially for drowsy poets to lie in and there intone aloud amid the steam and boiling ripples.'[39]

Scenes of reading have certainly changed, but the metaphor at work in Thomas's analogy remains a useful one if it helps to take the strain of the expectations we now bring to his vast body of work. While knowing that any standard of interpretation must have its elastic limit, the contributors to this volume have been sensitive to the idea that a certain degree of stretchiness in our reading is required if we in turn are to appreciate the flexibility of Thomas's writing. Taken together, then, the following chapters not only testify to the variety of his formal experiments – it's hard to think of a genre he didn't try his hand at – but also seek to articulate the ways in which those experiments might serve to complicate what it is we mean when we say we're reading Dylan Thomas. Counting syllables, comparing manuscripts, switching senses, mixing media, invoking voices – all of these modes of interpretative work amount to an experience of reading that will continue to expand as we come to appreciate Thomas's modernism.

Notes

1. *Under Milk Wood*, directed and produced by Douglas Cleverdon, Monday, 25 January 1954, *The Radio Times*, 1576 (22 January 1954), p. 19.
2. *Under Milk Wood*, directed by Pip Broughton, produced by Bethan Jones, Monday, 5 May 2014, *The Radio Times*, 4692 (3 May 2014), p. 64.
3. *UMW*, p. 9.
4. Ibid. p. 3. *Coronation Street* first screened in December 1960. For more on *Under Milk Wood*'s glancing relation to soap opera, see John Goodby, *The Poetry of Dylan Thomas: Under the Spelling Wall* (Liverpool: Liverpool University Press, 2013), p. 418.
5. *UMW*, p. 3.
6. Ibid. pp. 4–7.
7. Jed Esty, *A Shrinking Island: Modernism and National Culture in England* (Princeton and Oxford: Princeton University Press, 2004), p. 3.
8. Ibid. p. 61; *UMW*, p. 19.
9. Virginia Woolf, *Between the Acts*, ed. Frank Kermode, with introduction and notes (Oxford: Oxford World's Classics, 1998), pp. 3–5.
10. Ibid. p. 88.
11. Having allotted the original production a family-friendly slot, the BBC opted to repeat the production at a point in the schedule that would shortly come to be known as the watershed. See the listings, for instance, for Tuesday, 28 September 1954, *The Radio Times*, 1611 (24 September 1954), p. 24; Tuesday, 25 January 1955, *The Radio Times*, 1628 (21 January 1955), p. 25; Tuesday, 17 April 1956, *The Radio Times*, 1692 (13 April 1956), p. 25. The abridged version was first broadcast on 28 September 1954 on the Home Service: *The Radio Times*, 1611 (24 September 1954), p. 24.
12. *Under Milk Wood*, directed and produced by David J. Thomas, Thursday, 9 May 1957, *The Radio Times*, 135 [television edition] (3 May 1957), p. 19. The story of these early attempts to repurpose *Under Milk Wood* is told by Amanda Wrigley, 'Dylan Thomas' *Under Milk Wood*, "A Play for Voices" on Radio, Stage and Television', *Critical Studies in Television*, 9.3 (Autumn 2014), 77–88.

13. [Unsigned review], '"Under Milk Wood": B.B.C. Television', *The Times* (10 May 1957), 3.
14. Maurice Richardson, 'Television: Mother Wales', *The Observer* (12 May 1957), 15.
15. References to Pip Broughton's production are taken from *Under Milk Wood: A Unique Adaptation of Dylan Thomas' Play for Voices*, DVD (London and Cardiff: BBC Cymru Wales, 2015).
16. I borrow 'global village' from Marshall McLuhan's *The Medium is the Massage* (London: Penguin, 2008 [1967]), p. 63.
17. For details of prizes and sales figures, see Ralph Maud (with Albert Glover), *Dylan Thomas in Print: A Bibliographical History* (Pittsburgh, PA: University of Pittsburgh Press, 1970); for Thomas's influence on the burgeoning audiobook industry, and on Caedmon Records in particular, see Jacob Smith, *Spoken Word: Postwar American Phonograph Cultures* (Berkeley: University of California Press, 2012), pp. 49–78.
18. Robert Graves, 'These Be Your Gods, O Israel!', *Essays in Criticism*, 5 (1955), 129–50 (pp. 149–8). This was Graves's sixth and final talk in his Clark Lectures on *Professional Standards in English Poetry*, delivered at Trinity College, Cambridge, 1954.
19. Harold Macmillan, 'Most of our people have never had it so good', Bedford, 20 July 1957, repr. in *50 Speeches that Made the Modern World: Famous Speeches from Women's Rights to Human Rights*, ed. Andrew Burnet (London: Chambers, 2016), pp. 88–92 (pp. 91, 89).
20. Raymond Williams, *The Long Revolution* (London: Chatto & Windus, 1961), pp. 293–4.
21. Ibid. p. 294.
22. Ibid. pp. 240–1.
23. Ibid. p. 293.
24. Ibid. p. xi.
25. Raymond Williams, 'Dylan Thomas's Play for Voices', *Critical Quarterly*, 1 (1959), 18–26 (p. 24).
26. Ibid. pp. 22.
27. George Steiner, 'The Retreat from the Word', *The Kenyon Review*, 23.2 (1961), 187–216 (p. 207).
28. Ibid.
29. See, for instance, John Goodby, 'The Critical Fates of Dylan Thomas', in *The Poetry of Dylan Thomas*, pp. 1–49; and Randall Stevenson, *The Oxford English Literary History*, vol. 12: *1960–2000: The Last of England?* (Oxford: Oxford University Press, 2004), pp. 165–89 (p. 166).
30. A. Alvarez, 'The New Poetry, or Beyond the Gentility Principle', in *The New Poetry*, selected and introduced by A. Alvarez (Harmondsworth: Penguin, 1962), pp. 17–28 (p. 19).
31. David Holbrook, *Dylan Thomas: The Code of Night* (London: Athlone, 1972), p. 246. Rhian Barfoot deals at length with Holbrook's notorious reading of Thomas as a promiscuous *enfant terrible* in *Liberating Dylan Thomas: Rescuing a Poet from Psycho-sexual Servitude* (Cardiff: University of Wales Press, 2015).
32. Alvarez, 'The New Poetry', p. 19.
33. Goodby, *The Poetry of Dylan Thomas*, p. xii.

34. Ibid. p. 36.
35. The fifth notebook was acquired by Swansea University in December 2014. Goodby summarises his initial responses to '*N5*' in *Discovering Dylan Thomas: A Companion to the 'Collected Poems' and Notebook Poems* (Cardiff: University of Wales Press, 2017), pp. 2–4, 248–52.
36. Goodby, *The Poetry of Dylan Thomas*, p. 455.
37. See Stephen Best and Sharon Marcus, 'Surface Reading: An Introduction', *Representations*, 108.1 (2009), 1–21.
38. Dylan Thomas to Pamela Hansford Johnson, [early November 1933], *CL*, p. 59.
39. Ibid.

I. Bodies and Selves

Chapter 1

Wave Power: The Effacement of the Caesura in Dylan Thomas's Poetry

John Wilkinson

Declaring an interest, poetic or scholarly, in Dylan Thomas often brings a response which runs along the lines: 'I used to love Dylan Thomas when I was young but I haven't read him for years.'[1] It is commonplace that Dylan Thomas is an obscure poet with a popular readership, a technically disciplined poet who is also a byword for indiscipline and self-indulgence, and that his poems are loved by adolescents, a love frequently renounced in middle age. An example of such abjuring is the psychoanalyst Adam Phillips's shudderingly middle-aged revulsion from Thomas's 'slap-dash, slapstick, and apparently naively sophisticated Celtic fluency', renouncing the person Phillips was when he loved Thomas because, Phillips remembers or believes he remembers, Thomas 'seemed to be the apotheosis of "having a voice"'.[2] To renounce your first love seems ungrateful. Behind Phillips's repudiation lies the charge that Thomas's writing is masturbatory, and not far behind either in the light of the adjectives 'slap-dash, slapstick', otherwise so oddly applied to a poet of stringent technique; Thomas remained stuck with his stick, while Phillips grew into the adult world where intercourse and literature emerge as regulated practice out of the adolescent enjoyment of voice. Thomas is a writer who troubles us once we become literary, and Thomas's poetry may be popular in part because it disregards the bounds of propriety and the literary. His lyric practice dissents from lyric as intimate address overheard – a now-trite formulation investing poetry with a weird shame, as though eavesdropping were the foundation of generic individuality – and inclines rather to a lyric of a physical sonority made perceptible, almost palpable, through silent reading as well as listening. Thomas is not so much in love with his own voice as stroked into corporeal presence by his poetry's sonority, shamelessly.

Such thoughts are provoked by a submerged history of unrespectable poetry traced by Daniel Tiffany in his book *My Silver Planet*, but Tiffany's wide-ranging diagnosis of poetic kitsch does not quite apply to Thomas, as it would to the gaudier British surrealist and Apocalyptic verse contemporary with Thomas's.[3] This is because the plasticity of Thomas's poetry remains motivated, strongly attached to the actuality of a sea-scoured bay as well as the symbolic order of sea and land, and attached to a Welsh social and religious rhetoric; and although Thomas's poems may first sound nostalgic, a significant strain in kitsch, they fight nostalgia in reconstructing memory spatially and collapsing time. At his work's most formally radical – the poems in syllabics – extension of time into space presents a problem for vocal performance, especially for Thomas whose performance can transmute verses into ham; but these poems' inherent voicing and tone amass a wave power independent of performance. This chapter does not intend to set up a voice/text dichotomy in order to adjudicate for voice as opposed to the literary text, although it is clear that Thomas's work fell sharply from favour once New Criticism mandated a focus on the poem as isolated textual entity. But voice/text introduces a dichotomy challenged by Thomas's poetry, and a caesura it would deny. And the meaning of 'voice' in Phillips's dismissal needs specifying; if Thomas's recital manner has become embarrassing, yet it corresponds to a style conventional for its time, and by comparison with George Barker, for instance, and with his own practice elsewhere, Thomas is notably restrained in reading the syllabic 'Poem in October', distinguishing its syllables with a near-mimsy precision as though struggling against a rhythmic counter-force. But a poet's speaking voice has no priority over the internal voicings a poem proposes to a reader. That is to say, the sound of a poem is encoded phonemically, and a different performance can be heard pressing against the reader's restraint – both out of Thomas's oratorical propensity for strongly stressed rhythm, and the poem's wave power as it arises from the rhythmic ground of Thomas's poetry as a whole.

In describing the wave power of Thomas's verse, this chapter will explore the term 'caesura' and what it might mean for thinking about Dylan Thomas, and it will return often to 'Poem in October' (1945).[4] Caesura might be understood as *aporia* – that is, a gap out of which something might emerge, or which might cleave an entity violently and productively, while bearing in mind what it signifies more technically in metrics; but this translation would strip the term 'caesura' of a range of meaning rising about it like proud flesh about a wound. Moreover, the aim here is to advance a claim, that Dylan Thomas's poetry is driven by a compulsion to efface the caesura, and that this effacement is a poetic project which also goes well beyond the making of poems. Poetry is not merely an archive of literary texts and vocal performances. The story of Thomas's war on the caesura is the story of his refusal to be born, to acknowledge what Freud called the birth caesura, his refusal to submit his masturbatory delirium to heterosexual regulation, his refusal to submit his verse to drawing-room mannerliness, to a modest demeanour, and his refusal to die – death temporised from an ending to a caesura through a somewhat inchoate conception of an afterlife, resembling a return to the womb. This defiance of mortality has to be the more strenuous because rhythmic temporality is so insistent, so hard for Thomas to curb. His war on the caesura is the story of the riddled sea – the interminable sea riddled through its enigmatic sound, riddled in the sense of sieved through the latticework of waves which by metonymy catches bounty in its nets, riddled in the sense of multiply penetrated by the 'star-flanked seed' reflected in the sea's even and ever-surging surface.[5] Sky, sea and ground are as one. At their horizon, there can be no caesura.

What, then, is a caesura, metrically? Caesura introduces variable in-line breaks to avoid monotony in extended regular lines. As a syntactical pause, caesura differs from a performative pause which reading aloud might introduce at any point (however perversely). Then how does a caesura differ from a line-ending? A line-ending is a type of caesura, complicated by the fact that an enjambed line can work against expectations, refusing a syntactical pause; it might also bring rhyme into accordance or discordance with syntactical pause or not-pause. Internal rhyme and assonance can complicate in-line caesura too. Granted these qualifications, the importance of caesura is that it represents both break and continuity, modifying what comes before and what comes after. 'Caesura. An event that simultaneously unites and disunites.'[6] Assuming, that is, a thread which can be picked up again does indeed follow: the fear for Dylan Thomas, to cite the final phrase of a horrifying early poem, is that the conclusion of the poem itself coincides with a temporally collapsed orgasm and birth as a 'gross catastrophe'.[7] But leaving aside line endings and the special case of poem endings, shifts in regular stress introduced by caesuras increase tension and so enhance one's experience of the poem as an event. In her lecture 'The Caesura', Isobel Armstrong waxes rhapsodic; she asserts that the caesura,

> rather than the beat of ictus, creates the poem's temporal self-awareness, its felt time, by holding up, often for a breath, the momentum of rhythm. [. . .] The gap sets the sensoria in motion. The gap sets desire in motion. Yet the caesura does not represent anything.[8]

Effacement of such syntactical pauses therefore might throw emphasis on the formal contours of the poem; it might contribute to a sense of a poem as an object rather than event, should the poem be regular in

meter and lineation. Such, however, is not the effect of suppression of
the caesura in Thomas's poetry, and particularly not in the limit case of
his poems written in syllabics, despite their reified textual appearance.
Thomas's reading of 'Poem in October' dramatises the contradiction
that results.[9] His determination to find a reading style that holds to syllabics is sustained against an irrepressible rhythmic urgency. The poem's
formal structure – its elaborate and closed-off stanzas, its mathematically determined lines, its rhyme scheme – seeks to defeat the experience
of temporality concomitant on following a poem from start to finish, a
poem in this case obsessed with the passage of time from its title forward.
If suppressing the caesura is one strategy in a war against mortality, the
beat of time in 'Poem in October' is audibly undefeated, pulsing within
the poem's constraints. What this evidences is that rhythm is entered
into; it does not begin, neither does it end. The caesura of birth is always
already effaced; as Derrida writes of rhythm, '[i]t therefore begins before
beginning. That is the incalculable origin of a rhythm.'[10]

Nonetheless, Thomas's attraction to verse syllabics partakes of a compulsion to obliterate the caesura manifest in his repeatedly expressed
disgust at parturition, as well as comprising a stage in his struggle to
contain his rhetoric formally; as Édouard Glissant writes of the baroque,
'it recognises only the rigors of form, precisely because it is confront-
ing excessiveness.'[11] The confrontation works at every level – affective
excess and rhetorical excess as well as rhythmic – all engrained in the
organ voice that causes Adam Phillips to recoil. This is despite the
tendency of Thomas's syllabics described by John Goodby in *The Poetry
of Dylan Thomas: Under the Spelling Wall*, where he writes of the late
syllabic verse: 'These poems (and despite Thomas's own recorded performance of them) eschew emphatic, regular rhythms and distribute
meaning more equally among their words, giving a levelling effect, both
at the level of signification and the sonic web.'[12] This levelling effect, as
Goodby implies, tends to a merger of text and voice which Thomas's
vocal performance struggles to sustain while resisting alike both rhythmic impetus and the seduction of expressive stress which would redirect
voice towards an audience open to passive reception.

Equal distribution is indeed the salient characteristic of syllabic verse
in English, exemplified by Marianne Moore and the formal ability of her
verse to incorporate passages of quasi-scientific prose.[13] Although sty-
listically Thomas's 'Poem in October' lies a country mile from Moore's
zoological domain, both poets replicate stanzas of lines varying in length
and use insets or tabs to make replication unmistakable, whereas French
syllabic verse demands linear regularity and has adopted conventions
enabling the incorporation of caesuras in longer lines. If French syllabics

are all about temporal regulation, with every line theoretically occupying the same time in performance, Moore and Thomas alike seem bent on averting any danger that the ear might recognise a recurrent syllabic count.[14] Syllabic composition becomes apparent only to a reader viewing the textual pattern, and both poets are drawn to figuratively shaped stanzas that advertise an artifice hard for the ear to discern.[15] Elaborately shaped stanzas insist on a textuality that would immure voice and rhythm in typography aspiring to assign a poem to the condition of objecthood. Objecthood would extricate a poem from time, allowing it to be approached as though a sculptural mobile. Isobel Armstrong's reading of Marianne Moore's syllabic poem 'The Fish' draws out this quality and links it explicitly to visual caesuras – that is, to line-breaks enforced by a syllabic patterning regardless of semantic logic or rhythmic diktat, and contriving a prismatic textual object.[16]

When reading as well as hearing 'Poem in October', one is struck by the poem's resistance to punctuation other than pauses enjoined by line-breaks. Punctuation is punctilious in Moore and obstructs any possibility that her poems might concede to emergent cadence; although John Hollander writes charmingly that 'her unrolling, idiosyncratically periodic syntax overflows the frequently tightly syllabic cups and basins of her stanzas', his identification of her particulate poetry's 'lepidoptery' better conveys its odd meticulousness.[17] Thomas's suppression of punctuation departs also from its usual association in late-modernist American poetry with parataxis and optional syntax; the device encourages multiplicity in linking, and asks the reader to distribute stress in relation to what William Carlos Williams called the variable foot.[18] Make your own rhythm is the offer, according to individual breath and ear, but tentatively, mindful at every juncture that this is a choice. Moore's syllabics and Williams's variable foot therefore point in markedly different directions, in the one case towards Language writing, and in the other towards the poetics of banter in the New York School and the poetics of breath formulated by Charles Olson and subsequently acknowledged by Williams. The acme of breath poetics can be found in poems by Robert Creeley where scarcely a syllable passes unstressed, each rotating in a virtual space and throwing out a line to every other syllable. Thomas's poetry, however, is far more syntactically complex, its skeining made harder to untangle by an absence of punctuation which in verse both marks stresses and acts as a guide to semantic relations. Abjuring diacritical enforcement does not thereby extend permission to the reader (or, from another angle, demand choice) in the manner of breath poetics; rather it strives against the always-incipient pressure of cadence. Here are the poem's opening two stanzas:

It was my thirtieth year to heaven
Woke to my hearing from harbour and neighbour wood
And the mussel pooled and the heron
Priested shore
The morning beckon
With water praying and call of seagull and rook
And the knock of sailing boats on the net webbed wall
Myself to set foot
That second
In the still sleeping town and set forth.

My birthday began with the water-
Birds and the birds of the winged trees flying my name
Above the farms and the white horses
And I rose
In rainy autumn
And walked abroad in a shower of all my days.
High tide and the heron dived when I took the road
Over the border
And the gates
Of the town closed as the town awoke.[19]

The first stanza of 'Poem in October' withholds punctuation, to the extent of suppressing hyphens where they would be called on in regular usage; word formations which beg for hyphens proliferate here. The suppression of hyphens is assertive. It enables a pun like 'mussel pooled', which anticipates as it were through physical stimulus the morning and its beckoning, where if hyphenated the phrase would be pinned down as adjectival. But the main consequence of de-hyphenating is the equitable distribution Goodby refers to, rendering this stanza's tangled but conventional syntax, spatial rather than temporal. The spine of its long unfolding sentence can be tracked in the phrases 'woke to my hearing [. . .] The morning beckon [. . .] Myself to set foot', but the verbs do not make for a brisk walk; indeed, what this poem strives to bring about and 'set forth' is a personal history about a revolving axis, a history written upon the landscape.

Such an account might seem paradoxical, for a hyphen, contrary to a caesura, is a mark whose Greek origin announces that it yokes two elements together 'under one'. But a hyphen thereby asserts a distinction from the unhyphenated words surrounding it; the at-oneness of the hyphenated expression would break from the semantically defined relatedness of words in the ordinary course, to be yoked in its assertive unity to the noun or verb it modifies. Poetry, however, is not an ordinary course of words, and the effect of suppressing hyphens along with this poem's befuddling syntax is to hyphenate every word in the stanza, to distribute hyphenation equally across the would-be stressless landscape.

This effect is exaggerated by the divorce of ordinarily compound words (for instance, 'sun light'), by the reactivation of compound words (such as 'singingbirds' for 'songbirds'), and by a practice of enjambement often carried forward by 'and', the weakest and least stress-bearing of conjunctions, here equivalent to a hyphen. Linkage in 'Poem in October' is persistent, multiple, open to disentanglement, unemphatic and horizontal. It might be described as chained. Further, it would scarcely be an exaggeration to assert that the process of linkage is more important than what is linked – that poetic thinking here reverts to intra-uterine proto-mental processes marked by the dominance of rhythm whose encounter with separate mentality, across the caesura of birth, can be felt to threaten catastrophe. Rhythmic voice produces an intoxicating restoration, which Thomas resists so as to spare his developed sense of self even while inventing elaborate, quasi-mechanical verse instruments for overcoming the caesura between two systems of thinking.[20]

'Poem in October' connects its words in quite a regular way, grammatically, but makes syntax hard to follow through real time – syntax has to be mapped on the page. If every word is implicitly hyphenated, it follows that caesura must be impossible: indeed, theoretically, caesura *is* impossible in English syllabic verse, which is why syllabics are most often used in a compromise formation with accentual verse, as in Thomas's own earlier practice.[21] The *Princeton Encyclopaedia of Poetry and Poetics* comments that '[w]hen poets of other langs. tried to adopt Fr. Syllabic metrics, they faced the problem of word stresses in midline, which interfered with the reader's perception of the syllabic pattern. Hispanic and It. poets used these midline stresses to produce a variety of rhythms in their lines, but Eng. poets used them to create regular patterns – that is, accentual-syllabic verse.'[22] Thomas, however, wishes to level out word stresses while mystifying the syllabic pattern unless in sight of the text, so that its control feels integral to its vocal production rather than an imposition on it; he incorporates the poem as a sustainable event, he makes it audibly substantial, through what Goodby felicitously calls its sonic web or Simon Jarvis calls its 'phonotextual clusters' (thus distinguishing textual phonemes from performed phonetics).[23]

De-hyphenating in order to hyphenate is only one paradoxical strategy Thomas uses to restore proto-mental linkages without dissolving identity into primordial rhythm. Thomas's poetry is obsessed by the interrupted and broken, but through negation; it would heal or at least suppress or disguise fractures even if it risks creating monstrosities in the process. Although sharing with late-modernist disjunctive verse a sensitivity to the oppressive coherences which determine our conscious lives, Thomas's would not challenge the mind-forged manacles with scrap. Instead of arranging fragments of a shattered linguistic armature, freeing the mind to sport and sharpen its political-critical consciousness, Thomas's poetry aspires to produce novel coherences, universes. Or, more specifically, it creates and populates a single universe, instantiated in each poem, although verse techniques are brought ever more firmly under conscious control.[24] In Heideggerian terms, 'world worlds', but its upsurging becomes less dependent on 'having a voice'.[25]

From the start, Thomas was never able to tolerate discontinuity, a catastrophe beginning for him with expulsion from the womb and recurring throughout his life, life experienced as a sequence of losses. Consider the first poem in the Buffalo notebook, dated 3 November 1930, when Thomas had just turned sixteen, which begins 'I know this vicious minute's hour'.[26] 'You have offended, periodic heart', the poem proclaims, going on to anticipate 'Poem in October' in describing 'reality, whose voice I know / To be the circle not the stair of sound.' A stair is periodic, as are the heart's periodics destined either to ascend to glory or descend to the loam, '[e]ach silver moment chimes / in steps of sound'. This draft falls apart after asserting the circularity of the real; how will the poem end if there is no place at which to arrive, no teleology? How will the last caesura be overcome? The young Thomas had no answer; but the circle of sound is what his poems will later convene rather than merely describe. Yet the contradiction in writing poetry, a lineated art, so as to overcome periodicity cannot be gainsaid. How might the fateful stair of sound be flattened? The sonic reality of 'Poem in October' is distributed through the lamination of sea, earth and sky; the boy's infant whisper '[t]o the trees and the stones and the fish in the tide' percolates through the universe which '[s]ang alive / Still in the water and singingbirds', and must continue to do so. The pun on 'still' is precise; activity remains still and unsuperseded, it persists in time like a wave. But this whispering and singing occurs descriptively; we still need to understand how the poem extends sonic reality to its limits and beyond.

Universing poetry, worlding poetry, is to be distinguished from fictive, science fiction, narrative or surrealist poetry because the poem's binding principle does not depend on temporal progress or external allusion. It can go nowhere, but to go nowhere may be the poem's mission. Such poetry does not need to be intellectual in tenor or rhetorically gorgeous; it can be as brilliant as John Ashbery's, as erudite as J. H. Prynne's, or as sensuous as Édouard Glissant's, but often can be recognised through its uncanny mood, something pre-conscious sensed as the determining undertow of a poem's surface reticulation. Universing *poiesis* creates a possible place whose interconnectedness incorporates readers within its linguistic field, not explicitly but as participant in its articulations.

A reader does not overhear but is invoked. Psychic interiority becomes identical with an elaborated world structured as a domain of being, thinking and feeling, and especially through the poem's rhythm and its phonotext, a thick sonic reality which overcomes any tendency towards commentary, towards the parade of self and its views, for the poem does not depend on externalities even if individual and political forces call on the shaping poem. The interchangeability of elements within Dylan Thomas's verse, a feature ridiculed by Thomas's contemporary Geoffrey Grigson, and the re-assignability of phrases within a complete poetical universe, accords with this poetic logic.[27] Rhythm and phonotext may be primary modes of access to a poem's universe, but Thomas pointed the way to a poet as different as J. H. Prynne in seeking, against his own astonishing facility, to make a poetic universe through different contrivances – even if the worlding of his syllabic poems continues to be sustained by the voice from which a new autonomy for the poem is sought.

'Poem in October' hovers about the present participle sonically, as in its peculiar past-in-present tense, irresistibly turning to singing; although the phonotext is a tightly implicated web, its dominant feature is a chime around the word 'sing'. 'Sing' could imagine performance while not itself a performance, for performance must cease in time, and end in silence. In its singing this poem unifies air, earth and sea to achieve a singularity structured as phallic in the first three stanzas. In the first, birds perform a weaving through the elements (the echoing near-rhymes of 'wood', 'rook' and 'foot' associate 'rook', a most unethereal bird, with the terrestrial) and likewise through hearing, in order then to settle in '[m]yself to set foot' – a movement performed in a densifying flock of short *e* sounds. A fourth element, fire, stays in reserve for the last stanza of the poem. Alongside, present participles continue to sing, together with the noun 'morning' masquerading as a participle. This movement repeats in the second stanza but in a more overtly sexualised landscape. Again, birds weave between the elements in the first two lines, as does the pun on 'white horses', at once farm animals and breakers in the bay. The name of the previous stanza is scattered in the air visibly, in phonemes, falling to fertilise the earth through the erection and ejaculation indexed in the lines, '[a]nd I rose / In rainy autumn / And walked abroad in a shower of all my days.' 'Shower', here, has its premonition in 'water praying' now audible as 'spraying'. Detumescence follows: 'high tide and the heron dived when I took the road', and again the poem returns to the settled 'I'.

The script is less blatant in the third stanza, but visible and audible nonetheless:

> A springful of larks in a rolling
> Cloud and the roadside bushes brimming with whistling
> Blackbirds and the sun of October
> Summery
> On the hill's shoulder,
> Here were fond climates and sweet singers suddenly
> Come in the morning where I wandered and listened
> To the rain wringing
> Wind blow cold
> In the wood faraway under me.[28]

Once more, birds swerve between air and earth, not so watery this time; they are 'sweet singers' whose singing runs through the first two lines in 'springful', 'rolling', 'brimming', 'whistling'. While 'the rain wringing' parallels 'a shower of all my days' in a more depressive tone, here the descent falls tellingly on the ear, audible in the short *u* sounds of 'sun', 'summery', 'suddenly' and 'under', a thread that ends in the resolution of the dominant past-in-present tense of the poem (a past tense modified by insistent present participles) with that terminal simple past of 'sung'. What subsequently merges into and must modify the phallic rise and fall, subsuming its repetition into a various continuity, into the stillness of ocean self-expressed as a wave, here is brought about through synchronic meteorological and seasonal change. 'My birthday', as a definite point of temporal punctuation, can be marvelled away as 'the weather turned around' instead of the self turning in its surveying, and this shift governs the further reaches of the poem. The dialectic of this poem brings penis and womb into universe making without the catastrophe of birth. The universe is already-created, has already survived its unliving.

After three further stanzas, fire is reserved to the last, with that element's association with dead autumnal leaves and blood earlier consecrated by Shelley's 'Ode to the West Wind' and Hopkins's 'The Windhover', in a tradition of Lucretian poetry reshaping the womb of life out of rot and physical damage. The poem's end falls and rises in fire and youth: 'And the true / Joy of the long dead child sang burning / in the sun.' A bloody sunset lies underfoot at the same time, the same place, in fallen leaves – also the leaves of this poem itself, from which 'my heart's truth' will '[s]till be sung', rising anew from dead words, at once level with the streets of the town and surmounting 'this high hill':

> And there could I marvel my birthday
> Away but the weather turned around. And the true
> Joy of the long dead child sand burning
> In the sun.
> It was my thirtieth

Year to heaven stood there then in the summer noon
Though the town below lay leaved with October blood.
    O may my heart's truth
      Still be sung
On this high hill in a year's turning.[29]

There is no interruption by death, there is no interruption by birth. The poem would eradicate the caesura identified by Freud in *Inhibitions, Symptoms and Anxiety* when he speculates that '[t]here is much more continuity between intra-uterine life and earliest infancy than the impressive caesura of the act of birth allows us to believe.'[30] The end-caesura or 'gross catastrophe' of death is challenged in some of Thomas's most celebrated poems, 'And death shall have no dominion' and 'Do not go gentle into that good night' – a gross catastrophe which is the key to Thomas's Christ obsession, defended by William Empson in a splendid riposte to a critic who

> works up his denunciations [. . .] to the point [. . .] of accusing the jealous Thomas of telling Jesus to get back into the womb because he wants to be the Messiah himself. The idea that any man can become Christ, who is a universal, was a major sixteenth-century heresy and has been kept up among the poets [. . .].[31]

In keeping with this heresy and Thomas's Unitarian background, Christ's incarnation represents the general catastrophe of birth in the early 'Before I knocked', a poem written in metronomic, knocking four-beat sexains.[32] Catastrophe is both performed and countered by powerful rhythm, and the poem's delirious orality both expels and revels through language's forming, breaking waves. The swing of the poem between castration anxiety and assertive phallicism, between phallicism and the oceanic womb (expounded in Lacanian terms in Rhian Barfoot's reading), anticipates resumption on the far side of any break.[33] The poem imagines the protoplasm of incarnation entering the womb as well as suffering its expulsion, and puts immaculate conception under blasphemous pressure: conception has no ovular and spermatozoic origin, but shapes the poetic embryo out of a lifespan physical to the extent that it includes its own ordure, while ghostly evoking what precedes life and follows it in a 'last / Long breath' that might carry this poem towards its reader. Even '[b]efore I knocked and flesh let enter, / With liquid hands tapped on the womb', intra-uterine life has compounded a full ontogenesis:

I knew the message of the winter,
The darted hail, the childish snow,
And the wind was my sister suitor;

Wind in me leaped, the hellborn dew;
My veins flowed with the Eastern weather;
Ungotten I knew night and day.[34]

This is followed by two and a half stanzas of premonitory decay and mortality before the staggering final line, '[a]nd doublecrossed my mother's womb.' Both birth and death do violence to the pre-parturient 'molten form', neither internalised nor expelled by the mother. Here is the creation, victim and expression of a Blakeian Godhead swinging the exemplary caesura of '[t]he leaden stars, the rainy hammer', knocking Christ and himself into shape (theologically they are one). Sonically, God's hammer swings relentlessly across the heavily stressed line-breaks. So, also, the double-crossing violence of sexual intercourse is enjoined on the male position in order to defeat the caesura of birth as well as the male/female caesura – for beyond male is female and beyond female, male. As W. R. Bion expresses it in his brief, late text 'Caesura' (1975):

> How is one to penetrate this obstacle, this caesura of birth? Can any method of communication be sufficiently 'penetrating' to pass that caesura in the direction from post-natal conscious thought back to the pre-mental in which thoughts and ideas have their counterpart in 'times' or 'levels' of mind where they are not thoughts or ideas? That penetration has to be effective in either direction. It is easy to put it in pictorial terms by saying it is like penetrating into the woman's inside either from inside out, as at birth, or from outside in, as in sexual intercourse.[35]

But when intercourse in Thomas's poem repeatedly double-crosses the threshold, it knocks against it time and again, an intolerable periodicity. How shall the threshold be crossed without this insistent encounter with the break – without this encounter with the male/female caesura? The poem is saturated with disgust at the flesh, flesh phallically alone in the universe or womb-like in comprising the universe, and intercourse might fill the missing middle between such phallicism and fecundity: but that is not the path taken, a path that would recognise prior and future generations and, by extension, sociality. On such a path, the caesura of birth would continue to mortify. So the one overtly celebratory stanza in 'Before I knocked' instead permits 'my mortal creature' to drown in uterine oceanic feelings, 'the salt adventure / Of tides that never touch the shores.'[36] A rare enjambement hints at the levelling of thresholds to follow in the later syllabics.

The enjambement prepares, then, for 'Poem in October', where flesh dissolves into a sensorium of delight, notwithstanding the caesura of birth and the social world beyond 'the gates / Of the town' that still threatens to breach the poem's sphere, obtruding checkpoints which must be trespassed across, before, and after, or made nugatory. The poem dreams that 'all the gardens / Of spring and summer were blooming in the tall tales / Beyond the border' – beyond, rather than before – so that 'my birthday' can be marvelled away and time organised prosodically across space. Lest such protraction be reckoned abstract, part of the poem's force comes from its undergirding by a specific and precisely observed place, Laugharne in Carmarthenshire; indeed, in a letter of 26 August 1944 to Vernon Watkins, Thomas refers to 'Poem in October' as 'the first place poem I've written', despite giving it a calendrical title.[37] To anyone who knows how Thomas's poems had been nourished by Swansea and its bay, this sounds disingenuous, but the comment signifies a new ability to tolerate what syllabics perform, secure in simultaneous rise and fall so that dispersal 'in the water and the singingbirds' can coexist with '[i]t was my thirtieth / Year to heaven stood there then in summer noon / Though the town below lay leaved with October blood.' It is possible now to survive the labial stasis of 'below lay leaved' and to cast out upon the waves. Swansea Bay may be audible and discernible in earlier poems such as 'Before I knocked', but there, landscape was internalised; this new universal erases the caesura between internal and external. The psyche and the landscape become identical, not through the one-way vector of pathetic fallacy, but through the coincidence of rise and fall, the exchange of continuous breathing. So the restored middle is breath. The threshold-levelling device of syllabics conforms with the prevalence of mood as opposed to distinct and violent emotions of desire, rage and ecstasy; the pre-separation affective formation of mood, common to mother and infant, suffuses the world and acknowledges no boundaries between self and other. It changes like the weather – '[t]he weather turned around'.

Crossing and recrossing the caesura threatens to accomplish only its thickening into a barrier; to overcome it is unintentionally to reassert it. Thomas's irregular rhymes as well as the irregular line-lengths of this poem contrive to satisfy and deny expectations of pause and stress at once. Rhyme cannot be allowed to sign off a sonic completion; Thomas's rhymes are leaky even for assonantal rhyme, leaking between 'wall' and 'forth', to take a telling example from the poem's first stanza. Thomas's running stitch of birds mediates between sea, sky and earth without reaffirming the elements' separation in so doing. Barriers fade into wave patterns, each stanza a wave-form as waves conform to a bay. Rhyme does its stitching job without calling attention to itself; this is invisible mending, inaudible mending within a prosody whose regularity is imperceptible. Neither, despite his frequently religious diction, could Thomas be a poet of transcendence. What Hölderlin calls the 'utterly unbound', the transport of the tragic and the mystical, paradoxically would require caesura:

> In the rhythmic sequence of representations, in which the tragic transport exhibits itself, that which one calls the *caesura* in poetic metre, the pure word, the counter-rhythmic interruption, is necessary; precisely in order to counter the raging change of representations at its summit so that it is no longer the change of representations but the representation itself which appears.[38]

But Thomas's job is one of universing, where the raging change of representations rotates and unifies to comprise his poetry's sphere. Sexual compulsion and disgust, but also his poems' seasonal synchrony, are alike driven by a pressure to efface that must itself confront the reiteration of difference on the way to effacement. Historical time, marked by birth and death, must yield to repetition: but how to repeat without starting again? Through such universing. Each stanza must suture time and times musically in its waves, an expansive present, an unceasing present. Lyric poetry is the one literary form which dreams of simultaneity, although haunted by the fate of becoming its own memorial; it must resist capturing and freezing, in its artifice it must live illuminated within the sphere it creates. Hence Thomas's elegy 'A Refusal to Mourn the Death, by Fire, of a Child in London': more than a meditation on the inadequacy of elegy, it surges affectively as another negation of endings, a memorial that dissolves itself.[39]

W. R. Bion ends his paper on 'Caesura' with a rephrasing of Freud's reference to the birth caesura as follows: 'There is much more continuity between autonomically appropriate quanta and the waves of conscious thought and feeling than the impressive caesura of transference and counter-transference would have us believe.'[40] What can Bion mean by 'autonomically appropriate quanta', and indeed, what is the relationship between Freud's comment and Bion's rephrasing, including a translation from birth to transference and counter-transference? A further exegetical rephrasing might read: 'There is much more continuity between mobile and clustering phonemes and suprasegmentals of speech (in other words, prosody) and the waves of time, space, mood, and a poet's linguistic reservoir, than the impressive caesuras of the poem's beginning and ending would have us believe.' And this leads to another claim to which this chapter has already gestured. That is, each poem by Thomas rises as a wave just as Heidegger describes it in his lecture on 'Language in the Poem'. David Nowell Smith provides a commentary in his book on Heidegger's poetics, *Sounding/Silence*, thereby explaining the sense of resumption that attends a Thomas poem:

The 'veiled essence' of rhythm lies in the 'source' of the wave – in, that is, the very impetus into movement through which the poetic site articulates itself in an individual poem; in this, it echoes the movedness [. . .] that, in 'The Origin of the Work of Art,' characterized the artwork's engagement with the limits of its medium.[41]

With Bion and Heidegger in mind, it may be said of 'Poem in October' that it rises from a poetic site that feels familiar to anyone even slightly acquainted with Thomas's poetry. For all its recognisable matrix, it seems less divorced from the material world and the independently memoried poet, than previous poems by Thomas. All signs are motivated: 'And the mystery / Sang alive'. This poet's song, human song, and the song of the earth are one, but the achievement encompasses an outward orientation. Listen to the weather:

> It turned away from the blithe country
> And down the other air and the blue altered sky
> Streamed again a wonder of summer [. . .][42]

The long vowel sweep of 'blithe' and '[s]treamed' snatches up the short *u* sounds, rushing the particles forward until calmly suspended at the end of '[f]orgotten mornings when he walked with his mother'. The particles become visible and audible in 'parables / Of sun light', parabolas of sunlight audible in language as 'wonder of summer' and 'walked with his mother'. Here is the '"veiled essence" of rhythm' as the poem gathers itself rhythmically out of the song of the earth in its wave, in its parabola, in its parable. The poem's singing is visible too – particularly in the last stanza where it is leaved, spread out in text as summer's passing lies displayed in the fallen leaves. Such unsurpassed intensity of sound and vision are reminiscent of Bion's speculations on foetal mental life, starting embryologically with the early development of optic and auditory pits.[43]

'Though I sang in my chains like the sea.' Everything in this chapter seems to lead to the celebrated last line of 'Fern Hill', written in 1945, a year later than 'Poem in October'.[44] The movedness of the poem, to use a Heideggerian term, meaning a kind of buckling against the limits of language marked in rhythm, produces a further magnificent wave out of the same site as 'Poem in October'. It would be easy to point to apples and owls and the rest of the stock shared between the poems, but the wave gathers phonemically, more than in the things it sweeps up, and more powerfully through its linkages than the things linked. 'Parables / Of sun light' in the earlier poem lead to 'legends of green chapels' in another *reading* of the natural world, and audible again in 'Fern Hill' as 'the sabbath rang slowly / In the pebbles of the holy streams' at the end of its second stanza, paralleling the first stanza's 'daisies and barley / Down the rivers of the windfall light.'[45] 'Windfall' falls out of apples – apples and pebbles, apples and parables. 'Fern Hill' too gathers in syllabics and, like 'Poem in October', is notable for its lexical simplicity, eschewing Latinate words, its lines stretching longer than in the earlier poem, but with few commas and only eight full stops in fifty-four lines. These are the chains in which the poem sings, a continuous song, each song identical and a variation, precedented and unprecedented. Thomas's off-rhymes chain or stitch through his poems while skirting repetition. The signifying chains lap like waves. Signifying waves, however, are shaped by the geography of a particular coast, much as an infant's language is shaped by her mother's gestural and linguistic embrace. A coast is land and sea both, a place of exchange, of outerness and innerness; so the waves sound like the land and like its people's speech (the word 'lovely' sounds as delectable in a Welsh accent as it sounds complacent in an English one), and the waves shape like verse against its line-endings. After the rivers and streams at the start of 'Fern Hill', the sea is reached only in its last line, opening out and curtailing at once; yet reaching the sea feels inevitable, for we were hearing it all along, beyond Fern Hill and the farm, moving through the poetic site of Dylan Thomas, bringing each poem into hearing and vision, and stretching past the caesura of the poem's ending – which also precedes its beginning.

Such is the wave power of Dylan Thomas's verse. Every poem's semantic and affective wave participates in Thomas's obliteration of the caesura. Owing to the trauma of birth, things have gone to smash already, and the amelioration Thomas imagines is for breaks and resumptions to succumb to waves, in a prosody without end stops or caesuras, pulling back and forth in its chains like the sea. Such a description harkens back to Adam Phillips's charge against Thomas, restaging the routine condemnation of Thomas's poetry as masturbatory. The shame of lyric poetry which others would overcome, would efface, through proclamations of political and ethical solidarity and sympathy is flaunted, on the contrary, by Dylan Thomas time and again:

> The seed-at-zero shall not storm
> That town of ghosts, the trodden womb
> With her rampart to his tapping [. . .]

Rather, the seed-at-zero will spill across the universe:

> Through the rampart of the sky
> Shall the star-flanked seed be riddled,
> Manna for the rumbling ground,
> Quickening for the riddled sea;[46]

The sin of Onan seeds the phonemic universe, across sky, ground and sea. What is effaced is not lyric shame, as by a conventional resort to social acceptance and identification with a self-conscious subject, but the caesura. Recall, however, how Bion shifts from the caesura of birth to the caesura of transference and counter-transference. Where might this poem eventuate again in relation to the reading presented here? Is it possible, after the exchange of a reading, even to refer to 'this' poem, using an untroubled deictic? The 'autonomically appropriate quanta' criss-cross between Thomas's poetic universe and a reader's ingestion and exposition.

But there is something to be said in favour of Adam Phillips too. The containment of wave power within the maternal bay is a limitation Thomas could not overcome, using his resources of technical detachment. Universing has to be open to influx, not restricted to the shape of one bay. Dylan Thomas was a poet of London and New York City as well as of Laugharne and Swansea, but you would scarcely know it, with the signal exception of the wartime London poems collected in *Deaths and Entrances* (1946). Indeed, you would scarcely know that Swansea was a port, open to other worlds; Laugharne, too, up to the sixteenth century. A bay is a mouth, language as abstraction shaped through individual corporeality. But a mouth takes in as well as gives forth. Thomas's universe may have been too small. But in a universe that has indeed become limited, limited in a deadly irony by the illimitability of human aspirations, limitation proposes the stakes. The impulse to epic must be contained, not only in poetic practice, but also confounding the totalising figures of the local, the national, the racial, while still taking in, still breathing. Universing within limits must be the poetic and human imperative, and reading Thomas suggests as much, even as it affords a shameless pleasure.

Notes

1. The first version of this chapter was delivered as a plenary lecture at *Dylan Unchained: The Dylan Thomas Centenary Conference, 1914–2014* at Swansea University, September 2014. My thanks to John Goodby for his invitation, and to Neil Reeve. A lightly revised version was delivered in the 'History and Forms of the Lyric' lecture series at the University of Chicago in October 2014. My thanks to Richard Strier.
2. Adam Phillips, contribution to 'A Symposium on Forsaken Favorites', *The Threepenny Review*, 117 (Spring 2009): <http://www.threepennyreview.com/samples/phillips_sp09.html> (last accessed 1 September 2014).
3. Daniel Tiffany, *My Silver Planet: A Secret History of Poetry and Kitsch*

(Baltimore, MA: Johns Hopkins University Press, 2014), see especially chapter 1.

4. 'Poem in October', first publ. in *Horizon* and *Poetry* (Chicago), February 1945; repr. in *CP14*, pp. 160–2. John Goodby traces the poem's composition to the summer of 1944, but follows previous editors in admitting the possibility of an earlier date (*CP14*, p. 385).

5. I'm referring here to 'The seed-at-zero', *CP14*, pp. 87–8.

6. Paulo César Sandler, *The Language of Bion: A Dictionary of Concepts* (London: Karnac, 2005), p. 97.

7. 'Now the thirst parches lip and tongue', *NP*, pp. 117–18 (p. 118). Or in another early poem of heterosexual intercourse, 'Their faces shone under some radiance', which ends a little more subtly: '[t]he suicides parade again, now ripe for dying' (*CP14*, pp. 19–20 (p. 20)).

8. Isobel Armstrong, 'The Caesura', lecture given at the conference *The Languages of Literature: Attridge at 70*, University of York, May 2015. My thanks to Isobel Armstrong for providing me with her lecture notes.

9. Several recordings of 'Poem in October' survive on the Caedmon Records label. For instance: 'Poem in October', *Dylan Thomas Reading Complete Recorded Poetry*, TC 2014 (1963); and 'Poem in October', *An Evening with Dylan Thomas*, TC 1157 (1963). Both of these tracks are excerpted on the box-set, *Dylan Thomas: The Caedmon Collection*, intro. Billy Collins (2002).

10. Jacques Derrida, *Monolingualism of the Other; or, The Prosthesis of Origin*, trans. Patrick Mensah (Stanford: Stanford University Press, 1998), p. 48. Qtd by David Nowell Smith, *On Voice in Poetry: The Work of Animation* (Basingstoke: Palgrave Macmillan, 2015), p. 65.

11. Édouard Glissant, 'Open Circle, Lived Relation', in *Poetics of Relation*, trans. Betsy Wing (Ann Arbor: University of Michigan Press, 1997), p. 200.

12. John Goodby, *The Poetry of Dylan Thomas: Under the Spelling Wall* (Liverpool: Liverpool University Press, 2013), p. 389.

13. It could be argued that *any* performance of syllabics in English necessarily introduces a stress pattern: 'Though Auden often expressed a crude bias against Gallic culture, [. . .] he seems rather to emphasise how alexandrines inevitably get lost in translation, even when read in their original form, for Anglophone speakers who cannot "share a common cosmos" with Francophone ones, despite their best efforts. But such a judgment might also be taken as spelling doom for any attempt to write syllabic verse in English: if Anglophone readers cannot help imposing stresses on syllabic lines written in a largely atonic language such as French, how will they avoid doing so in relation to comparable lines as written in their own tongue?' (Richard Hillyer, 'Let Me Weigh the Counts: Auden's Horatian Syllabics', *Versification*, 5 (2010), 11–26 (p. 25)). But this underlines the crucial distinction between the phonetics of performance and the phenomenology of phonemic patterning.

14. Specifically, 'Poem in October' 'has seven ten-line stanzas with a syllabic count of 9, 12, 9, 3, 5, 12, 12, 5, 3, 9', as Alan Bold notes in *Dylan Thomas: Craft or Sullen Art* (London: Vision Press, 1990), p. 160.

15. Cf. Northrop Frye in *Theory of Genres* (1957): 'A poem of Marianne Moore's, *Camellia Sabina*, employs an eight-line stanza in which the

rhyming words are at the end of the first line, at the end of the eighth line, and at the third syllable of the seventh line. I doubt if the most attentive listener could pick this last rhyme up merely from hearing the poem read aloud: one sees it first on the page, and then translates the visual structural pattern to the ear.' (Excerpted in Virginia Jackson and Yopie Prins (eds), *The Lyric Theory Reader: A Critical Anthology* (Baltimore: Johns Hopkins University Press, 2014), pp. 3–9 (p. 38).)

16. Armstrong, 'The Caesura'.
17. John Hollander, 'Marianne Moore's Verse', in *The Work of Poetry* (New York: Columbia University Press, 1997), pp. 250–70 (pp. 261 and 257).
18. Leaving 'variable foot' to variable definition. But 'Dr. W. C. Williams once remarked to me in a letter that free verse was to him a means of obtaining widely varying speeds within a given type of foot.' (Yvor Winters, 'THE INFLUENCE OF METER ON POETIC CONVENTION', in *In Defense of Reason*, 3rd edn (London: Routledge & Kegan Paul, 1947), p. 120.) 'Speed' is an effect of distribution of stress.
19. 'Poem in October', *CP14*, pp. 160–2 (p. 160).
20. This account of the caesura and systems of thinking is indebted to W. R. Bion and to the exposition of his ideas offered in James S. Grotstein, *A Beam of Intense Darkness: Wilfred Bion's Legacy to Psychoanalysis* (London: Karnac, 2007). See especially chapter 24, 'Fetal mental life and its caesura with postnatal mental life', pp. 256–8.
21. Thomas's tendency had been to default to pentameter. In a well-judged contemporary review subsequently reprinted in a monograph on Thomas, Henry Treece decided that '[t]his poem is remarkable also for some exquisite allusions to the landscape and activities of childhood; and, perhaps more important still, for a long stanza-form of ten lines, containing a regular pattern through the poem of long and short lines of varying rhythms. This technical advance, together with the poem *Vision and Prayer*, marks a definite moving away from the rhythmic monotony of the pentameter line, to which the poet has adhered for so long.' (Henry Treece, *Dylan Thomas*, 2nd edn (London: Ernest Benn, 1956), p. 103.)
22. 'Syllabic Verse', in *The Princeton Encyclopaedia of Poetry and Poetics*, 4th edn (Princeton: Princeton University Press, 2012), pp. 1388–90 (p. 1389).
23. 'This is not the claim that there could somehow be a natural palette of vowel-sounds, each bearing its appropriate thematic or semantic coloration. There is no such natural correspondence. But there can, instead, be what one might call clouds or mists of such associations, clouds whose force is not necessary or natural but is rather a kind of prosodic weather formation gathering in the poet's peculiar handling of verbal music. And I would want to argue that phonotextual clusters can with sufficient attention and power become something more permanently established in the *reader's* repertoire of response, too.' (Simon Jarvis, 'Why Rhyme Pleases', *Thinking Verse*, 1 (2011), 17–43 (p. 36).) I am grateful to Eric Powell, who illuminated for me the significance of Jarvis's discussion.
24. Another idea of this universing might be gained from the career of John Ashbery, where a switch from obtrusive fragmentation in *The Tennis Court Oath* (1962) to an ever-unfolding universe-creating practice is clearly evident – and not unlike Thomas in its universing being braced on

a childhood landscape, even if Ashbery's pastoral is less cartographically located.

25. 'The Origin of the Work of Art', in Martin Heidegger, *Off the Beaten Track*, ed. and trans. Julian Young and Kenneth Haynes (Cambridge: Cambridge University Press 2002), especially p. 23.

26. 'I know this vicious minute's hour', *NP*, p. 48; repr. *CP14*, pp. 4–5.

27. Geoffrey Grigson, 'How Much Me Now Your Acrobatics Amaze', in *Dylan Thomas: The Legend and the Poet*, ed. E. W. Tedlock (London: Heinemann, 1963), pp. 155–67 (p. 164). '(Here perhaps I should interpolate that the second, just-construable piece which I quoted from Mr Thomas, is one made up by myself of disconnected lines from three stanzas of one poem [. . .] it reads, I am convinced, as authentically as most of Mr Thomas's stanzas.)' Needless to say, it doesn't.

28. 'Poem in October', *CP14*, p. 160.

29. Ibid. pp. 161–2.

30. Sigmund Freud, *Inhibitions, Symptoms and Anxiety*, in *The Standard Edition of the Complete Psychological Works of Sigmund Freud*, vol. 20, trans. James Strachey, in collaboration with Anna Freud, assisted by Alix Strachey and Alan Tyson (London: Vintage, 2001 [1925–6]), pp. 87–156 (p. 138).

31. Cited in John Haffenden, *William Empson. Volume II: Against the Christians* (Oxford: Oxford University Press, 2006), p. 485.

32. 'Before I knocked', *CP14*, pp. 38–9.

33. Rhian Barfoot, *Liberating Dylan Thomas: Rescuing a Poet from Psycho-Sexual Servitude* (Cardiff: University of Wales Press, 2015), see pp. 59–62; Barfoot's reading in relation to the 'pre-historic "mother–father conglomerate"' results in a different emphasis from the attention to thresholds and breaks in the reading here.

34. 'Before I knocked', *CP14*, p. 38.

35. W. R. Bion, 'Caesura', in *The Complete Works of W. R. Bion*, 16 vols, ed. Chris Mawson and Francesca Bion (London: Karnac, 2014), X, pp. 33–49 (p. 40).

36. 'Before I knocked', *CP14*, p. 39.

37. Thomas to Vernon Watkins, 26 August 1944, *CL*, p. 580. Writers differ in the seriousness with which they regard Thomas's assertion. Andrew Lycett feels licensed to represent 'Poem in October' as a 'neat, personalised description of the changing Carmarthenshire weather pattern', a startling inept description, in *Dylan Thomas: A New Life* (Woodstock and New York: Overlook Press, 2005), p. 213; while Barbara Hardy has reasons of her own for a categorical and erroneous denial – '"Poem in October" uses a primal scene of childhood and landscape but in a way which is only incidentally and implicitly Welsh' – in *Dylan Thomas: An Original Language* (Athens, GA: University of Georgia Press, 2000), p. 24. This is erroneous because Laugharne was not Thomas's 'primal scene of childhood and landscape'.

38. Friedrich Hölderlin, 'Remarks on *Oedipus*' (1803), trans. Stefan Bird-Pollan, in J. M. Bernstein (ed.), *Classic and Romantic German Aesthetics* (Cambridge: Cambridge University Press, 2003), pp. 194–202 (p. 195).

39. 'A Refusal to Mourn the Death, by Fire, of a Child in London', *CP14*, pp. 172–3.

40. Bion, 'Caesura', p. 49.
41. David Nowell Smith, *Sounding/Silence: Martin Heidegger at the Limits of Poetics* (New York: Fordham University Press, 2013), p. 52.
42. 'Poem in October', *CP14*, p. 161.
43. 'The embryologist speaks about "optic pits" and "auditory pits". Is it possible for us, as psychoanalysts, to think that there may still be vestiges in the human being which would suggest a survival in the human mind, analogous to that in the human body, of evidence in the field of optics that once there were optic pits, or in the field of hearing that once there were auditory pits? Is there any part of the human mind which still betrays signs of an "embryological" intuition, either visual or auditory? [. . .] are we to consider that the foetus thinks, or feels, or sees, or hears? If so, how primitive can these thoughts, or feelings, or ideas be?' (Bion, 'Caesura', p. 38.)
44. 'Fern Hill', *CP14*, pp. 177–9.
45. Ibid. pp. 177–8.
46. 'The seed-at-zero', *CP14*, p. 87.

Chapter 2

Nosing Around: *Portrait of the Artist as a Young Dog*

Rod Mengham

In a letter written to Pamela Hansford Johnson on 15 April 1934, Dylan Thomas describes what she means to him in terms that identify their interdependence and separation from the rest of humanity with a reimagining of the link between spirit and body:

> And you were a tiny spirit floating around the room, flying faster and faster till you became invisible, & I could hear only your wings. It was a very quiet, monotonous sound, and came from a tail-less mangy dog which limped across the room.

The room contains two lovers, an airborne spirit, and a mangy dog, but the relationship between all these things is curiously indefinite and mutable:

> I know you weren't the mangy dog, dear. But who was? That's the worst of writing without thinking: you write more than you think. I must have been the mangy dog, but I don't feel at all self-pitiful today. Damn the nonsense. Forget it.[1]

Writing without thinking, Thomas instinctively connects the figure of the dog with access to another plane of existence, one in which vision is merged with audition, the spiritual with the animal, the one lover with the other. In the everyday world of the young freelance journalist, this is 'nonsense', but in the insistent clairvoyance of Thomas's poetry, it is a thoroughly characteristic transformation; one that turns to the figure of the dog quite naturally, as the photographs of Pentti Sammallahti do (Figure 2.1). John Berger's essay 'Opening a Gate' examines the work of the Finnish photographer in order to come to terms with the kind of secret knowledge it seems to impart. Berger himself owns a number of Sammallahti's photographs and observes, 'In each of these pictures there is at least one dog.' Dogs gradually become the focal point of the essay, which ends by placing the photographs to one side in order to concentrate on the significance of the special relationship between canines and humans. For Berger, this relationship invites us to recognise the validity of other, non-human ways of experiencing the world:

> Our customary visible order is not the only one: it coexists with other orders [. . .] Children feel it intuitively, because they have the habit of hiding behind things. There they discover the interstices between different sets of the visible.
>
> Dogs, with their running legs, sharp noses and developed memories for sounds, are the natural frontier experts of these interstices. Their eyes, whose message often confuses us for it is urgent and mute, are attuned both to the human order and to other visible orders. Perhaps this is why, on so many occasions and for different reasons, we train dogs as guides.
>
> Probably it was a dog who led the great Finnish photographer to the moment and place for the taking of these pictures. In each one the human order, still in sight, is nevertheless no longer central and is slipping away. The interstices are open.
>
> The result is unsettling: there is more solitude, more pain, more dereliction. At the same time, there is an expectancy which I have not experienced since childhood, since I talked to dogs, listened to their secrets and kept them to myself.[2]

In his childhood, Berger had imagined a collaborative relationship with dogs that involved partaking of secrets that adults could not share. Both dogs and children are only partly socialised; they are 'attuned to' adult forms of behaviour and communication but receive the signals given by adults after their own fashion. Berger's emphasis on simultaneous attunement to human and 'other' orders, to adult and childish forms of experience, could be used to guide an approach to the reading of *Künstlerroman* writing projects that are specific to the twentieth century; and it is especially suggestive for the reading of Dylan Thomas's *Portrait of the Artist as a Young Dog* (1940). Thomas's title borrows its shape from Joyce's earlier novel, precisely because the Joycean protagonist undergoes the evolution of a sensibility that ends up rejecting, and literally departing from, the available forms of socialisation. By exchanging *dog* for *man*, Thomas's own title offers to portray a different degree, indeed a different order, of departure from the norm. The keenness with which Thomas's writing accesses and deranges the information received by the sensorium is in some sense the transcription of a different, which is to say non-human, order of experience. The historical pressure behind this refocusing of the perceptual apparatus is exact but diffuse because it is part of a very gradual process, slow in building, that involves a fundamental change in the relationship between humans and animals. By the twentieth century, and with few exceptions, animals had disappeared

Figure 2.1   Pentti Sammallahti, 'Solovki, White Sea, Russia' (1992).

from our everyday lives, only to reappear as pets or as representations whose function is to reflect the preoccupations of their owners or users. In Berger's own terms, the twentieth-century animal was confined to the family home, or to the *spectacle*.[3]

This essay will triangulate *Portrait of the Artist as a Young Dog* with the work of two other writers for whom the exploration of a 'doggy' outlook is undertaken as a thought-experiment with an ethical motivation. It might well be objected that Thomas's collection of stories isn't really about dogs, and in one sense this is unarguable, except that dogs are referred to here and there, and more importantly, doggy attributes and characteristic forms of behaviour – dog-like ways of doing things and perceiving things – are built into the fabric of the writing. But first I would like to consider the purposeful way in which Franz Kafka and Stefan Themerson make the projected, the imagined, point of view of the dog the basis of their attempts to identify and situate the limitations to human ways of being in and operating in the world. The texts in question are Kafka's 'Investigations of a Dog' and Themerson's *Wooff, Wooff, or Who Killed Richard Wagner* and *Critics and My Talking Dog*.

Kafka's text amounts to an extraordinary investigation – ostensibly *by* a dog, but, more crucially, *of* a dog – in order to uncover the experience of an animal drawn inexorably into the condition of the spectacle. Most extraordinary of all is the poignancy with which the narrator is denied access to the hermeneutic code available to the reader. For the narrator is an old dog still trying to understand his experiences as a young dog; and this retrospection turns his account into another kind of portrait of the artist as a young dog. In effect, Kafka's dog has spent most of his life trying to understand and come to terms with an epiphanic event that struck him and bewildered him at the beginning of his so-called 'career':

> I had run in darkness for a long time, up and down, blind and deaf to everything, led on by nothing but a vague desire, and now I suddenly came to a stop with the feeling that I was in the right place, and looking up saw that it was bright day, only a little hazy, and everywhere a blending and confusion of the most intoxicating smells; I greeted the morning with an uncertain barking when – as if I had conjured them up – out of some place of darkness, to the accompaniment of terrible sounds such as I had never heard before, seven dogs stepped into the light [. . .] They did not speak, they did not sing, they remained all of them, silent, almost determinedly silent; but from the empty air they conjured music. Everything was music [. . .].[4]

The epiphanic event seems to unlock the young dog's senses – from having been 'blind and deaf to everything', he suddenly becomes super-aware of 'intoxicating smells', a whole range of different light levels, and a variety of different sounds, as well as an awareness of the *absence* of sound. The event awakens his senses and disarranges them. The central paradox of the story, as of other Kafka stories such as 'A Report to an Academy', which is narrated by an ape, is the use of a rational apparatus, of the procedures of inference and deduction, to arrive at a satisfactory explanation of the meaning and purpose of the experience, whose meaning and purpose nevertheless remain obscure. The animal uses human methods of analysis to grasp the nature of the event, but these lead nowhere. The music has been 'conjured' out of the air by a power that is immune to reason. We assume that behaviour reasonable to humans may feel unreasonable to dogs. But just how reasonable is it from a human point of view? The narrator has stumbled across a circus act performed by a troupe of acrobatic dogs – a spectacle that seems as counterintuitive to the canine onlooker as the spectacle of starvation as entertainment must seem to the reader of Kafka's 'The Hunger Artist'. Both are debased forms of art that represent a withdrawal from the customary transactions of the everyday material world. The Hunger Artist refuses to ingest anything from the world to which he belongs, while the acrobatic dogs suppress their instincts to conform with the logic of a routine that remains wholly mysterious to them and to the dog-narrator. The passage quoted conjures up the evidence of the senses, not to coordinate it, but to scramble it.

The relationship between physical experience and the sense that can be made of it is least straightforward for those positioned between cultures, between languages, between ethnicities, between classes. Kafka was a middle-class Yiddish-speaking Jew in Prague, writing in German at night and working by day in an insurance office serving working-class Czech-speakers. Another middle-class Jew, Stefan Themerson, was a Polish experimental film-maker exiled in 1940 to London, where he began the process of transforming himself into an essayistic novelist writing in English. In his first published novel, *Bayamus* (1949), the protagonist's subjectivity is caught up in a wholesale scrambling of meaning when, in 1940 – the critical year for Themerson – his head is transplanted onto another man's body, while the other man's head is transplanted onto *his* body.

The divorcing of 'reason' from 'flesh' – Themerson's terms – the rehousing of memory and sensibility within an alternative sensorium, is logically absurd if carried out literally, but ethically productive if carried out imaginatively. In a realistic fiction, the surgical operation would be replaced by geographical and cultural dislocation; the anatomical grafting, by second language acquisition. The historical situation of

Themerson, a Polish exile in London, generates a series of thought-experiments in which incongruous discourses, conventions of thought, and structures of feeling are forced into congruity with each other. This goes beyond an ethics of cosmopolitanism – although the scope of such an ethical project is taken very seriously – in order to test the limits of what is knowable or perceptible in relation to any given language, discourse, medium. After *Bayamus*, Themerson moved on to a shorter project in which he considered the epistemological syncopation between art and science, this time through the even wilder conceit of cross-species intervention:

> The bit of brain dogs receive their visual patterns with is nothing better than a piece of cheddar. And so is the bit of brain we receive odorous patterns with. In short, I came to the conclusion that if we could so to speak *see* what dogs smell, or if they could so to speak *smell* what we see, it would result in a better understanding between our two species.[5]

The absurd premise is characteristic of Themerson, and it should not be forgotten that one of the chief advantages of, and motivations for, installing it at the heart of any project, is the stimulus it gives to satirical wit and subversive humour. The narrator of this philosophical 'shaggy dog story' is clearly taken aback by the rapidity and sophistication with which his dog, Brutus, learns to process and interpret visual information. Brutus appreciates that interpretation is impossible without the recognition of organising principles in nature which he refers to as 'regularities'. The history of 'regularities' is the history of taxonomic systems, of the changing criteria for classifying data in one way rather than another, according to shifts in ideological or disciplinary priorities. Brutus's most significant observation is that epistemological breaks occur when art proposes new forms and relations, new ways of tracing patterns in the data, new 'regularities':

> 'I can prove to you that the regularities the physicists are finding in nature were first discovered by painters [. . .] and if the painters hadn't discovered them first, the physicists couldn't possibly have recognised them as regularities even if they were gaping at them through their telescopes and microscopes for bloody centuries! [. . .] And the nameless regularities painters are discovering today, scientists will be discovering tomorrow [. . .]'[6]

Artists introduce paradigm shifts by allowing the visionary to take precedence over the visible, by exploring the irregular rather than hugging the coast of the regular, by risking the irrational rather than plotting their course according to clear, rational, common-sense criteria. The results can mean disorientation, compass failure, even reversal of the earth's magnetic poles. Artistic experimentation can render the world wholly unrecognisable in familiar terms, as seems to be the case at the end of *Critics and My Talking Dog*, where even a walk down the street can resemble a voyage into the unknown:

> The street is soot black and sodium-light yellow. Both the carriage-way and the foot-way. Bicycles and bipeds, quadricycles and quadrupeds, move along in the black and yellow darkness and display their applications of some few regularities in nature. I look at the base of a lamp-post, and realise that ever since his nose has got connected with the less developed part of his brain, Brutus is not able to tell a bitch from a dog until he *sees* her.[7]

We usually expect dogs to adapt to our way of seeing the world, to learn human priorities and revise their own; we reward them for being subservient, for being loyal, which is why our generic name for them is Fido: 'I am faithful'. But this dog is called Brutus, and Brutus was famously unfaithful, treacherous in fact. Themerson's final paragraph forces the narrator and reader to adapt to the dog's way of seeing the world. The night is divided into two colours, soot black and sodium-light yellow, for no perceptible reason, since dogs do not associate lamp-posts with light sources, but with opportunities for territorial marking of a particularly odorous kind; they are interested in the base of the lamp-post, not the top. Humans seem to have more in common with bicycles than with other mammals, since both touch the ground at two rather than four points. The number of legs or wheels is the primary basis of classification for all objects moving down the street, although motion itself gives rise to distinctive variations that provide a secondary basis of classification, in respect of 'some few regularities in nature'. For the dog, the world is understood chiefly in terms of territoriality and species survival. Themerson's thought-experiment breaks down the boundaries between adjacent territories and inhabits a series of low-key extinction events, in which dogs forget how to be dogs and humans forget how to be humans. The text ends with a note of misgiving about the results of the thought-experiment and more than a twinge of regret that the experiment cannot be reversed and the results undone.

What is remarkable about both Kafka's and Themerson's texts is the consistency with which they sustain the barrier of untranslatability between human and canine languages, taking language in its broadest sense as a system of relations, with subject positions and predicates that determine the forms of our perception of the world and the meanings it has for us. This principle of untranslatability is mostly absent from literary experiments attempting to grasp the nature of canine existence, even when the attempt is being made by a writer as skilled and resourceful as Virginia Woolf, in her playful biography of Elizabeth Barrett Browning's dog, named Flush. Woolf is sensitive to the value and potential depth of companionship between human and animal – 'Broken asunder, yet made in the same mould, each, perhaps, completed what was dormant in the other' – yet this sensitivity is expressed as a sentiment only, in a text which mostly assimilates the canine to the human point of view; the biographical narrative is a tongue-in-cheek *Bildungsroman*, which sees Flush acquiring wisdom of a conventional sort (he adapts readily to the sorting of both humans and animals by class) and emotions suitable to the average melodrama.[8] The narrative point of view is indulgent towards its protagonist, but it is the indulgence of an adult towards a child, and can be patronising. The condescension this leads to is more than a little risky, politically and ethically, as when Flush's childish fear of Mr Barrett is compared to that of a 'savage': 'So a savage couched in flowers shudders when the thunder growls and he hears the voice of God.'[9] The elision of children, dogs and supposedly unsophisticated native peoples is both uncomfortable and extrinsic to any serious thought-experiment aimed at testing the boundaries between human and canine structures of feeling and understanding. Perhaps more to the point for the present discussion, Woolf's attempt to imagine the dog's interaction with its surroundings through smell uses periodic sentence structure and a sustained epic simile that actively draws attention away from the dog's own 'flooded' nerves to dwell at length on the comparison with a 'scholar who has descended step by step into a mausoleum'.[10] The incongruity between scholar and dog is equalled only by the lack of fit between Woolf's own rhetorical techniques and the phenomenological events they displace. Woolf was to be more systematically rigorous in her last novel, *Between the Acts*, which came out in 1941, one year after *Portrait of the Artist as a Young Dog*, and one year after the pivotal events in Themerson's *Bayamus*. One of several referents for the title is the description of what happens between the acts of a village pageant, in an empty hall; empty of humanity, but filled by the activity of several other species, whose own concerns are placed centre stage. Another referent is provided by frequent narrative excursuses into prehistory, inciting the recognition that humanity itself is only a momentary presence in evolution, occurring between the acts of a drama played out by species such as those that catch our attention during the interval in a village pageant.

Thomas's writing does not zoom out in this fashion, in order to render visible the larger contexts for its interest in species differentials; if anything, it zooms in, up close, in order to focus on the granular evidence for the behaviour proper to one species being displaced onto that of another. What I want to suggest about Dylan Thomas is that the governing point of view in *Portrait of the Artist as a Young Dog* undergoes an experiment that is almost the reverse of that experienced by Themerson's Brutus. Brutus acquires the habits of thought, the 'regularities' of perception and expression, of a human being; Thomas's protagonist seems to be caught up in a process of unlearning them, while acquiring the behaviour patterns, the forms of association, the instinctual priorities, even, of a small dog. The conventional modes of registering, and ordering, sense data are simply redundant. In Thomas's short stories, the focaliser is effectively defocused. In the story 'Just Like Little Dogs', he describes himself as a 'lonely nightwalker and a steady stander-at-corners. I liked to walk through the wet town after midnight, when the streets were deserted and the window lights out, alone and alive on the glistening tramlines in dead and empty High Street under the moon.'[11] And, throughout the volume, a high proportion of the writing is concerned with seemingly perpetual motion, with wandering around Swansea and its suburbs, and the Gower Peninsula, with a compulsive drifting in the service of sexual desire, with a strong territorial attachment – in this version of Swansea, the *flâneur* cocks his leg more often than not – and with a peculiarly open-ended form of sensory curiosity. Although I am making something of a joke out of the frequency with which the protagonist urinates in *Portrait of the Artist as a Young Dog*, this – the most common method by which the dog marks its territory – can actually be deployed in the writing to powerful effect. In the final story, 'One Warm Saturday', the protagonist sees and is attracted to a girl sitting in the Victoria Gardens in Swansea, but he is too shy to speak to her; he later sees her in a nearby pub and does manage to speak to her, after which they both go to her lodgings. Quite oddly, he then pulls away from intimacy with her and leaves the room in order to use the toilet; except that he does not use the toilet; he climbs instead to another floor in the lodging house, goes to what is described as 'the dead end of the passage', and 'makes water' on the floor.[12] This very pointed, and very striking, marking of territory is expressed neutrally, in matter-of-fact terms, as if it were quite unexceptional. Its seeming inevitability in the sequence of events is owing partly to the dreamlike atmosphere that settles on the last two pages of the story and of the book, but partly also to the rivalry between the narrator and 'Mr O'Brien', who compete with one another for the favours of the girl, Lou, with an almost instinctual doggedness – if I can be forgiven the pun.

The story 'Just Like Little Dogs' revolves around issues of natural selection. It gets its title from a phrase used by the magistrate dealing with two paternity orders brought against two brothers, named Tom and Walter, who have 'coupled' with two girls, named Norma and

Doris. Tom is attracted to Norma, Walter is attracted to Doris, but at the last moment they switch partners before having sex – for purely instinctual reasons. '"But why did you change over, if you loved her?"' the narrator asks Tom. '"I never understood why," said Tom. "I think about it every night."'[13] This irrational compulsion the two brothers give way to prompts the magistrate to compare their behaviour to that of small dogs, but this is in fact an incidental comparison that rounds off a more sustained exploration of the sensory vigilance that accompanies the territorial alertness of the narrator and the two brothers alike. For much of the story, the three figures are seen lurking under a railway arch keeping watch, although 'keeping watch' does not cover the range of senses being deployed. They hover there, on the lookout with ears pricked, like biological recording mechanisms:

> We stood in the scooped, windy room of the arch, listening to the noises from the muffled town, a goods train shunting, a siren in the docks, the hoarse trams in the streets far behind, one bark of a dog, unplaceable sounds, iron being beaten, the distant creaking of wood, doors slamming where there were no houses, an engine coughing like a sheep on a hill.[14]

The sounds they hear are 'unplaceable', and I think this is characteristic of the way that Thomas's prose writing resounds – or re-sounds. The clauses and sentences that contain them are in no particular order, while the sounds encompassed by these sentences are both never enough and more than enough to complete the grammatical task of the sentence, which unfolds with no particular goal in view, except to be impressible: open and receptive to the evidence of location. And this prose which listens is the medium of an habitual mode of being in the world, a condition of walking and standing-at-corners that is automatic to those who perform it nightly, but which cannot be accounted for in terms of ordinary human domesticity. The agents of this form of attention do not understand why they behave this way, although they feel a continual obligation to succumb to it:

> Why was he humped here with a moody man and myself, listening to our breathing, to the sea, the wind scattering sand through the archway, a chained dog and a foghorn and the rumble of trams a dozen streets away, watching a match strike, a boy's fresh face spying in a shadow, the lighthouse beams, the movement of a hand to a fag, when the sprawling town in a drizzle, the pubs and the clubs and the coffee-shops, the prowlers' streets, the arches near the promenade, were full of friends and enemies?[15]

In the familiar phrase, these men all do have families to go to, complex social relationships to negotiate, and yet their blind need is to repeat, time and time again, the rudimentary survival tactics that enable them to sort: friends from enemies, safe places from exposed places, promenaders from prowlers, chained dogs from stray dogs.

In his brilliant analysis of the discourses of panic surrounding the parallel conditions of stray dogs and 'unowned' women at the beginning of the twentieth century, Geoff Gilbert identifies the fear of rabies and of venereal disease as decisive pretexts for the various campaigns being mounted to impound and domesticate both. It is a striking aspect of this episode in the history of social discipline that the diagnosis of both rabid and syphilitic conditions should dwell on the symptoms of sensory derangement or, as one commentator expresses it, 'chaotic disturbance of sensibility':

> Hearing, sight, taste, and even smell itself, are intensely acute, being exaggerated to the point of pain, and but broken and falsifying media to the mind. The sudden opening or shutting of a door, a brusque tone of talk, a sip of water or beef-tea, a sudden flash of light as from the opening of a hunter's watch or from the light of a mirror, the merest sniff of ammonia; any of these trifling irritants of sensibility never fails to bring on convulsions.[16]

This extreme perceptual alertness is being attributed to a human patient suffering from rabies, the disease that properly belongs to the dog. Its tendency to magnify the smallest sensory event and be open to a multitude of impressions all at once, bears a close relationship to the hyperactive attentiveness of Thomas's feral protagonist, and to the hair-trigger reactions of his prose. The vigilance of this prose is effectively unending, it does not employ a sentence structure that ever feels complete, it simply pauses for rest. And I think there is a politics of a sort to this canine syntax, which Thomas lays out in inimitable fashion in his first letter to Henry Treece of July 1938, responding to Treece's accusation about the lack, in Thomas's poetry, of 'any social awareness'. Thomas bridles at this and insists that there is a kind of politics of attention in his work, which he distinguishes from the politics of planning that could be linked to the poetry of Auden and his associates:

> You meant, I know, that my poetry isn't concerned with politics (supposedly the science of achieving and 'administrating' human happiness) but with poetry (which is unsentimental revelation and to which happiness is no more important – or any other word – than misery) [. . .] You are right when you suggest that I think a squirrel stumbling at least of equal importance as Hitler's invasions, murder in Spain, the Garbo-Stokowski romance, royalty, Horlick's [*sic*], lynchlaw, pit disasters, Joe Louis, wicked capitalists, saintly communists, democracy, the Ashes, the Church of England, birthcontrol, Yeats' voice, the machines of the world I tick and revolve in, pub-baby-weather-government-football-youthandage-speed-lipstick, all small tyrannies, means tests, the fascist anger, the daily, momentary lightnings, eruptions, farts,

dampsquibs, barrelorgans, tinwhistles, howitzers, tiny death-rattles, volcanic whimpers of the world I eat, drink, love, work, hate and delight in – but I *am* aware of these things as well.[17]

Again, you get the syntax without measure, the registering of disparate items of information and sensory impressions, the lack of an order of importance, a lack of sequence; nothing in the sentence occupies a particular place; anything could be placed anywhere; nothing shows evidence of planning; and information derived from the media gradually gives way to information derived from the organs of observation, hearing, smell and taste. Thomas's very choice of title for his 1940 volume of short stories, *Portrait of the Artist as a Young Dog*, tells us that he has been thinking about a mode of apprehension of the world that is mobile, resourceful, omnivorous, only semi-domesticated, smelly, noisy and completely without prejudice in its assessment of the grounds for helping friends and harming enemies. It's a jokey title that hides an insistence – 'but I *am* aware of these things as well' – on a serious need to see, hear, taste and smell the world with heightened senses requiring an equivalent linguistic form of shape-shifting. I believe that in 'superpower' parlance, this is referred to as 'species-shifting'. Among contemporary writers, Donna Haraway has gone perhaps further than any other in her insistence on the need for 'companion-species relating'.[18] Her emphasis is not on a one-sided imaginative projection, but on systematic mutual interaction:

> Earth's beings are prehensile, opportunistic, ready to yoke unlikely partners into something new, something symbiogenetic. Co-constitutive companion species and co-evolution are the rule, not the exception. These arguments are tropic for my manifesto, but flesh and figure are not far apart.[19]

Thomas's writing in *Portrait of the Artist as a Young Dog* is conspicuously prehensile; its rhythm and syntax are those of an endlessly renewed form of attentiveness, testing the air and the lie of the land without preconception, reviewing the familiar with a thoroughly reformed order of priorities. Because of its alertness to the materials of language and the mouthing of its words, it brings life to the figure and almost literally embodies it in flesh. Perhaps inevitably, Haraway's professed favourite among the tropes she employs in her polemical writing is *metaplasm*, a term used in poetics to indicate alteration in the form of a word, through addition, subtraction or substitution of letters or sounds; Haraway uses it to denote the remodelling of relations between species rather than between verbal elements, the long-term aim of her advocacy being to 'remould kin links to help make a kinder and unfamiliar world'.[20] The strenuous obliqueness of Thomas's writing prevents him from making any such claim, but the unfamiliar world he uncovers in poetry and prose is a very local and familiar one in which we no longer feel ourselves, but something akin.

Notes

1. Thomas to Pamela Hansford Johnson, 15 April [1934], *CL*, pp. 139–40.
2. John Berger, 'Opening a Gate', in *The Shape of a Pocket* (London: Verso, 2001), pp. 5–6.
3. John Berger, 'Why Look at Animals', in *Why Look at Animals* (London: Penguin, 2009), p. 25.
4. Franz Kafka, 'Investigations of a Dog' [1922; published in translation by Willa and Edwin Muir in 1933] (London: Everyman, 1993), pp. 422–3.
5. Stefan Themerson, *Critics and My Talking Dog* (Black River Falls, WI: Obscure Publications, 2001), unnumbered pages [p. 1]. The publisher states in the colophon that 'It is believed this story was written around 1950.'
6. Ibid. [pp. 20–1].
7. Ibid. [pp. 23–4].
8. Virginia Woolf, *Flush*, ed. Kate Flint, with introduction and notes (Oxford: Oxford World's Classics, 1998), p. 105.
9. Ibid. p. 31.
10. Ibid. p. 16.
11. 'Just Like Little Dogs' (1939), *CS*, p. 182.
12. 'One Warm Saturday', *CS*, p. 241.
13. 'Just Like Little Dogs', *CS*, p. 184.
14. Ibid. p. 180.
15. Ibid. pp. 180–1.
16. David Sime, MD, *Rabies: Its Place among Germ-Diseases, and Its Origin in the Animal Kingdom* (Cambridge: Cambridge University Press, 1903), p. 42, cited in Geoff Gilbert, *Before Modernism Was: Modern History and the Constituency of Writing* (Basingstoke: Palgrave Macmillan, 2004), p. 127.
17. Thomas to Henry Treece, 6 or 7 July [1938], *CL*, p. 359.
18. Donna Haraway, *The Companion Species Manifesto: Dogs, People, and Significant Otherness* (Chicago: Prickly Paradigm Press, 2003), p. 20.
19. Ibid. p. 32.
20. Donna Haraway, 'Introduction', in *The Haraway Reader* (London: Routledge, 2003), p. 2.

Chapter 3

Staircases, fires; bombs, milk, wombs, wax, hangmen, sleep, rabbits, stew; a Mars Bar, pinpoints; lovely peaches

Deborah Bowman

> *D: What did you mean by a conversation having an outline? Has this conversation had an outline?*
> *F: Oh, surely, yes. But we cannot see it yet because the conversation isn't finished. You cannot ever see it while you're in the middle of it. Because if you could see it, you would be predictable — like the machine. And I would be predictable — and the two of us together would be predictable.*[1]

'Littérature, ou – la vengeance de "l'esprit de l'escalier"', formulated Paul Valéry: let's call literature the revenge of 'staircase wit', or 'the spirit of the staircase', 'a retort or remark that occurs to a person after the opportunity to make it has passed' when already you've left the hot salon or saloon, descending to your coat, the door, the chill air of the way home thinking of that thing you might have said, if only you had said it.[2] But writing, Valéry's *aperçu* suggests, means always being able to say it: get home, pick up the pencil, sit at the typewriter, open the laptop, make it new, and again, and again there will be time for the last word (even if that *mot*, like Valéry's, is going to fake a retake, or – a correction). Revenge is a fifth draft best served chilled, a revision can always trump a vision, and the literary world becomes a party where everyone's always already perfectly poised out here on the staircase all the time, saying our if onlys.

Reading them, too. Valéry's next aphorism considers 'Le plaisir ou l'ennui causé à un lecteur de 1912 par un livre écrit en 1612' – the enjoyment or annoyance sparked in the reader of a book written three centuries ago – and in doing so points to the way in which his eternal staircase is above all the haunt of readers who are all of us *esprits de l'escalier*, will not ever have been there when it happened and the brilliant *re* hit the mark or the page or the presses, but compensatingly have had and will have all the time in the world to make it out.[3] Our thoughts all are afterthoughts, but look,

> what often happens when a piece of writing is felt to offer hidden riches is that one phrase after another lights up and appears as the heart of it; one part after another catches fire, so that you walk about with the thing for several days.[4]

Cinders, we *shall* have gone to the ball.

* * * *

What shall we have read?

> The conversation of prayers about to be said
> By the child going to bed and the man on the stairs
> Who climbs to his dying love in her high room,
> The one not caring to whom in his sleep he will move
> And the other full of tears that she will be dead,
>
> Turns in the dark on the sound they know will arise
> Into the answering skies from the green ground,
> From the man on the stairs and the child by his bed.[5]

The first poem in Dylan Thomas's 1946 *Deaths and Entrances* – this is its opening – revolves around speech, its effects, and their relations in time. Its first line makes you wonder about what 'conversation' and 'prayers' have to do with each other, and then about the status of each when 'about to be said', for a conversation cannot 'turn' in advance of itself, and saying words is only part of saying prayers: any good child might go upstairs knowing that he's moments away from asking God to bless Mummy and Daddy and Auntie Ann and perhaps believing and wanting it just as much here and now on the stairs as he will in a minute there on his knees beside his bed; but he also knows, with J. L. Austin, that intentions alone be they ever so good will get you nowhere or worse, and that consequently he will have asked no such things until he's put his little hands together and his well-meanings into a certain form of words; has hereby said his prayers.[6] A conversation of prayers-about-to-be-said, then, emphasises that praying is, like promising and betting, a speech-act; and the way in which its speech may pre-exist its act, turned over in the mind and mouth beforehand, is crucial to this poem's tricks with time, which synchronise its events with and then pivot them on (and in, and about) the time of reading.

Or rather, times. Praying is a speech-act like promising and betting, and its *hereby*, like theirs, cannot but imply, because it seeks to inflect, a hereafter (at least one): speech-acts, then, are forms of words which in their focus on a present performance are also unavoidably entangled with future states. And in that they also resemble, as Emily Dickinson saw, poems:

> A word is dead, when it is said
> Some say –
> I say it just begins to live
> That day.[7]

As the suspicion of new auditory life quickens in the rhyme between 'dead' and 'said', and grows through 'say' to 'say' to 'day', saying slips from rumour ('Some say') to decree ('I say'). Dickinson's poem enacts both formally and logically the way in which the relation between 'Some say' and 'I say' is governed by a performative asymmetry which makes of any conversation between them something other than the music-hall patter of he-said-she-said; for while the indefinite subject 'some' retreats towards a generalised background of 'express[ing] the common or widespread belief that', the definite subject 'I' advances towards a foregrounded 'utter[ing], speak[ing]; [. . .] express[ing] in words, declar[ing]'.[8] 'I say' is always *I hereby say*. And the self-awareness of Dickinson's poems frequently turns, like Thomas's 'The conversation of prayers', on the way in which this performativity – the written first person's constant *hereby saying* – means that a future is already springing from the present even as you're not quite noticing it, so reading, you have always to be re-begetting your bearings:

> Could mortal lip divine
> The undeveloped Freight
> Of a delivered syllable
> 'Twould crumble with the weight.[9]

The way in which 'un*developed*' kind-of maps onto '*delivered*' feels the temptation to assume that an instance of verbal delivery coincides with the arrival of its full meaning; only kind-of maps, though, which, together with the way in which when you think about it 'Freight' and 'delivery' develop *develop*'s own etymological baggage – 'to open out (something folded or rolled up) [. . .]. Also: to remove the covering or wrapping from; to unwrap' – reminds you that delivery is just a beginning, for words once spoken are likely to open out into further significance in their interpretative futures: upon being, as you might say, as some might say, 'unpacked'.[10] As is the case, for example, with the last word in the phrase 'mortal lip divine', which, whatever you do with it on arrival (yours and its), is likely to gain at least another meaning as you read on. Should you have understood it as an adjective paying 'mortal lip' an oxymoronic compliment, the lack of a verb at the end of line 3 will send you back to unfold it into a verb meaning 'guess, intuit'; and should you have taken it, initially, as that verb, the fourth line's emphasis on mortality will open out its adjectival meaning 'immortal' to counterpoint what 'crumble with the weight' implies: not only structural weakness but Ozymandian temporal decay from the weight of waiting. (After a bit you might notice, too, the pressure exerted backwards by the F of Freight on *divine*'s *v*, suggesting, in among all this and as a commentary on all this, that, while to see one or another meaning at one time or another might be mortal, what's divine is overseeing and distinguishing among all of it in timeless now, like the dictionary, as *f* reaches back weightlessly simultaneously to *v* in the line before it: to define.)

(As somewhere along the while 'lip divine' could *develop* into *divinelip*.)

The time of a poem's saying, then, like that of any prayer, can be felt at once as corresponding to a present performance and as comprehending a long uncertain future. As in lines 9–12 of 'The conversation of prayers':

> The sound about to be said in the two prayers
> For the sleep in a safe land and the love who dies
>
> Will be the same grief flying. Whom shall they calm?
> Shall the child sleep unharmed or the man be crying?

Four lines are hesitating across the stanza-break at the poem's centre, between two eight-line sections each of which begin with 'The conversation of prayers about to be said'; and one and a half of them come straight at you, now, here, saying: 'Whom shall they calm? / Shall the child sleep unharmed or the man be crying?' Well? Shall they? Say which. *Say*: it's as if your word could be acted upon instanter, a choose-your-own-adventure bedtime story. A future comes up for grabs or air; but even as you're asked what's to happen, something has already, as 'his dying love' became 'the love who dies': not as those around her can see or might pray now to help, but like a character in a film you've seen ('*Which one is she?*' – '*The love who dies.*'), seen at a taxonomic distance through the wrong end of an affective and grammatical telescope. These lines are a caesura, a fault and a glimpse peeking at the long view of what it might be to read perfectly synchronically – each word simultaneously displaying its entire cargo of possible meaning – while at the same time suggesting not only the miseries but also the splendours of diachronicity; of feeling the weight of your reading gather in time; of guessing, missing, having missed, realising, returning, re-meaning. Of the versions of the self conversion considers; of the devil on the stairs; of saying what just begins to live this day, or die.

And of interpretation's long perspectives, which on Valéry's staircase stretch the development of each delivered syllable's Freight to infinity and so extend poetic unpacking from the most inspired or slapdash or naive or topically informed to the most painstakingly researched or profound or contextually ignorant or derivative apprehension conceivable. This scale has featured prominently in Thomas's critical reception: the poles of gut reaction and infinite reflection have both been advanced as its most appropriate and rewarding responses, and discussions of his work have polarised his own 'saying' as inspired, slapdash, naive, topically informed, painstakingly researched, profound, contextually ignorant and derivative. All rest on opinions about the extent to which in and around Thomas's writing *l'esprit de l'escalier* has been, or is, or should be, given the run of the house; about how and when and where and by whom and for what reason and to what effect the Freight of its delivered syllables is, might, should, shouldn't, could, can, can't be developed.

Because although

> what often happens when a piece of writing is felt to offer hidden riches is that one phrase after another lights up and appears as the heart of it; one part after another catches fire, so that you walk about with the thing for several days,

it's also true that

> Le plaisir ou l'ennui causé à un lecteur de 1912 par un livre écrit en 1612 est presque un pur hasard. [. . .] La gloire d'aujourd'hui dore les œuvres du passé avec la même intelligence qu'un incendie ou un ver dans une bibliothèque en mettent à détruire ceci ou cela.[11]

Out on this staircase – we're still here – our thoughts which all are afterthoughts are perhaps not very much like thoughts at all, and what that reader of 1912 finds lighting up in a years-old volume is a matter almost of pure chance. Today gilds the works of the past with only accidental intelligence: your discovery or mine of a poem's 'hidden riches' is like an act of God, one part after another catching fire randomly as flames or worms may consume. What Empson and Valéry put up again is something else always and undecidably for grabs: the location of the staircase, where fire, illumination, infestation, and gilding are slippages between library, book, and reader: 'one part after another catches fire', but 'you walk about with the thing for several days', smouldering yourself; look again and writing '*is felt* to offer hidden riches' and phrases '*appear* as the heart of it'. What shines on the edge of the page is the book's gilding (but who put it there?), and it comes off on your fingers and in the sunlight; shelves rarely self-combust, what a reader finds is '*presque* un pur hasard' (which cuts both ways), and even the common book- or paper-louse can be found to prefer, and to do so as a result of others' preferences; for

> we find in books not just what is in them but what we need from them – or what we need most, as the *Trogium pulsatorium* [. . .] feeds off the molds and other organic matter found in ill-maintained works in cool, damp, and neglected areas of archives and libraries.[12]

*   *   *   *

'Not just what is in them but what we need from them'; they are endless and/or we are insatiable. Empson put his finger prepositionally on the problem of that *and/or* in Thomas's poems:

> The difficulty about trying to give the meaning *in* prose is that the critic seems to be reading an unreasonable amount '*into*' the passage [. . .]. The extra meanings *are in* the detail all right, but they *are being put in* all the time, as part of the style.[13]

Meaning may appear 'in' your prose, but you are 'reading [it] into' the poem; meanings 'are in' there already but 'are being put in' at the same time, all the time you read. The thing about Thomas's poems, that is, is that they turn out to have more in them than is in them, and you don't know how it got there; which is true of poetry more generally, and is what Edwin Denby meant when he wrote that 'the difference between the "Ode on a Grecian Urn" and a letter on the editorial page of the *Daily News* isn't so great if you look at both of them without reading them. Art is certainly even more mysterious and nonsensical than daily life.'[14] He added that it was also 'a pleasure much more extraordinary than a hydrogen bomb is extraordinary'; Denby was writing in 1954, the year the United States tested initially in secret a hydrogen bomb which from a cylinder 179.5 inches in length and 53.9 inches in diameter mysteriously, nonsensically unpacked its fallout into seven thousand square miles of the Pacific Ocean and an international outcry. Twenty years earlier, Thomas's remarks on literary yield had pointed out more innocently a related absurdity: 'None of us today want to read poems which we can understand as easily as the front page of the *Express*, but we all want to get out of the poems twice as much as we ourselves put into them' (that was the year before Desmond Hawkins described *18 Poems* as 'the sort of bomb that bursts not more than once in three years', feeling the threat in unsolicited abundance).[15] And, earlier still,

William Empson had put over a page of *Seven Types of Ambiguity* into exploding five words of newsprint over a page of *Seven Types of Ambiguity*, pointing out that 'ITALIAN ASSASSIN BOMB PLOT DISASTER' operated, as do many poems, by 'convey[ing] its point [. . .] with a compactness which gives the mind several notions at one glance of the eye [. . .] with a force like that of its own favourite *bombs*'.[16]

Which explode, *OED: v.* 5.a. intr.: 'expand violently [. . .] under the influence of suddenly developed internal energy.' As Empson's headline and book demonstrated, literary works frequently detonate like this, a word or phrase 'develop'ing several meanings felt all at once – when '*Bomb* and *plot* [. . .] can be either nouns or verbs, and would take kindly to being adjectives, not that they are anything so definite';[17] or when 'conversation' means 'verbal exchange' but is also 'conversion' + 'say', and contains the word 'converse' meaning 'opposite', and the sound of the word 'verse' which means 'poetry' and 'a line of poetry', and comes from the Latin *vertĕre*, to turn (as might a staircase or a fate or a faith); and also contains (in a poem in which death hovers and the tomb) the French *ver*, worm – has that gone too far? have I? has Dylan Thomas? Because 'suddenly developed internal energy' may be generated by the ingredients in the shell-case or their exposure to and combination with an environment, or both; 'part of the style' is also what develops in my kind of reading. And the greater the suddenness of the development, the greater the suspicion that it can't all have been in there in the first place: that 'the critic seems to be reading an unreasonable amount "into" the passage'. Just as you might say the atmosphere contributes an unreasonable amount of oxygen to the explosion.

Thomas often described his writing process as one of putting-in: poems are '"watertight compartments"'; he was 'tightly packing away everything I have and know into a mad-doctor's bag'.[18] An early play draft casts 'The Spirit of Poetry' as a grocer in the 'Metaphysical Stores' where Thomas has 'used up all the available milk, wombs, wax, hangmen and sleep'.[19] *18 Poems* does include five milks, eight wombs, three waxes, one hangman and sixteen sleeps; but beyond a half-embarrassed, half-boastful awareness of his own verbal tics, Thomas's shopping list shows his interest in those elements of his poems which once combined could get out of his control, for all are ingredients which might in imagination swell, increase, and multiply not only themselves but into other things: wombs create babies which milk engrosses past infancy; to 'wax' is to grow, hangmen produce '*dead* flesh' which allows Thomas to, as he wrote, 'build up a *living* flesh from it', and for him, as for Goya, *The sleep of reason produces monsters* and dreams and tomorrow.[20] He 'let' his images, he wrote, 'breed', 'contradict' and 'conflict'.[21] And transcribing a 'steady scheme of consonantal rhyming' in a letter, he continued: 'I never use a full rhyme, but nearly always a half rhyme. [. . .] But perhaps this elaborate explanation has been a waste of time. You may have noticed it all before, for it has a strange effect.'[22] His qualificatory hedging ('nearly always', 'perhaps', 'may') both hints at near-rhyme's now-you-hear-it-now-you-don't quality, and adds into the mix the losses, interruptions and contingencies liable to intervene between a 'steady scheme' in composition and a 'strange effect' in reading.

His critics have been less cautious, both when asserting that Thomas's poems lack 'intelligent or intelligible control' (Empson summarises this as his having been 'attacked for (in effect) tossing the juice around so smudgily', neatly smudging cause and consequences, alcohol, inspiration and ink), or when rebutting it:[23] 'the regular form of ['Over Sir John's hill']', remarks Goodby, 'is visible at a glance (in fact, its five 14-line stanzas maintain an intricate regular syllable count of 5, 6, 14, 16, 5, 1, 15, 5, 14, 5, 14, 14 and an *aabccbdeaedd* pararhyme scheme).'[24] But this, like Alan Bold's claim that 'preference for the syllabic count instead of accentual verse enabled [Thomas] to construct his poems with a scrupulous attention to their aural impact', fails scrupulously to attend to English poetry and its readers, speakers and listeners; for English ears – unlike, say, French ones – are usually unbothered by anisosyllabism, and so, as Derek Attridge points out, 'most readers' of regular syllabics in English 'would probably not notice if one of the lines had a syllable more or a syllable less (though the counting of syllables may have been important in the creative process)'.[25] It's a telling parenthesis: to claim that syllabics are finely adjusted to 'aural impact' in English, or 'visible at a glance' (and how do you see a syllable?) not only ignores the evidence of their own readings – Bold's and Goodby's glances at 'Over Sir John's hill' yield different syllable-counts – but in a particular way elides 'intelligent' with 'intelligible control', making a claim that compositional effort can and will be losslessly appreciated.

This seems the point of such assertions: 'intelligible' writing justified as the nice echo of 'intelligent' design – that is, it must have been the poet and not the critic what done it. The cross-rhyming in 'The conversation of prayers', for instance, points to an architect's plan, beams which cannot exist in the eye of the beholder alone. The critic cannot have smuggled them in secretly prior to some triumphantly staged discovery, and that's reassuring, or something, to readers like Ralph Maud who anxiously 'believe that there is always, or almost always, one meaning given by the context which rings true', steeling themselves to be 'positively *Puritan*' when dealing with 'an abundance of alternative meanings'.[26] Look at them, look *there*, formal features are indisputably *in* the poem, not *in* my head.

They are stew, not rabbits.

What?

Rabbits first, in I. A. Richards's account of the genesis of *Seven Types of Ambiguity*:

> Taking the sonnet ['Th'expense of spirit'] as a conjurer takes his hat, [Empson] produced an endless swarm of lively rabbits from it and ended by saying 'You could do that with any poetry, couldn't you?'[27]

How do the rabbits get into the sonnet-hat? The conjuror-critic had them up his sleeve, to create only the effect of magic (and – which might be by the bye and might not – shame, and waste, and spirit, and lust in action – *lively* rabbits). With sufficient technique in sleight of hand you could do that with any hat, couldn't you? But the first chapter of *Seven Types of Ambiguity* sees this, which you couldn't:

> one may know what has been put into the pot, and recognise the objects in the stew, but the juice in which they are sustained must be regarded with a peculiar respect because they are all in there too, somehow, and one does not know how they are combined or held in suspension.[28]

Attending to ambiguity as Empson does involves recognising that all juices are to some extent smudgy, and that what Matthew Fort calls the 'polite exchange of flavours, [. . .] the fundamental principle of all stews and braises', applies to the words in a poem as to the ingredients in a pot; so that in the lines '[t]he sound about to be said in the two prayers / For the sleep in a safe land', 'sound' and 'sleep' and 'safe' come to taste of each other and different things too, the phrases 'sound asleep' and 'safe and sound'.[29] That example, though – like most noticings about literature – is a possible rabbit, in that you can't show that these associations were put in by Thomas and not pulled out of my sleeve. The advantage, to a certain critical mind set, of paying attention to formal features is that I'd have more difficulty doing that with a rhyme-scheme.

But if syllables might count 5-6-14-14-5-1-14-5-14-5-14-14, or it might be 5-6-14-16-5-1-15-5-14-5-14-14, and if what I hear with my little English ear is more like *short-short-long-long-short-reallyshort-long-short-long-short-long-long*, and if sometimes the 14s are 13s or 15s, and if *aabccbdeaedd* rhymes only with half-rhymes – how much can I taste at all of it as I read it, and how much does that matter? It's in this respect that Keith Selby likens Thomas's formal patterns to Sylvia Plath's as described by Eric Homberger, finding that '[m]any are just exercises'.[30] What's happening in Thomas's work, this suggests, is what William Gass saw in *À la recherche du temps perdu*, where

> there can be no doubt [Proust's] tapestry is intricate and cunningly worked;
> yet much of the so-called form [. . .] is meaningless [. . .] It placates critics
> who chase relations like lawyers trying to settle rich estates. An unfeelable
> form is a failure.[31]

Mid-century poetry in English, though, liked its forms both immediately feelable – Plath's brassy jingles, all those Movement villanelles and bouts of *terza rima* – and less so, from Thom Gunn's and Marianne Moore's invisible syllabics to Philip Larkin's late 'The Building', whose interfering patterns of seven-line stanzas and eight-line rhyme-scheme are further muffled by enjambement and half-rhyme.[32] But look! I felt those, didn't I, or else I couldn't describe them now, and neither could Gass have judged the cunning of Proust's needlework, or critics been placated; words dead when said might be still possessed of an ongoing life long as a Chancery suit in everlasting probate.

For – remember the staircase – who's to set the deadline by which you must have felt a form? No form even calculable is unfeelable. I may not receive any shock of rhyme-apprehension as I encounter the second word of a rhyme-pair many lines distant – the middles of the first and last lines of 'The conversation of prayers', say – but after noticing them whenever I do, my reading is charged and changed by knowing that they are all in there too, somehow, and one does not know how they are combined or held in suspension through their long stewing which was and is and after a while starts to feel that it increasingly will be my stewing over them. One does not know.

Thinking through the systems theory which was developing through the 1940s and 1950s as a way of knowing about things not immediately perceptible, Gregory Bateson reflected that:

> life depends upon interlocking circuits of contingency, while consciousness
> can see only such short arcs of such circuits as human purpose may direct.
> [. . .] – and love can survive only if wisdom (i.e., a sense or recognition of the
> fact of circuitry) has an effective voice.[33]

The much-commented-upon patterns and processes, systems and cycles and circulations of Thomas's poems are of their time in their preoccupation not only with 'the fact of circuitry' and its interlocking, but with its frequent hiddenness from first human sight and remove from apparent human purpose; under which circumstances to claim their intricacy as a defence against accusations of compositional carelessness is one thing, relevant, but to claim their at-a-glance visibility to a reader quite another, not. When in 1947 Empson came to revise *Seven Types of Ambiguity* for its second edition, his preface returned to criticisms that he'd refused to say, finally, whether ambiguity was located in the poem or the reader's mind, asking who, anyway, was the reader, for 'the point I am trying to make is that this final "judgment" is a thing which must be indefinitely postponed.'[34] That what will survive of us is love has to remain an almost-instinct only and merely almost true as far as we can see and hear and feel it, *so that* we can see and hear and feel it, and 'some say' come back to tell 'I say' about other ways of reading than this present moment; which may indeed feel remote from the hereby saying of human purpose. Gass is wrong, then, to doubt whether

> the fuses of [Proust's] involuntary memories [. . .] really set off the rest of the text; otherwise we should have to believe that, when those little powdered strings are lit, a miracle of physics occurs – one in which the boom blows up the bomb.[35]

For mortal lip rereading can divine and define from the wise *OED* that *bomb* is a translation of the 1588 Spanish 'bomba de fuego "a ball of wilde-fire"', which derives from 'bombo "a bumming or humming noise"', which is from 'Latin *bombus*. The word is thus ultimately identical with boom.'[36] Literature is a staircase and a circuit where the boom is forever blowing up the bomb.

*   *   *   *

And the force that through the green fuse drives the flower; or, in another word, promise: what today says it has undelivered and unde- veloped in it of tomorrow. Reading Thomas – dealing with Thomas too, by most accounts – was always about that. Empson remembered him, unemployed in wartime, 'telling me how frightening it was always to have nothing to do next day: sometimes, he said, "I buy a Mars Bar, and I think tomorrow I will eat that, so then I can go to sleep, because I have a plan".'[37] Tomorrow's Mars Bar gives you today's plan, which makes imaginable tomorrow; what's come to be called Thomas's 'process poetic' would be better termed a 'promise poetic', for promise was what for him made all the processes in the world go round: 'Just as a live body has its rhythms and its patterns and its promise (promise is perhaps the greatest thing in the world), so has a dead body [. . .] A dead body promises the earth as a live body promises its mate.'[38] Promise, in this circuit-diagram as in his remark to Empson, is what for Thomas produces futures out of presents. He counted on it often: his letters beg promises of pounds, shillings, and forgiveness, and themselves promise to deliver, write, repay, reform, turn up; the presence in his writing of what he termed elsewhere 'the huge, electric promise of the future' was complexly involved with the electrifying promise of his life as a famously promising poet.[39] The explosive possibility Desmond Hawkins had detected in *18 Poems* was revealed when he saw it as 'not merely a book of unusual promise; it is more probably the sort of bomb that bursts not more than once in three years' – and Robert Graves read Thomas's early poems thinking that 'poetic prodigies are [. . .] ill-omened [. . .] there is only promise, not performance' (his damning catching the faint shape of Edith Sitwell's praise: 'I could not name one poet of this [. . .] generation who shows so great a promise, and even so great an achievement').[40]

As these double-edged compliments suggest, one difficulty (promise being perhaps the greatest thing in the world) is that you have to get (it) out of the brackets to show it was there; inside them still it's only *perhaps* the greatest thing, and only perhaps describable as *in* the world. (My early promise, in order to have been itself, must be greater than itself but fulfilled only with something contained already within itself. Extraordinary like a bomb.) Thomas, who often reused or developed his own juvenilia, was sensitive to poetic perhapses and promises, as for example when lines from an early notebook poem – 'Some life, yet unspent, might explode / Out of the old lie burning on the ground' – find not only 'life' sprouting from 'lie', but suspect that Wilfred Owen's hissing shrapnel might still be live, if not alive. (Listen to it: 'The old Lie: Dulce et decorum est / Pro patria mori': *est*, *esssst*, it *is*.)[41] This is sharply aware of the way in which both propaganda and allusion – like Thomas's own early plagiarism and near-plagiarism – rely on the potential of some past charge which though possibly a dud might in new air catch and blow everything sky-high.[42]

But explosion ('issuing forth') could be a hope; when Thomas described his locked mad-doctor's bag it was in despair about unfulfillable promise:

> all you can see is the bag, all you can know is that it's full to the clasp, all you have to trust is that the invisible and intangible things packed away are – if they *could* only be seen and touched – worth quite a lot.[43]

But it might be a dud; all you can see is the bag, and 'what is said in Mr Thomas's poems', complained Julian Symons, 'is that the seasons change; that we decrease in vigour as we grow older; that life has no obvious meaning; that love dies. His poems mean no more than that. They mean too little.'[44] After Thomas's death, Empson noticed in critics 'a growing irritation with his poetry, caused by a belief that it is a hoax, not really meaning anything'. But what makes Empson a good reader is how he continues: 'A great deal of it, I confess, I have never cracked, and when people make sense of it I feel: "This is not enough".'[45] That is, he takes his initial observation that Thomas's 'early verse turns on rather few fundamental ideas, so that once you know what to expect you can find them with less effort' as merely a practical preliminary.[46] Symons found 'no more' in Thomas than his own paraphrase; what is 'not enough' for Empson isn't Thomas's writing but reductive critical glosses: criticism which elevates notes about the poem's 'fundamental ideas' into a finished article, preening itself upon its disappointed discrimination at having found so little.

The heresy of paraphrase is just that, to claim that it – and not its subject – is enough; promise and implication meanwhile never can be, and they know it. Seamus Perry notes that

> Faced with a poem that begins 'Light breaks where no sun shines; / Where no sea runs, the waters of the heart / Push in their tides', Glyn Jones, a sceptical friend, ventured that it 'probably expresses something pretty trite and commonplace, in prose terms, about the foetus and the pre-natal state'. That puts it harshly, but Jones was shrewd to pick up on the feeling in the lines, in which different possibilities somehow co-exist in a riddling state of as yet unrealised potentiality.[47]

Perry shrewdly picks up on the simultaneous under- and over-whelm of reading Thomas, the way in which his poems' fascination with and awed response to 'as yet unrealised potentiality' is always also 'something pretty trite and commonplace'. That's where, as Empson said, you start. Unborn babies just do have, just *are*, potential, but you try explaining one; potential is by its very definition a containment of the complex within the simple, and the formula of 'putting the complex into the simple' is itself one of the simplest versions of pastoral: aphoristically it asks and claims a That's all? which is at the same time That's *all*.[48] Pastoral turns Symons's yawn into also a gasp at 'unrealised potentiality', which is what Empson had seen as he looked into the poem-stewpot with 'a peculiar respect': it was 'the respect', he added, 'due to a profound lack of understanding for the notion of a potential', a phrase wondering at not only the mystery of things to come but the mysteriousness of the very idea that they will. This is what made Empson so perceptive about what Thomas called 'the invisible and intangible things packed away' in writing: his generosity towards and patience with the future, which lets it get there by itself while observing in his present self the effects of its uncertainty. 'There is still a lot of [Thomas's] poetry where I can feel it works and yet can't see why', he explained, but when a line 'seems very good [. . .] I assume on principle that there is something there which I feel and can't see, but could see'.[49] Could see … if what? That conditionless conditional is maddeningly accurate in its apprehension of how the future can look from now, for you can well believe a thing to be seeable without being at present able to foresee it or even its visibility to some other person; it does not thereby follow that you ought to stop looking.

Later, developing ambiguity into pastoral, Empson would call this position a 'sense of richness (readiness for argument not pursued)'.[50] His parentheses keep faith with, as in glossing they unfold but still hold in unpursued, the term's – and his own – promise, understanding that 'lack of understanding' can be profound in more than one way, and the job of a critic be to sound out those depths or as it may be shallows in herself, holding back from pursuit: (promise is perhaps the greatest thing in the world). Parentheses can do that: mark a different world and time, as in mathematics brackets indicate material for separate expansion. It was an analogy which Empson had tested:

> When Dr Johnson went to the Hebrides he took with him Cocker's *Arithmetic*, because (he said) you get tired of any work of literature, but a book of science is inexhaustible. When I was refugeeing across China (in 1937–39) I too had a little book of school Problems Papers, but it was worth carrying the poems of Dylan Thomas as well because they were equally inexhaustible.[51]

Confined to his chamber when he felt his fancy disordered, Johnson passed the time calculating the national debt as a girdle of silver (Mrs Thrale forgot how broad) around 'the globe of the whole earth, the real globe'; what Empson termed 'the concentration needed for poetry' makes promising poems just as handily expansible and absorbing, for in the absence of kindling what you want on the boat-train or in the airport's an infinitely unpackable tinderbox of a text so that you can walk about with the thing for several days or weeks or months, one part after another catching fire in you on your travels.[52] Brackets empty themselves over the books Empson travelled with into lengthy algebraic workings-out – his copy of Angela Thirkill's *August Folly* teems with polynomial equations – whose solutions were in there all the time, as-yet unseen; his 1947 comparisons of ambiguity's 'hidden riches' and 'teasing out the meaning of the text' to doing anagrams were written out of this same experience of travelling with few books and much time to fill.[53] 'One could spend a whole essay on the analysis of a few lines (any few lines)' by Thomas, noted Nicholas Moore;[54] Empson not only had patience with this promise but played patience with its difficulty, an activity which, while enjoyable, nevertheless admits the possibilities of boredom, frustration and wasted time, the detachment of parenthetical living; an undated notebook jotting – 'like Dylan Thomas – the pointless idea hanging about hoping for a point' – feels the tetchy *longueurs* of waiting to get on with things, but also sees the point of hanging about hoping.[55]

As does Thomas's 'Request to Leda (Homage to William Empson)'.[56]
Written as 'Request to Leda', an Empsonian parody in a pastiche detective story, the parenthesis added to its title upon the poem's first publication reappoints it to a new double life, in which Thomas's dense allusiveness can be played as knowing winks to Empson's style, and at the same time taken straight, as allusion:

> Not your winged lust but his must now change suit.
> The harp-waked Casanova rakes no range.
> The worm is (pin-point) rational in the fruit.[57]

What this nine-line poem knows about both writers could expand through pages of notes; its title and first two lines alone can tell that Empson wrote 'Invitation to Juno' and 'Homage to the British Museum', and about an affair ('suit') in Japan, using the refrain '[t]he heart of standing is you cannot fly', before flying back to Britain before the war;[58] that Thomas was born in and often left Wales ('harp-waked'), philandered ('Casanova', 'rake'), and was judged unfit for military service ('rakes no range' in a 'suit' of civvies, un'winged'). All these things happened.

But a 'Request' is as concerned with the future as an 'Homage' is with the past, and this poem with what isn't yet there as what was, its brackets wormholes from now to soon. For if this poem were the villanelle it promises to become, '(pin-point)' would eat through alternate stanza-ends like a Very Hungry Worm until lines one and three closed as jaws in a final couplet. This poem is not the villanelle it promises to become, but the first stanza of even a potential villanelle will imagine for you its last couplet, ready or not:

> Not your winged lust but his must now change suit.
> The worm is (pin-point) rational in the fruit.

As refrains will, 'Now change' has changed: a Metamorphosis into a metamorphosis, making an insect fable of the villanelle's certain promising, for insects' predictable life-cycles wing them for mating; 'change' first marked Thomas's alteration into Empson, but now suggests a need to emerge, as from pupation, into something else again, ugly duckling into swan. And other consequences play out and in other futures: Leda slept with her husband too, and the end of that night was two eggs and four babies, some proportion (a rational number, but stories vary) wormy with immortality. Helen is always said to be the child of Zeus. Parodies, requests and homages are fruitful with another's promise, but as parasites, are also worms in someone else's fruit; and Thomas's word-worm *rational* is or has an Empsonian mathematical maggot in the brain, 'a perverse fancy or desire; a streak of madness or insanity'.[59]

Now change. Crawled from the (pin-point) of a hole and the speck of an egg, a desire, an idea, their consequences like brackets, their contents opening like wings.

What can you know about that (pin-point)? That there's a 'pin-point' in Empson's 'Arachne'; that there's a 'pin's point' in Thomas's 'My world is pyramid'.[60] That nobody knows how many angels can dance there; no, more, that discussion of them stands for 'simply a debating exercise' and a dance of *as ifs* about unknowing.[61] But to pin-point is accurately to locate, as I. A. Richards did – remembering the whole of *The Meaning of Meaning* 'talked out' with C. K. Ogden between 23:00 and 01:00 on 11–12 November 1918, on the staircase of 1 Free School Lane, Cambridge, England – when he called this 'a curiously pin-pointed starting point'.[62] All the contents of a book in two hours on a staircase and how many angels in how little room? These are the same question, and

> [t]he answer usually adjudged correct is [. . .] they may have location in space but not extension. [. . .] Thus, if your thought is concentrated upon one thing – say, the point of a needle – it is located there in the sense that it is not elsewhere; but although it is 'there' it occupies no space there, and there is nothing to prevent an infinite number of different people's thoughts being concentrated upon the same needle-point at the same time.[63]

Or the same imagined ending of a villanelle occupying no space on any page. A parenthesis in it which 'may be thence without any detriment to the rest' as if not there.[64] And the point at its centre which mathematically 'is conceived as having position but no extent, magnitude, dimension, or direction'; all the things you might do or not do, or think dancing in or on all your futures and promises; and ambiguity, expanded in the second edition of 1947 into 'any verbal nuance, however slight, which gives room for alternative reactions to the same piece of language', room however many should happen and to whom, at the same time and in all later others.[65] A mad-doctor's bag which can now (you see?) hold open any of its and my and your contents and discontents. A promise in all its yets as-yet invisible. What's inside a tin of peaches unopened in a story by Dylan Thomas.

* * * *

The narrator's aunt has been 'keeping it for a day like this', teased by cousin Gwilym; '"a large tin of peaches"', she calls it, and again, "They're lovely peaches"', she says; to her visitor, '"you must"', '"just one"', '"they're lovely"'.[66] But they're refused, and later the boy in bed hears talk downstairs: '"Mrs Williams," she said, and "motor car," and

"Jack," and "peaches." I thought she was crying for her voice broke on the last word.'[67] That innocently relayed voice-break marks something which you can feel but know you could never prove, so that unknowing spills out from the narrator into the possibilities of the whole story's world like the loveliness of the peaches from the unopened tin with no boundaries breached and the mad-doctor's bag still intact.

In 'The Peaches', the child narrator's naive descriptions repeatedly suggest both that something is happening (as you realise), and that the child doesn't realise it; but the child will then seem perhaps to realise; or perhaps not. This device needs more complex a name than that blunt instrument 'unreliable narration', for what this proposes, like other stories in *Portrait of the Artist as a Young Dog*, is not the unreliability but the unrelatability of all internally focalised narration: that true internal focalisation would be as blankly incomprehensible as external focalisation. Insides and outsides, it insists, are not that simple; people are often radically incomprehensible to themselves, as when the couples in 'Just Like Little Dogs' have sex in the dunes, then swap, and marry in two wrong, loveless, pairings: they 'never understood why' any more than they can determine their babies' paternity.[68] 'The Peaches' is the epicentre of this blankness, in which speech-acts of a usually elucidatory nature – admission, explanation, confession – collapse into opacity. Does the narrator understand what it means to say that Uncle Jim is like a fox, or what his cousin is doing in the outside lavatory 'reading a book and moving his hands'? (While his description suggests he doesn't, his reaction – '"We can see you!"' – might or might not.[69]) Did he commit all or any of the crimes he lists, unspeechmarked, before saying out loud he has nothing to confess?[70] Is the hangman's house inhabited (a light is on) or abandoned (as Uncle Jim claims)?[71] Contained, out of sight, the indeterminable: in the pub, in the dark, in a house in the dark, in an outside lavatory, in a barn, in the secrecy of your past misdeeds or imaginings, downstairs when you're upstairs in bed; in the tin of peaches. Her voice broke on the last word.

For he did describe his poems as '"watertight compartments"', but Thomas later explained it otherwise: 'The best craftsmanship always leaves holes and gaps in the works of the poem so that something that is *not* in the poem can creep, crawl, flash, or thunder in.'[72] These holes and gaps are what Gass tries the boundaries of in Gertrude Stein's *Tender Buttons*:

> the text is, I think, overclued [. . .]; nevertheless, the 'total altogether of it' remains cryptic, and we are likely to feel that our interpretations are forced unless they are confirmed by readings from another direction. [. . .] Thus this is certainly not an airtight text. It leaks. But where? and why should we care?

It will not tell us what day the bridge is to be bombed, the safe rifled, or buck passed. We must set to work without reward or hope of any.[73]

What writing 'will not tell' remains resiliently intact, untouched and even protected by what it invites into itself, a collected corroboration which lets in doubt even as it plugs the background with one more pixel (*They are gathered at the point of delicious ripeness*, boasts a marketing leaflet from 1938, the year of 'The Peaches', *and a few brief hours after being picked the fruit is cooked and sealed in cans, secure from injury or contamination, and then remains ready for long months, even years, to be opened for the pleasures of the table*).[74] And these are also those holes and gaps in criticism which Empson defends when, commenting on a student's essay on Hart Crane – a poet he compared with Thomas – he writes: 'I think your analysis is right as far as it goes but if completed leaves no word which is at all meaningless.'[75] *But*, not *and*.

Completion, reward, hope of it, fulfilment are then threats as well as promises, and rewards and hopes of setting to work, for what so often creeps, crawls, flashes or thunders into interpretation is suggested by John Berger's account of reading a photograph: 'Meaning is dis-covered in [. . .] what cannot exist without development. Without a story, without unfolding, there is no meaning [. . .]. Certainty may be instantaneous; doubt requires duration; meaning is born of the two.'[76] Berger's description is another dance of knowing with unknowing, and the unknown value is occupied by time. A phrase or a tin of peaches, however you might think it preserved, is subject to and develops in all the pleasures which might even dwell on and implicate it, injured and contaminated, treasured since you found it, saved for a day like this. But Berger's elegantly aphoristic formulation lets in too little and seals itself up too quickly, as if meaning happened once, and I were looking back through all duration to the instant it certainly began, as if it weren't starting all around and about me now. What Wayne Koestenbaum calls the 'glaze' produced in and as reading – a finish, a drivel, a syrupy transparent addition, an interpretation which is its own distraction – corrects this: 'I depict glaze as the realm of throttled enigma [. . .] but also with a fantasy-life given free rein to meander and to amplify its own overtones.'[77] I can't get over myself, is what this surface reflects, and I have all the time in the world not to do it. Which is all, as Berger elsewhere more suggestively indicates, that a reading, like writing, like a photograph, might promise: 'The minimal message [. . .] may be less simple than we first thought [. . .]: *The degree to which I believe this is worth looking at can be judged by all that I am willingly not showing because it is contained within it*.'[78] I think your analysis is right as far as it goes but if completed leaves no word which is at all meaningless. Thus this is certainly not an airtight text. It leaks. They're lovely peaches.

Notes

1. Gregory Bateson, 'Metalogue: Why Do Things Have Outlines?' (1953), in *Steps to an Ecology of Mind* (Chicago and London: University of Chicago Press, 2000), pp. 27–32 (p. 32).
2. Paul Valéry, *Rhumbs*, in *Tel Quel*, 2 vols (Paris: Gallimard, 1944), II, pp. 7–101 (p. 70); 'esprit, *n.*, 2.c.': all definitions and etymological references are from the *Oxford English Dictionary* online (*OED*): <http://www.oed.com> (last accessed 15 March 2016).
3. Ibid. p. 70.
4. William Empson, 'Preface to the Second Edition' (1947), in *Seven Types of Ambiguity* (London: Chatto & Windus [1930; 3rd edn, 1953]; Harmondsworth: Penguin, 1995), pp. vii–xv (p. xi).
5. 'The conversation of prayers', *CP14*, pp. 171–2, ll. 1–8.
6. See J. L. Austin, *How to Do Things with Words*, ed. J. O. Urmson (Oxford: Oxford University Press, 1962).
7. Emily Dickinson, F278A.1, *The Poems of Emily Dickinson*, ed. R. W. Franklin, 3 vols (Cambridge, MA, and London: Belknap Press of Harvard University Press, 1998), I, p. 297.
8. *OED*: 'say, *v.*1 and *int.*' 9.a; I.
9. Dickinson, F1456B, *The Poems*, III, p. 1277.
10. *OED*: 'develop, *v.*', 2.†a.
11. Valéry, *Rhumbs*, pp. 70–1.
12. 'The Impossible Bookshop', *Dublin Review of Books Blog* (27 February 2013): <www.drb.ie/blog/the-book/2013/02/27/the-impossible-bookshop#sthash.DjcOUHSQ.dpuf> (last accessed 15 March 2016).
13. William Empson, 'To Understand a Modern Poem' (1947), in *Argufying: Essays on Literature and Culture*, ed. John Haffenden (London: Chatto & Windus, 1987), pp. 382–6 (p. 383 [my italics]).
14. Edwin Denby, 'Dancers, Buildings, and People in the Streets' (1954), in *Dance Writings*, ed. Robert Cornfield and William MacKay (London: Dance Books, 1986), pp. 548–56 (p. 556).
15. Thomas to Glyn Jones, [c. 14 March 1934], *CL*, p. 122; Desmond Hawkins, 'Poetry', *Time and Tide*, 45.6 (9 February 1935), 204.
16. Empson, *Seven Types of Ambiguity*, p. 236.
17. Ibid. p. 237.
18. Thomas to Henry Treece, 16 May 1938, *CL*, p. 344; Thomas to Vernon Watkins, [20 April 1936], *CL*, p. 249.
19. Thomas to Pamela Hansford Johnson, [January 1934], *CL*, p. 117.
20. Thomas to Johnson, [c. 21 December 1933], *CL*, p. 89; Francisco Goya, *El sueño de la razón produce monstruos* (1799) [Etching, aquatint, drypoint and burin]. Metropolitan Museum of Art, New York.
21. Thomas to Treece, 23 March 1938, *CL*, p. 328.
22. Thomas to Johnson, [early November 1933], *CL*, p. 58.

23. *CL*, p. 297 (see also Geoffrey Grigson, 'How Much Me Now Your Acrobatics Amaze', in *Dylan Thomas: The Legend and the Poet*, ed. E. W. Tedlock (London: Heinemann, 1963), pp. 155–67); William Empson, review of *Collected Poems* and *Under Milk Wood*, *New Statesman and Nation*, 15 May 1954, repr. in *Argufying*, pp. 391–5 (p. 391).

24. Goodby, *The Poetry of Dylan Thomas*, p. 14. See also, for example, Jacob Korg, 'Dylan Thomas's Concept of the Poet', in *Dylan Thomas: Craft or Sullen Art*, ed. Alan Bold (London: Vision Press, 1990), pp. 15–34 (p. 21); and, in the same volume, Gareth Thomas, 'A Freak User of Words', pp. 65–88; and Alan Bold, 'Young Heaven's Fold: The Second Childhood of Dylan Thomas', pp. 156–74.

25. Bold, 'Young Heaven's Fold', p. 157; Derek Attridge, *Poetic Rhythm: An Introduction* (Cambridge: Cambridge University Press, 1995), p. 107.

26. Ralph Maud, *Where Have the Old Words Got Me? Explications of Dylan Thomas's Collected Poems, 1934–1953* (Cardiff: University of Wales Press, 2003), pp. xvi, xvii.

27. I. A. Richards, 'William Empson', *Furioso*, 1.3 (1940), [n.p.].

28. Empson, *Seven Types of Ambiguity*, p. 6.

29. Matthew Fort, *Sweet Honey, Bitter Lemons* (London: Ebury Press, 2008), p. 304.

30. Keith Selby, 'Hitting the Right Note: The Potency of Cheap Music', in *Dylan Thomas: Craft or Sullen Art*, pp. 89–111 (pp. 101–2).

31. William H. Gass, 'Proust at 100', in *The World within the Word* (New York: Basic Books, 2000), pp. 145–57 (p. 155).

32. Philip Larkin, 'The Building', in *Collected Poems*, ed. Anthony Thwaite (London: Faber, 2003), pp. 136–8.

33. Bateson, 'Style, Grace, and Information in Primitive Art' (1967), in *Steps to an Ecology of Mind*, pp. 128–52 (p. 146).

34. Empson, *Seven Types of Ambiguity*, p. xv.

35. Gass, 'Proust at 100', p. 155.

36. *OED*: 'bomb, *n.*'.

37. Empson, *Argufying*, p. 407.

38. Thomas to Johnson, [25 December 1933], *CL*, p. 97.

39. Thomas to Johnson, [week of 11 November 1933], *CL*, p. 73.

40. Robert Graves, *The Crowning Privilege: Collected Essays on Poetry* (Harmondsworth: Penguin, 1955), p. 154; Edith Sitwell, 'A New Poet', *The Sunday Times*, 15 November 1936, 9.

41. 'I have longed to move away', *CP14*, p. 20, ll. 12–13; Wilfred Owen, 'Dulce et Decorum Est', in *The Complete Poems and Fragments: Volume I: The Poems*, ed. Jon Stallworthy (London: Chatto & Windus, 2013), p. 140, ll. 2–8.

42. See Jeff Towns, '"Borrowed Plumes" – Requiem for a Plagiarist', in *Dylan Thomas: A Centenary Celebration*, ed. Hannah Ellis (London: Bloomsbury, 2014), pp. 42–61.

43. Thomas to Watkins, [20 April 1936], *CL*, p. 249.

44. Julian Symons, 'Obscurity and Dylan Thomas', *The Kenyon Review*, 2.1 (Winter 1939/40), 61–71 (p. 71).

45. Empson, *Argufying*, p. 405.

46. Ibid. p. 391.

47. Seamus Perry, 'Everything is good news', *London Review of Books*, 36.22 (20 November 2014), 5–8 (pp. 5–6).
48. William Empson, *Some Versions of Pastoral*, reissued with 'Preface to 1974 edition' (Harmondsworth: Penguin, 1995 [1935]), p. 25.
49. Empson, *Argufying*, p. 393.
50. Empson, *Pastoral*, p. 118.
51. Empson, *Argufying*, p. 392.
52. Hester Lynch Thrale, cited in George Birkbeck Hill (ed.), *Johnsonian Miscellanies*, 2 vols (Oxford: Clarendon Press 1897, repr. London: Constable, 1966), I, p. 200; Empson, *Pastoral*, p. 25.
53. Empson, *Seven Types of Ambiguity*, p. 10.
54. Nicholas Moore, 'The Poetry of Dylan Thomas', *The Poetry Quarterly*, 10.4 (1948), 229–36 (p. 231).
55. (MS Eng 1401) 1105, William Empson Papers, Cambridge, MA, Houghton Library, Harvard University.
56. I discuss the text printed in *Horizon*, 5.30 (1942), 6, and Dylan Thomas and John Davenport, *The Death of the King's Canary* (Harmondsworth: Penguin, 1978), pp. 18-19; Goodby prints the unexplained variant 'The harp-waked Casanova wakes no change', *CP14*, p. 129, l. 2.
57. 'Request to Leda (Homage to William Empson)', ll. 1–3.
58. *The Complete Poems of William Empson*, ed. John Haffenden (London: Allen Lane, 2000), pp. 12, 55, 69–70.
59. *OED*: 'worm, *n.*', 11.†b.
60. Empson, 'Arachne', *The Complete Poems*, p. 34; 'My world is pyramid', *CP14*, p. 65.
61. Dorothy L. Sayers, 'The Lost Tools of Learning' (1947), in *The Poetry of Search and the Poetry of Statement* (London: Gollancz, 1963), pp. 155–76 (p. 162).
62. B. Ambler Boucher and John Paul Russo, 'An Interview with I. A. Richards', *The Harvard Crimson* (11 March 1969): <http://www.thecrimson.com/article/1969/3/11/an-interview-with-i-a-richards/?page=1> (last accessed 15 March 2016).
63. Sayers, 'The Lost Tools of Learning', pp. 162–3.
64. George Puttenham, *The Art of English Poesy* (1589), in *Sidney's 'The Defence of Poesy' and Selected Renaissance Literary Criticism*, ed. Gavin Alexander (London: Penguin, 2004), p. 153.
65. Empson, *Seven Types of Ambiguity*, p. 19.
66. 'The Peaches' (1938), *CS*, pp. 126–42 (p. 134).
67. Ibid. p. 141.
68. 'Just Like Little Dogs', *CS*, pp. 179–85 (p. 184).
69. 'The Peaches', *CS*, p. 138.
70. Ibid. p. 139.
71. Ibid. p. 135.
72. 'Poetic Manifesto' (1961), *EPW*, pp. 154–60 (p. 160).
73. Gass, 'Gertrude Stein and the Geography of the Sentence', in *The World within the Word*, pp. 63–123 (pp. 89–90).
74. 'Delicious Australian Canned Fruits', October 1938: <http://www.hub-uk.com/specials/special0020.htm> (last accessed 15 March 2016).
75. William Empson, Bernard Heringman and John Unterecker, 'Three Critics

on One Poem: Hart Crane's "Voyages III"', *Essays in Criticism*, 46.1 (1996), 16–27 (p. 23). Undated draft exam questions by Empson substitute Crane's name for Thomas's, and suggest 'Compare Crane with Dylan Thomas' ((MS Eng 1401) 1050, Empson Papers).

76. John Berger, *Understanding a Photograph*, ed. Geoff Dyer (Harmondsworth: Penguin, 2013), p. 64.
77. Wayne Koestenbaum, *Notes on Glaze: 18 Photographic Investigations* (New York: Cabinet, 2016), p. 13.
78. Berger, *Understanding a Photograph*, p. 21.

Chapter 4

Dylan Thomas: 'On out of sound'

Peter Robinson

Dylan Thomas liked to generate poetic sense by the vertical substitution of related lexical items in familiar phrases. The last line of the third verse of 'The hunchback in the park' takes 'out of sight' and 'sight and sound' and produces the original, but oddly familiar, '[o]n out of sound'.[1] Five years later, he adapted the same phrase in the 1946 BBC Wales radio broadcast 'The Crumbs of One Man's Year', describing a Fifth of November scene in which the Guy 'was a long time dying on the hill over the starlit fields where the tabby river, without a message, ran on, with bells and trout and tins and bangles and literature and cats in it, to the sea never out of sound.'[2] Thomas was criticised for the 'sound and fury signifying nothing' side of his poetry, as for instance when Bernard Spencer reviewed *Twenty-five Poems* in the Christmas 1936 issue of *New Verse*: 'These poems strike one immediately because of their resonance (sometimes their rhythm is monotonous), their swirl of vigorous images, and, even before they are understood, their flavour of psychology and metaphysics.' The reviewer adds that they 'divide more or less clearly into sense and nonsense-poems', and he concludes by praising ones where the poet's 'fertility and remarkable sensitiveness to words does really ring the bell', poems such as 'The hand that signed the paper' which 'has concentrated the peculiar horror and mindlessness of modern politics.'[3] The distinction is arbitrary and the line hard to draw, but it shadows an evolution in Thomas's work suggested by the poet himself.

'The hunchback in the park' might seem such a 'sense' poem, unusually straightforward and quotidian in its setting, yet, understood even as it is being read, it too has 'resonance' and 'swirl' and a 'flavour of psychology and metaphysics'. It also confuses any simple evolution from 'nonsense' to 'sense', given that it derives from an early notebook sketch. Reflecting on the May 1932 draft poem, I identify weaknesses to be addressed in the July 1941 rewriting. The aim in this chapter is, then, to relate the character and action of that rewriting process to Thomas's contextualising of the poem in 'Reminiscences of Childhood' (1943). I further suggest that the 'sound' of Thomas's poetry is an unusually successful attempt to combine a personally obsessional exploration with widely applicable cultural significance.

'The hunchback in the park': 9 May 1932

William Empson, best and most stalwart of Thomas's early critics, thought the 1941 sale of the notebooks to Buffalo a good sign:

> One had heard that his first two volumes of poetry were drawn, though with some changes, from notebooks compiled before he was twenty; but it is news (to me at any rate) that he sold the talisman on reaching the age when Keats died ('It's lovely when you burn your boats. They burn so beautifully'), so that the poems written after 1941 proved to him that he could do without it. Surely, it is tiresome to hear critics upbraid the 'infantilism' of a man who could do that? Some of the early poems I think are the best, but some of the later ones undoubtedly have his full power.[4]

'The hunchback in the park' was (excepting a few lines mined for 'Holy Spring') the last work Thomas revised from his early notebooks before selling them. It stands at a watershed between the early and later poems. Sight-filled spaces and sounds in 'The hunchback in the park' evoke limits and continuities, which reach on 'out of' or are 'never out of sound.'[5] Being 'out of sound' locates the no-longer hearer firmly in one place, while the 'never out of sound' evokes what Seamus Heaney named 'Dylan the Durable', a permanent presence in the culture.[6]

The colloquial source of that 'sound' phrase concludes the first stanza of the 9 May 1932 draft. Square brackets introduced by Ralph Maud indicate notebook deletions:

> The hunchback in the park,
> A solitary mister
> Propped between trees and water,
> Going daft for fifty seven years,
> Is [getting] dafter,
> A cripple children call at,
> Half-laughing, by no other name than mister,
> They shout hey mister
> Running when he has heard them clearly
> Past lake and rockery
> On out of sight.[7]

Here 'running [. . .] out of sight' takes the poem's focus further on with the children beyond the sight of the hunchback, while 'out of sound' keeps us nearer to him and his senses. The first three lines above appear exactly, though without end punctuation, as the opening of 'The hunchback in the park'. The faltering rhythmic impulse in '[g]oing daft for fifty seven years' is relieved in the work dated 16 July 1941 (subsequently published that October in *Life and Letters Today*) by means of the six-line verse structure with its irregular rhymes and flexible rhythms ranging between five, four, three and two stresses. Such a faltering rhythm aptly qualifies the 'figure without fault' that the hunchback is imagined to make 'inside his hanging head' in the 1932 draft, or 'straight and tall from his crooked bones' in the 1941 poem.

The middle two verses of the early draft outline the poem's main action:

> There is a thing he makes when quiet comes
> To the young nurses with the children
> And the three veteran swans,
> Makes a thing inside the hanging head,
> [A] figure without fault
> And sees it on the gravel paths
> Or walking on the water.

> The figure's frozen all the winter
> Until the summer melts it down
> To make a figure without fault.
> [It is a poem and it is a woman figure.][8]

Drawing on the deleted 'It is a poem and it is a woman figure', which spells out a metaphorical strand implicit in the revision, the 1941 work shapes an identification of the poet with the hunchback.[9] The romantic image of a damaged poet compelled to seek perfection in imaginatively creative projections is reinforced by two other identifications in the symbolising modes of Thomas's verse. That the hunchback in the revision makes the flawless woman figure from 'his crooked bones' recalls God creating woman out of Adam's rib, while the 1932 notebook draft's having the hunchback see this figure 'on the gravel paths / Or walking on the water' conjures up the second Adam's exploit on the Sea of Galilee. These biblical associations help sponsor identification, also made by John Goodby, in his further notes to the poem, of the park with the Garden of Eden – its opening a creation myth, its closure seeing fallen man expelled at the tolling of the bell, the memory of a created-perfect woman preserved until the next morning.

There's little harm in such large meaning promotion, though 'The hunchback in the park' also resists it in a number of ways – by not preserving the walking on the water idea, or the overt identification between hunchback and poet in the removal of the painfully literal metaphor linking the imagined woman to 'a poem'. This resistance may be a response to an evident failure of inspiration in the 1932 draft. Its final seven lines are about the transformation of the hunchback's taunting into a compensatory indication of happiness or inner strength:

> Mister, the children call, hey mister,
> And the hunchback in the park
> Sees the figure on the water,
> Misty, now mistier,
> Hears it's [*sic*] woman's voice;
> Mister, it calls, hey mister,
> [And the hunchback smiles.][10]

The deletion of this final line suggests that the 1932 poet's attempt to tease meaning from the poem's occasion failed to satisfy. One problem the draft illustrates is, then, that key lyrical trajectory of a movement from sponsoring occasion to drawn-out significance. The poet attempts to adopt the hunchback as a means for transforming humiliated imperfection into inner muse-inspired resilience. The woman's voice speaks to the hunchback here, echoing the taunting boys, but with a transformed implication – one the hunchback's smile aims to underline. Yet the draft ends at the point where it lamely asserts what it can't embody. It thus feels wishful because its conclusion is an assertion unsupported by the deed of rhythmic or metaphoric performance.

Before touching on how Thomas addressed these problems in his 1941 rewriting, I turn now to Jon Silkin's view of this passage in the 1932 draft. 'But in noticing', he writes, 'the almost declarative tone in such accessibility in the received version we might (I do) regret the loss of the lovely sonic play' in the last five lines of the notebook text. The poem's revision

> is wonderful writing, yet 'writing' (I say this with much hesitation) is what it has become, sacrificing the intimate interjection of 'Misty, now mistier' and the extreme delicacy of its punning with 'Mister'. For isn't this the point of both poems, that the crooked man daydreams his exact wishful restorative opposite; and so this interlinking pun does it in a way that the later substituted, more declarative, simplicity doesn't.[11]

Silkin's points are all valuable, but I disagree about the pun. To my ear, it doesn't have 'extreme delicacy'. Rather, it needs treating with extreme delicacy to work as Silkin wishes. The pun itself draws attention to what is wishful about the draft's offered solution to the hunchback's plight, by making it turn upon the misty figure on the water being able to call to the mister, or be heard to call by him. The entire shift from the everyday description of the park and its inhabitants to the transformative fiction, the art of the poem, hinges on this pun. The sleight of hand and mind upon which the draft depends is shown to be a trick – by having it rest upon the joke that the superlative of 'misty' and 'mistier' is not mistiest, but 'Mister'. Thomas could see that it didn't work, not least because there was no art concealing art here, rather a show of how precariously joking, not delicately so, was the thread that leads to the gesturing close of the hunchback's smile – a smile that is self-satisfying, a word which can't help bringing in the anxiety that the imagined woman is a projection from sexual fantasy.

Silkin notes that this creation of a 'wishful restorative opposite' is 'the point of both poems'; but commenting on the cancelled last line of the 1932 draft, he draws attention to another level of point, and points, that casts a retrospective doubt over the eighteen-year-old poet's idea of how the ordinary could be made significant:

> In the first version the smiling depends only upon himself. The ending of the ultimate version, however, shows Thomas's fine capacity to open the poem out beyond interlocutions with himself (*pace* his hostile critics) to the mister's relationship with society – boys, dog, nurses, swans, and park keeper (authority). One notices that the syntax and meaning need little punctuation, and that only the minimum of full stops is provided – with the exception of punctuational stanza spaces.[12]

The poem opening out beyond a notional self-satisfaction that produces the smile appears, in the conjunction of Silkin's sentences, to be related to the rhythmic, stanzaic and punctuational strategies of the revision. If the compensatory imaginative effort of the poem, its imagining the woman for the hunchback, is to be identified with the poet, and the revised poem moves beyond this to 'the mister's relationship with society', then this implicates the theme of the poet's own relation with society. It implies that the revised poem is also significantly qualifying the necessary relation of this compensatory activity to the larger social space that Silkin both identifies and goes on to justify when he associates it with the time in which the revision was made: 'the poem was rewritten in the midst of war', and 'what this experienced dimension of war finely adds is that of the confrontational element between the children's mockery and the hunchback's loneliness and vulnerability.'[13] It will be important to bear in mind, though, that the revised poem's inner dynamic, however worked upon by the wartime circumstances of returning to and selling the notebooks, depends upon the poet's and readers' identification with both the mocking boys and the isolated hunchback.

'The hunchback in the park': 16 July 1941

The first thing Thomas had to do in July 1941 to make his old draft work was to develop the side of the poem that recalls a real park and the poet's real childhood, his being a boy and seeing the hunchback, delaying the imaginatively transformative action of the poem, and refraining from any overt statement of what this imaginative creation might mean or do for either the hunchback, the poet, or readers of the poem. In his transcription of the revision, Maud prints the first four of the poem's seven verses as a single block, suggesting that the stanzaic structure was only realised in the course of the more securely rhythmical rewrite:

> The hunchback in the park
> A solitary mister
> Propped between trees and water
> From the opening of the garden lock
> That let the trees and water enter
> Until the (church-black) bell at dark (Sunday sombre)
> Eating bread from a newspaper
> Drinking water from the chained cup
> That the children filled with gravel
>   In the fountain basin where I sailed my ship
> Slept at night in a dog kennel
> But nobody chained him up.
> Like the park birds he came early
> Like the water he sat down
> And mister they called hey mister
> The (mitching) boys from the town (truant)
> Running when he had heard them clearly
> [Past lake and rockery]
> On out of sound[.]
> Past lake and rockery
> Laughing when he shook his paper
> Through the (Indian ambush) of the willow groves ([wild] loud zoo)
> Hunchbacked in mockery
> Dodging the park keeper
> With his stick that picked up leaves.[14]

It seems unlikely from this transcription that the poet in his craft and sullen art had already decided on the six-line stanza, not least because of the accumulated clauses separating the subject named 'The hunchback in the park' in line 1 from its main verb '[s]lept' in line 10. Introduction of the stanza breaks creates some initial construal difficulties for the poem. The firm full stop after 'chained him up' suggests an initial idea of twelve-line stanzas, while the deletion of the full stop after '[o]n out of sound', and the deletion and transfer of the line '[p]ast lake and rockery' from the position it held in the 1932 draft to its place as the first line of the fourth verse, suggests a realisation that it is settling into six-line groups. The revision of 'church-black' to 'Sunday sombre' in line 6 may relate to the same awareness, for the additional weak syllables in the substituted phrase lengthen the line to a pentameter, rounding off that group and sustaining the bell chime of the bracketing rhyme on 'park' and 'dark'.

From this point on, the transcription reports the establishment of a stanzaic pattern:

> And the old dog sleeper
> Alone between nurses and swans
> While the boys among willows
> Made the tiger jump out of their eyes
> [Apes – danced] To roar on the rockery stones
> And the groves were blue with sailors
>
> Made all day until bell time
> A woman figure without fault
> Straight as a young elm
> Straight and tall from his crookèd bones
> That she might stand in the night
> After the lock and chains
>
> All night in the unmade park
> After the railings and shrubberies
> The birds the grass the trees and the lake
> Had followed the hunchback
> And the wild boys innocent as strawberries
> To his kennel in the dark.

Daniel Jones reports that an 'earlier poem, dated 9th May 1932 in the *Buffalo Notebook*, was transformed by extensive revision into a new composition; this final version, copied into the same Notebook, is dated 16th July 1941 by Thomas himself.'[15] But Maud's transcription of the redrafted poem is, in a number of respects, not the final version, for in the final verse the penultimate and antepenultimate lines would need to be reversed. This ability to revise by reversing the order of lines in what would be the third stanza and the final one points to the rhythmical and syntactic shape of 'The hunchback in the park', its movement and additive structure formed around the cadences of coherent single lines. The revised poem grows out of the original draft by mending the rhythmical hesitations of the earlier text, responding to the rhythmic and rhyming suggestions of the youthful attempt so as to develop a responsively echoic shape – making the fully worked-out poem from a broken-backed torso. Yet the syntax of the final poem, with its verbs hung at intervals on the one stated subject, strains the spine of 'The hunchback in the park' almost, though finally not quite, to breaking point, and this strain, or fragility, in the structure of the poem is key to its value.

With a letter headed 'Laugharne, Tuesday' and speculatively dated '[1941, probably]' by Vernon Watkins, Thomas enclosed 'Among those Killed in the Dawn Raid was a Man Aged a Hundred' and 'The hunchback in the park', writing: 'Here are two poems of very different kinds. That is to say, here are two poems. Do tell me at *once* what you think of them.'[16] Sadly, whatever Watkins replied is not included in the collection of Thomas's letters to him, nor does Thomas refer in later letters to any such comments. Nor did he revise the poem, it would seem, once he had sent it to his friend. Nevertheless, the collocation of these two poems, completed at approximately the same time, does suggest that there may be connections between the two, and that 'The hunchback in the park' has its own unstated association of old men and threats from aerial warfare.

Cwmdonkin poems and 'pandemonium'

In a letter to Watkins of 29 December 1938, Thomas enclosed the thirteen-line 'Poem', published under the title of its first line 'Once it was the colour of saying', following it with '[t]his Cwmdonkin poem – minus pandemonium – *must*, please, be typed before read.'[17] Five lines in the middle of the poem develop its acceptance of others and their needs by taking it back to a memory of childhood behaviour:

> When I whistled with mitching boys through a reservoir park
> Where we stoned at night the close and cuckoo
> Lovers in the dirt of their leafy beds,
> The shade of their trees was a word of many shades
> And a lamp of lightning for the poor in the dark [. . .][18]

In the July 1941 rewrite of 'The hunchback in the park', Thomas had recalled the earlier poem: 'And mister they called hey mister / The (mitching) boys from the town (truant)'. He may have opted for the 'truant' reading, not because it avoids the West Wales colloquialism translated into standard English for this poem, but rather because he had already used the word in 'Once it was the colour of saying', published in *The Map of Love* (1939). In his next letter, postmarked 8 January 1939, Thomas writes:

I'm glad you like my last poem. I shan't alter anything in it except, perhaps, but probably, the 'close & cuckoo' lovers. The 'dear close cuckoo' lovers is a good suggestion. I can't say the same for 'halo for the bruised knee and broken heel' which is esoterically *off* every mark in the poem. I see your argument about the error of shape, but the form was consistently emotional and I can't change it without a change of heart.[19]

He did revise it, but not by taking up Watkins's suggestion. The definitive text has 'cold and cuckoo', underlining the discomfort of making love in the shadows of the park, rather than the either literally obvious or sentimentally interpretive 'close'.

'Once it was the colour of saying' has been interpreted by commentators as announcing the poet's turn away from the verbally driven, condensed symbolism of his earlier style in both poetry and prose, for '[n]ow my saying shall be my undoing / And every stone I wind off like a reel.'[20] He no longer wants to stone the lovers as he had when a boy. Now he will throw the stones at himself, undoing his older style and stoning the younger self that went with it. This development chimes with a widespread and long-term reaction to the Munich Crisis of September 1938, through which modernist techniques were increasingly adapted and domesticated to express ideas of community and continuity through local pieties, variously detectable in Louis MacNeice's *Autumn Journal* (1939), T. S. Eliot's 1939 lectures which became *The Idea of a Christian Society*, and Virginia Woolf's *Between the Acts* (1941). Thomas had mailed a letter to Watkins on 14 October 1938 in which he noted that 'A saint about to fall' was 'only provisionally called "In September", & called that at all only because it was a terrible war month'.[21] The association of Cwmdonkin Park with violence against love, as well as with war, had again arisen at the time when hostilities were narrowly averted two months before Thomas composed 'Once it was the colour of saying'.

The relationship of 'The hunchback in the park' to the First World War is spelled out in the first version of 'Reminiscences of Childhood' (1943):

This sea town was my world; outside, a *strange* Wales, coal-pitted, mountained, river run, full, so far as I knew, of choirs and sheep and story-book tall hats, moved about its business which was none of mine; beyond that unknown Wales lay England, which was London, and a country called 'The Front' from which many of our neighbours never came back. At the beginning, the only 'front' I knew was the little lobby before our front door; I could not understand how so many people never returned from there; but later I grew to know more, though still without understanding, and carried a wooden rifle in Cwmdonkin Park and shot down the invisible, unknown enemy like a flock of wild birds.[22]

There is a passing echo here from the opening to James Joyce's *Finnegans Wake* (1939), a book founded on a sin in the resurgent Phoenix Park, in that 'river run' epithet for Wales – a passing echo evocative of relationships between language, place, society and sense for the Thomas of 15 February 1943, when this talk was first broadcast on the BBC Welsh Home Service. His introduction of Cwmdonkin Park, the location of his poem, occasions its being read on the radio, and preserved in a differently punctuated version.[23] The First World War setting has him in the park with his toy rifle: where, in the poem, he will create something invisible, here he is shooting down an 'invisible, unknown enemy', compared to something beautiful and free, a flock of wild birds. He is destroying in fantasy what is figured as the opposite of a dangerous enemy. The 1932 draft constitutes an attempted amends for this violence brought into the child's life before he could understand it, and for his boyhood taunting of the 'parkee'. The 1941 poem finds more successful reparation in the contextualised childhood identification between outer and inner violence, by means of an idealised woman free from danger, preserved in the hunchback's fantasy.

The poem turns childhood memories into a reparative emblem for shame and guilt at injustices, both his own and those of what Silkin calls 'authority' – identified with the structures of adult social life, its constrictions and contained releases into leisure: the locks and suchlike of the park. Silkin is also helpful on its formal and thematic 'flow':

> And this unlocking or flowing out of the perfect image relates to one other meaning of lock, which is, of course, the mechanism that restrains, controls the level of, and admits, a body of water, into a lower stretch of itself. This meaning appears to be operative because 'the trees and water [that] enter' cause a reflection until nighttime, when reflections cease. Thus what is brought, pastorally, with water in the morning light corresponds with what is released from the hunchback in the creative restoration of himself by day, and which flows back to him at night when the 'woman figure' stands guard.[24]

Silkin's editorial insertion when citing 'the trees and water [that] enter' underscores the line's source in Auden's '[a]nd the full view / Indeed may enter / And move in memory as now these clouds do, / That pass the harbour mirror / And all the summer through the water saunter.'[25] A poem written for the promotion of tourism to the Isle of Wight, 'Look, stranger, on this island now' elaborates a period of left-leaning populism. Alluding to Auden helps evoke in Thomas's poem two ideas of the social order intuited by Silkin: structures that enclose and curtail, and an egalitarian totality, identified with water, fluidity and the seaside – whose Swansea version is also drawn upon in 'Reminiscences of

Childhood'. Caught up with the 'stones' and stoning in the 1938 poem, the poet's acknowledgement of ambivalence is key to the poem's success. In a letter sent on 21 March 1938, Thomas had written that he would like to see in Watkins's poems 'a little creative destruction, destructive creation'.[26]

So does the figure of the woman in the revised text serve as, in Silkin's words, an 'exact wishful restorative opposite'? What's more, if it is an exact and wishful opposite, can it really be restorative? Or is it rather a mere contrary, and a fantasy at that? Here is how this imagined woman figure appears in the collected 1941 version. The poem's subject-agent, named in its first line, the hunchback in the park, has

> Made all day until bell time
> A woman figure without fault
> Straight as a young elm
> Straight and tall from his crooked bones
> That she might stand in the night
> After the locks and chains
>
> All night in the unmade park
> After the railings and shrubberies
> The birds the grass the trees the lake
> And the wild boys innocent as strawberries
> Had followed the hunchback
> To his kennel in the dark.[27]

Unlike the 1932 draft, the female figure the hunchback has spent the day creating in the park is not related back to him, but left in the park after it has closed, like a piece of private municipal statuary. The imaginary object is placed within an enclosed, but shared, social space. What the hunchback creates out of his own material vulnerability and loneliness, to recall Silkin's terms, is an object projected as surviving in the park even when he is not there.

Silkin's description of the woman figure as being the 'exact [. . .] opposite' of the hunchback points towards what dooms it to failure in the 1932 draft. For such a conceptualisation finds this figure entirely and merely personally compensatory, an emblem of everything that he isn't, one seeming to abolish all that he is in that wishful-sounding smile at the draft's close. The 1941 revision doesn't only open the poem out to society, but keeps the woman figure within hearing distance of those social constraints, so that the 'figure without fault' – which the 1932 poet might have imagined as 'a poem' – is now embedded in a poem that is precisely not without fault, not perfect, because it contains the imperfections the figure is set against. The poem, in this sense, is a good enough object, containing within its space both the complex experiences of the park itself, with its real and imaginary acts of violence, and the need for a compensatory and wishful other – while not identifying that wishful other with the form of the poem.

So it has to be a woman figure, yes, but it must not also be the poem, for that way the poem is implicated in the flawed and limiting wish fulfilment. Because the social limits are inscribed within its poetic form, the reparative emblem can stand against the taunting of the hunchback and his doglike treatment, because rather than trying to wish it away, the poem acknowledges it in the process of setting up an image within the social space to stand against it. In this way, it catches up its own 'flaws', the slightly shaky, improvised syntax, delayed verbs all relating back to the initially stated subject, the interchangeability of ordering in the lines, the improvisatory rhythm in the casually varied six-line stanzas, the occasional rhymes from the strongly insistent ('mockery ... rockery') to the glancingly associative, as in the final stanza's 'park [. . .] lake [. . .] hunchback [. . .] dark'. These establish 'The hunchback in the park' as what Thomas has called 'an action': 'I can see the sensitive picking of words,' he wrote to Watkins, 'but none of the strong, inevitable pulling that makes a poem an event, a happening, an action perhaps, not a still-life or an experience put down, placed, regulated.'[28]

'Creative Politics'

In 'Squares and Oblongs', his 1948 collection of aphoristic remarks first published in a collection of essays called *The Poet at Work*, W. H. Auden writes:

> A society which really was like a poem and embodied all the esthetic [*sic*] values of beauty, order, economy, subordination of detail to the whole effect, would be a nightmare of horror, based on selective breeding, extermination of the physically or mentally unfit, absolute obedience to its Director, and a large slave class kept out of sight in cellars.[29]

Auden follows these highly contentious observations with an illustration, one taken from the manuscripts of 'Ballad of the Long-legged Bait', also bought by Buffalo at the same time that it obtained Thomas's notebooks. Auden doesn't specify who is '[t]he poet', as he calls this negatively exemplary figure, but the publishers had placed a facsimile of a page from those manuscripts as an illustration to his contribution, a page that doesn't appear to include all the changes the older poet reports:

The poet writes:

> The mast-high anchor dives through a cleft

changes it to

> The anchor dives through closing paths

then to

> The anchor dives among hayricks

finally to

> The anchor dives through the floors of a church.

The cleft and the closing paths have been liquidated and the hayricks deported to another stanza.

There's Creative Politics and Scientific Government for you.[30]

Auden's analogy here, which he drives metaphorically hard to make his polemical point, is at least as bullying as the supposed behaviour of the poet he alights upon in his un-contextualised and unacknowledged example. Thomas's line is the final one of the penultimate quatrain in his ballad made up of forty such verses:

> Land, land, land, nothing remains
> Of the pacing, famous sea but its speech,
> And into its talkative seven tombs
> The anchor dives through the floors of a church.[31]

The poem may be all at sea, as it were, but the line that has been achieved by what Auden considers tyrannical violence and force makes good enough sense in context. Again, there are the 'never out of sound' seas, all seven of them figured as tombs, which they can be, and as part of the creation. Thus a fishing boat's dropped anchor could dive through the floor of a church by a stretch of the imagination – one well prepared for by the style and substance of Thomas's ballad in its previous thirty-eight stanzas.

Auden's use of a line from Thomas is, then, a part of what would become the backlash against his mode from one of those older poets who had pioneered the style Thomas was reacting against. I am not inclined to credit Auden's idea that poets struggling with words to make affective shapes are behaving like absolute despots and petty tyrants, not least because such an extreme conception is of a piece with the idea that perfectly idealised opposites can compensate for damage in lived experience. The acts against persons with which the poetic revisions are compared have an inflated rhetorical power but limited descriptive illumination. If you liquidate persons in your purges they actually die, or if you banish them they disappear into exile possibly for ever, or if you enslave them they lose their freedom. When a poet does the supposed equivalents of these things with words, they do not die but remain in the language, continuing to influence by proximity or distance the words that have replaced them, and if 'banished', they remain in the writer's lexicon for use on another occasion, and similarly in the lexicons of others. What's more, if the words are not left free to form relations with other words in the minds of the writer and his fellow speakers, then the vocabulary of that writer and community will be permanently impaired. In such a light, no one would cut a word from a text, for fear that it ceased to exist for them and anyone else. If such were the case, either the language would quickly die, or any rewriting would be impossible. No such prospect, at least as far as this widely written and spoken language, English, is concerned, appears in the offing.

Thomas's revision of 'The hunchback in the park' bears little resemblance to the motiveless acts of wilful variation, ones not contextualised in light of the style and project of their poem 'Ballad of the Long-legged Bait', that Auden attributes to his supposedly exemplary, notoriously tyrannical poet. They bear little resemblance on both literal and metaphorical levels, as regards language and society. For the further point of Auden's polemical aphorisms, composed in the light both of European fascism and American corporatism, is to detach poets from social obligations and responsibilities, allowing them to hum along to themselves. This was how they would contribute to the preservation of freedom. He considers any explicit value in their motivations not only of no use to society, but positively dangerous if allowed to work beyond the realm of their own petty tyrannies, namely the poems they write and so ruthlessly revise.

But 'The hunchback in the park' was not produced by such a process, and, further, the poem in its development reaches towards a space of others' lives, comes into contact with the constraints of social life and natural fate, of childish prejudice and the fear of difference, whether it be the lovers in the shadows or the hunchback on his park bench. Silkin's comments on this poem point towards the conclusion that its belonging to the 'sense' side of Thomas's oeuvre is connected with the wartime conditions in which it was written, and with the greater need for social connectedness that knowledge of the war and his situation in it brought upon the poet. There is also the conventional identification of greater transparency with greater social reach, a natural assumption that was to be turned against Thomas's signature style, associated with assumptions about his lifestyle, as part of the Movement's reaction against his work in the years following his death.

Whether it be '[o]n out of sight' or '[o]n out of sound', Thomas's poem 'The hunchback in the park' concerns the limits of embodied human experience and how poetry's imagined shapes can work to enhance both. In his letter to Pamela Hansford Johnson of December 1933, Thomas had written that, while 'the life of the body is, perhaps, more directly pleasant, it *is* terribly limited, and the life of the non-body, while physically unsatisfying, *is* capable of developing, of realising infinity, of getting somewhere, and of creating an artistic progeny.'[32] His poem about the hunchback in the park and the woman created out of his bones transforms this self-thwarting contrast into a work of art because it accepts both and places them in a mutually supportive auditory experience. This is why, to recall Spencer's terms, the poem's 'resonance' and 'swirl', the 'flavour of psychology and metaphysics', lead us 'on out of sound' and even, perhaps, 'never out of sound'.

The work of revision in July 1941 brings the wishful into the auditory vicinity of the inevitable and necessary, catching into its shape the threats of violence both within individuals and from without in the association of Cwmdonkin Park with the Front in the First World War, or its lucky avoidance of serious damage in the Three-Night Blitz of Swansea in the February of that year. Thomas's responses to this bombing of his hometown throw into relief another of Auden's aphorisms in that same collage: 'All poets adore explosions, thunderstorms, tornadoes, conflagrations, ruins, scenes of spectacular carnage. The poetic imagination is therefore not at all desirable in a chief of state.'[33] Rather, the poetic imagination can be so exercised by such extremities because they outrage the imaginative work required for art.

Thomas's poetics had undergone a shift towards the communitarian in the aftermath of Munich, but it did not entail his adopting anything like the empirically plain style that would emerge some fifteen years later. Alongside other 1940s poets, Thomas had the example of Joyce's communitarian catch-all portmanteau language in *Finnegans Wake* – another dog he would partially house-train to his purposes. This is why the 'sound' of Thomas's poetry in 'The hunchback in the park' and elsewhere is an unusually successful attempt to combine a personally obsessional exploration with the widely applicable cultural significance of a social space and its inhabitants, both real and imagined. It has survived denigration by association with infantile tyranny and violence. Like the sea, Thomas's work has remained 'never out of sound' and, as he put it in 'Should lanterns shine' (1934), it has exemplified how '[t]he ball I threw while playing in the park / Has not yet reached the ground.'[34]

Notes

1. 'The hunchback in the park', *CP14*, pp. 138–9 (p. 139).

2. 'The Crumbs of One Man's Year', *TB*, pp. 151–7 (p. 155).

3. Bernard Spencer, 'Dylan Thomas', *New Verse*, 23 (Christmas 1936), 19=21. It is signed 'C. B. S.' [Charles Bernard Spencer], identified by Geoffrey Grigson and reported in Ralph Maud (ed.), *Poet in the Making: The Notebooks of Dylan Thomas* (London: Dent, 1968), p. 277. The editorial interventions that characterise *The Notebook Poems: 1930–1934* (1989) mean that, as Maud advises in his introduction, '[a]nyone who wants to know what words the young Thomas misspelled can consult the previous edition [*Poet in the Making*]; here the misspellings are silently corrected, as are obvious punctuation errors. [. . .] Where Thomas substituted words interlinearly, this edition either takes the later reading (and notes the deleted words only if they are interesting) or leaves the earlier reading in the poem (recording the changed reading in the notes)' (*NP*, p. xii). For reasons that will become clear, the text preserved in *Poet in the Making* is used in this chapter to comment on deletions independently of their being interesting or not to its editor.

4. William Empson, 'Dylan Thomas in Maturity', in *Argufying: Essays on Literature and Culture*, ed. John Haffenden (London: Chatto & Windus, 1987), p. 404.

5. Empson derives the affinity with Keats from Constantine Fitzgibbon, *The Life of Dylan Thomas* (London: Dent, 1965), p. 271. For details of the sale, see Maud, *Poet in the Making*, pp. 273–4.

6. Seamus Heaney, 'Dylan the Durable? On Dylan Thomas', in *The Redress of Poetry: Oxford Lectures* (London: Faber, 1995), pp. 124–45.

7. Maud, *Poet in the Making*, p. 155.

8. Ibid. p. 155.

9. John Goodby notes that both 'paper' and 'figure' in 'The hunchback in the park' carry associations with writing poetry. I am indebted to his showing me a longer note on 'The hunchback in the park' not used in the new *Collected Poems*, but which can now be read in *Discovering Dylan Thomas: A Companion to the 'Collected Poems' and Notebook Poems* (Cardiff: University of Wales Press, 2017), pp. 181–2.

10. Maud, *Poet in the Making*, pp. 155–6.

11. Jon Silkin, *The Life of Metrical and Free Verse in Twentieth-Century Poetry* (Basingstoke: Macmillan, 1997), p. 258.

12. Ibid. p. 259.

13. Ibid. p. 258. The Luftwaffe bombed Swansea in the Three-Night Blitz of 19–21 February 1941. Paul Ferris reports Thomas and his wife as in central Swansea 'on the morning immediately after the third and worst raid' where they met Bert Trick, who wrote: 'As we parted, Dylan said with tears in his eyes, "Our Swansea is dead."' (Cited in *Dylan Thomas* (Harmondsworth: Penguin, 1978), pp. 183–4.)

14. Maud, *Poet in the Making*, pp. 297–8.

15. Daniel Jones (ed.), *The Poems of Dylan Thomas* (New York: New Directions, 1971), p. 271.

16. Thomas to Vernon Watkins, [?15 July 1941], *Letters to Vernon Watkins* (London: Dent, 1957), p. 108.
17. Thomas to Watkins, 29 December 1938, *Letters to Vernon Watkins*, p. 52. Thomas alludes to a line from a poem by Watkins, 'Elegy on the Heroine of Childhood', written in memory of Pearl White: Vernon Watkins, *The Collected Poems* (Ipswich: Golgonooza Press, 1986), pp. 4–6. Watkins remembers 'trailing or climbing the railing, we mobbed the dark / Of Pandemonuim near Cwmdonkin Park' (p. 5); and his epigraph '… We died in you, and offered / Sweets to the Gods [. . .]' (p. 4) suggests that the internalised woman figure in Thomas's poem is related to this invulnerable film star famous for escaping from cliff-hanging dangers and disasters.
18. *Letters to Vernon Watkins*, p. 52.
19. Thomas to Watkins, [January 1939], *Letters to Vernon Watkins*, pp. 53–4.
20. *CP14*, p. 108. Walford Davies notes that against 'his early delight in form over content, Thomas hopes to claim, like Pope, "That not in fancy's maze he wandered long, / But stooped to truth and moralised his song"' (Dylan Thomas, *Selected Poems*, ed. Walford Davies (London: Penguin, 2000), p. 135).
21. Thomas to Watkins, [sent 14 October 1938], *Letters to Vernon Watkins*, p. 45.
22. 'Reminiscences of Childhood', *QEOM*, pp. 1–7 (p. 1).
23. The text printed in *Quite Early One Morning*, pp. 2–3, and attributed to *Collected Poems: 1934–1952* (p. 111), is much more heavily punctuated than the collected version, perhaps by a BBC typist, or by the poet to help with its on-air reading. This version of the text is preserved in *TB*, pp. 1–8 (pp. 4–5). For other references to Cwmdonkin Park in Thomas's letters, poems and stories, see James A. Davies, *Dylan Thomas's Places: A Biographical and Literary Guide* (Swansea: Christopher Davies, 1987), pp. 36–7.
24. Silkin, *The Life of Metrical and Free Verse*, p. 260.
25. W. H. Auden, *Look, Stranger!* (London: Faber, 1936), p. 19.
26. Thomas to Watkins, [envelope dated 21 March 1938], *Letters to Vernon Watkins*, p. 38.
27. *CP14*, p. 139.
28. Thomas to Watkins, [envelope dated 21 March 1938], *Letters to Vernon Watkins*, p. 38.
29. W. H. Auden, 'Squares and Oblongs', in *Poets at Work: Essays Based on the Modern Poetry Collection at the Lockwood Memorial Library, University of Buffalo* (New York: Harcourt, Brace and Co., 1948), p. 178. This text was revised into 'The Poet & The City', in *The Dyer's Hand* (London: Faber, 1963), p. 293; it is now collected in W. H. Auden, *Prose*, vol. 2, *1939–1948*, ed. Edward Mendelson (London: Faber, 2002), pp. 348–9. For some observations on this version, see Peter Robinson, 'W. H. Auden Revises a Context', in *In the Circumstances: About Poems and Poets* (Oxford: Oxford University Press, 1992), pp. 25–8.
30. Auden, 'Squares and Oblongs', pp. 178–9.
31. *CP14*, p. 137.

32. Thomas to Pamela Hansford Johnson, [about 21 December 1933], *CL*, p. 87.
33. Auden, 'Squares and Oblongs', p. 179.
34. 'Should lanterns shine', *CP14*, pp. 70–1 (p. 71).

II. Science and Media

'Lamp-posts and high-volted fruits': Scientific Discourse in the Work of Dylan Thomas

John Goodby

It is unusual, to put it mildly, to consider Dylan Thomas's poetry in terms of its relationship to science. The complaint made as long ago as 1947 by Leslie Fiedler, that 'nothing more modern than a ship' appears in it, still strikes a chord, with Thomas regarded by most as a poet purely of organic and cosmic fundamentals.[1] Supporters, as well as detractors, agree: Thomas's biographer Paul Ferris opined that 'He was an answer to the machine; his poems contain few images from the twentieth century.'[2] Thomas's poetry, to this way of thinking, is defined by its *opposition* to the modern, at the heart of which is the scientific world-view. It may be permissible for his work to have ignored politics, such arguments usually proceed, but to have erased from it interwar society, shaped as that was by sweeping technological change, was surely a major error of omission. Thomas, so this case goes, was a neo-Romantic who ignored his own times, and the fact that modernity signified the reign of science and its various outcomes. Hence, it is concluded, the narrowness of his work, for all its undoubted maieutic and rhetorical power.

Of course, as Ezra Pound once proposed, literature is '"news that STAYS news"', and such a critique often amounts to little more than a desire for the comfort of the standard overly sociological accounts of 1930s writing, a yearning for period references to Bakelite and chrome steel, the Comintern and Hitler.[3] It may, in some cases, also signify resistance to the Joycean revolution of the word to which Thomas so thoroughly subscribed. But, even if we discount these prejudices, it is, in any case, astonishingly easy to disprove the charge of technophobia. How was it possible for Fiedler and Ferris to miss, among many other items 'more modern than a ship', the likes of 'radium', 'carbolic', a ball-cock 'cistern', 'celluloid', 'arclamps', 'macadam', an aircraft 'hangar', car 'gears', 'allotments', coal-tips and oil-wells?[4] And, as Thomas rightly – if slightly dodging the issue – pointed out to Henry Treece, when he suggested that his poetry lacked 'social awareness', 'a good number of my images come from the cinema & the gramophone and the newspaper, while I use contemporary slang, cliché, and pun'.[5] In his correspondence Thomas is often alert, albeit unseriously, to technological and scientific developments; he is not un-Audenesque through lack of interest, as a November 1933 reference to the most famous 'helmeted airman' of the day, the American Wiley Post, shows.[6] Even the later poetry, distinctly pastoral as it is, registers the shadow of atomic weapons. And, far from being averse to technology in *propria persona*, Thomas embraced every new mass media form to appear in his lifetime: as writer and performer for radio, as film script writer, as near founding father of the spoken voice LP record industry in the United States, and as television presenter (the two programmes he made for the BBC have, alas, been lost). With good reason Marshall McLuhan noted how Thomas's cyborg energies traversed the 'thinning line between bucolics and cybernetics', and made him the exemplary electronic bard of his 'global village' in *The Medium is the Massage* (1967).[7] We know, moreover, that Thomas was an avid reader of popular science and sci-fi (he and Ray Bradbury were admirers of each other's work, for example); Ivan Phillips glimpses a 'premonition of *The Terminator*' in 'My hero bares his nerves', in which the body's inner 'wires' and 'box of nerves' are 'turned inside-out, [a lyrical representation] of visceral surfaces and superficial depths'.[8] His poems and stories appeared in generalist periodicals such as the *Athenaeum* and *The Fortnightly Review* which mixed literature and science articles, and he grew up in a home that took two daily newspapers (*The Times* and *The Telegraph*) at a time when stories such as Clyde Tombaugh's discovery of Pluto, or William Beebe's bathyscaphe descents into the depths of the Pacific Ocean, made the front page.[9]

Yet a 'subway' here or an 'antiseptic' there is the least of it. At the deepest levels – of subject, vision and style – there is compelling evidence that the 'process poetic' which Thomas forged in the twelve months from April 1933, and which informed all his work thereafter, was conceived of, and couched in, contemporary scientific terms; that is, in accordance with Darwinism and the new physics of the early twentieth century.[10] Change is its key thematic concern, apparent in a monistic focus on flux, the inextricability of creation and destruction, and the ultimate interconnectedness and simultaneity of all events and objects. Romantic pantheism and mutability are upgraded and supercharged in the light of cell biology and the creation of the universe; hence the fixation on drastic metamorphosis, whether in the human life cycle – conception, birth, adolescence, death – or its planetary and cosmic equivalents. But Thomas's poetry enacts this knowledge at the level of style, too, its incessant wordplay and intercutting images mimicking the incessant flux of the Einsteinian universe, just as the emphatic materiality of its language and its rhythms incarnate the processual, somatic rhythms of our bodies, of breath, heartbeat, feeding, sex. Physics and biology, respectively, offer the debate between relativism and determinism played out in the early poetry, although this is complicated by cultural repressions and neuroses, figured in the struggle between linguistic energy and the strictest of constraining metrical schemes. It is a far cry from the work of the 'Pylon Poets', who presented the sociological surfaces of their world overtly, often with great brilliance, but whose language subserves a discursive purpose, and whose pre-modernist forms simply act as containers for content rather than figuring a dialectical struggle with it.

And yet there are, of course, good reasons why readers might feel, even so, that Thomas's work is un- or even anti-modern. He almost squeezes the social world from his poems, and his lyric compression, wordplay and use of mythic method often make it difficult to detect science, technology or any mundane source. The preacher's *hwyl* of 'And death shall have no dominion', for example, will distract many from the poem's originating *mise-en-scène* of a naked body exposed in no-man's land. The deceptiveness is calculated, and the reader needs to be alert to it, and to the way it may affect every part and level of a poem; the modernity of 'arclamps' in 'Our eunuch dreams' is clear enough, but its reworking as 'ark-light' in 'Altarwise by owl-light' a year later reflects the way social and technological discourses are relentlessly, if playfully, subsumed and absorbed by those of religion and myth.

Cybernetic collocations

Thomas, his friend Daniel Jones once claimed, was uninterested in any studies 'with names ending in –ology, -onomy, -ography, -osophy, -ic, -ics, or even, to a large extent, just -y (history, botany)'.[11] Jones, however, was writing out of exasperation at the over-ingenious explicators who swarmed over the poetry after Thomas's untimely death in 1953, casting him as an expert in anything from Gnosticism to marine zoology. In reality, the threat (and less frequently the promise) of science and technology is a central subject of the early poems. 'Fuse', from the first line of the most famous of them, can be thought of as a key term in this regard. Chiefly a noun, but with verb-potential too ('the process of fusion'), it can be said to enact the proposition of Einstein's most famous equation – $E = mc^2$ – that energy and matter are intimately related. Moreover, it also pointedly yokes an organic and an inorganic sense, both plant stem and bomb timer, or circuit breaker, metapoetically describing the act of creating the many similar cybernetic collocations scattered throughout Thomas's first two collections, and which incorporate science and technology within the organic-cosmic round: 'oil of tears', 'milky acid', 'seaweeds' iron', 'motor muscle', 'girdered nerve', 'tufted axle', 'scythe of hairs', 'petrol face', 'man's mineral'.[12] Thomas himself presents such fusions as his *raison d'être* as a poet, indeed, in the summatory 'I, in my intricate image' (1935), a long lyric dialectically organised in three sections (as are several other early poems), in which he traces the adventures of a multi-layered cyborg 'ghost in metal' and exemplifies his 'habitual confusion of metal and flesh'.[13]

In relying so heavily on this trope, Thomas was of course reflecting a longstanding fear of human subordination to the machine. It had already appeared in the early notebook poem 'The ploughman's gone', of 28 March 1933, for example, in the form of a conventional lament for dwindling human contact with the natural world, symbolised by the replacement of the horse with motorised vehicles. Human beings, it concludes, are unwittingly making themselves functions of the machine: '[m]an who once drove is driven in sun and rain'.[14] By autumn that year, however, having perhaps absorbed the import of Hitler's seizure of power in January 1933 and what it implied for peace in Europe, Thomas had infused the idea of technological supersession with a generational dread of joining the 'riddled lads' who 'Cry Eloi to the guns' in a new world war.[15] The birth of this kind of mechanised slaughter is the subject of 'I dreamed my genesis', for example, in which the poet dreams 'my genesis and died again, shrapnel / Rammed in the marching heart, hole / In the stitched wound [. . .] muzzled / Death on the mouth that ate the gas.'[16] Such trench war technology suffuses *18 Poems* (1934) and *Twenty-five Poems* (1936): thus, a conceit on barbed wire images Christ's foreknowledge of his agony in 'Before I knocked', as 'flesh was snipped to cross the lines / Of gallow crosses on the liver / And brambles in the wringing brains.'[17] By late 1933 this had become a genuinely ambivalent quasi-futuristic vision, in part because Thomas's burgeoning socialism required a positive conception of 'the huge, electric promise of a future' in which science would be harnessed to human need.[18] In the unpublished 'We see rise the secret wind', for example, the modern city is that of Fritz Lang's film *Metropolis* (1927), a favourite of Thomas's, in which technology enslaves but could be 'saviour' to the 'wretched':

A city godhead, turbine moved, steel sculptured,
Glitters in the electric streets;
A city saviour, in the orchard
Of lamp-posts and high-volted fruits,

Speaks a steel gospel to the wretched
Wheel-winders and fixers of bolts.[19]

The poem which deploys cybernetic collocations most extensively is 'All all and all', written around ten months later, in early summer 1934. It balances the threat of the driver being 'driven' by the machine – being lost in the totality, or 'all', of cybernetic fusions – against the need to '[f]ear not the working world' of machinery and absorption in its 'synthetic blood', 'ribbing metal' and 'bridal blade'. Overcoming trepidation, the speaker comes to realise that his entry into the adult world of writerly and sexual empowerment entails acceptance of modernity's fusion of human and machine, and an embrace of the ambiguously 'mechanical flesh':

Know, O my bone, the jointed lever,
Fear not the screws that turn the voice,
And the face to the driven lover.[20]

The governing collocation of organic and inorganic in Thomas's work is that of the microcosm, the mapping of body and universe onto each other – although in his case the body *is* the universe, the universe the body. Writing to Trevor Hughes in January 1934, Thomas claimed that 'it is impossible for me to raise myself to the altitude of the stars, and [. . .] I am forced, therefore, to bring the stars to my own level and incorporate them in my own physical universe', and the movement is reciprocal: in the same letter he speaks of wanting to prove that 'the flesh that covers me is the flesh that covers the sun'.[21] The night sky in 'Light breaks where no sun shines' is a place '[w]here no seed stirs' but '[t]he fruit of man unwrinkles in the stars / Bright as a fig', semen constellating the seeded dark of the vaginal heavens.[22] This kind of conceit is a staple of ancient, medieval and Renaissance writing, of course, but here it is revisited in the light of the new physics of Planck, Rutherford and Einstein, as mediated through the works of popular science we know Thomas to have read, such as Alfred North Whitehead's *Science and the Modern World* (1926).[23]

Einsteinian bodies: 'lost in a big and magic universe'[24]

Ultimately, Thomas's poetic of process bespeaks an understanding that, for all its apparent solidity and stability, the physical universe is in a state of perpetual flux. Everything not only develops into its opposite but contains it, *is* it: 'The quick and dead / Move like two ghosts before the eye.'[25] The first proto-'process' poem, 'And death shall have no dominion', of April 1933, reveals the cosmological source of 'process' in its concluding lines:

> Heads of the characters hammer through daisies;
> Break in the sun till the sun breaks down,
> And death shall have no dominion.[26]

Here, the sun 'breaking down' is both an impossibility, a synonym for eternity (thus endorsing the Christian promise of resurrection), and something that will happen, according to modern cosmology, in five billion years' time. In this latter reading, we are promised only the cold comfort that, after death, we are 'resurrected' in so far as our molecules will 'push up the daisies' (the proverbial phrase which supplies the germ of the passage), re-joining the vegetation cycle until the Earth is swallowed by the sun's supernova. In the same vein, Thomas referred to 'our howls at [. . .] the destiny of the sun', and gave to his novel-in-progress the working title of *A Doom on the Sun*.[27] The actual physics of the life-cycles and deaths of stars had been calculated not long before by the astronomer Arthur Eddington, and publicised in bestsellers such as his *Stars and Atoms* (1926).[28] Crucially, 'And death' allows itself to be read as simultaneously upholding Christian belief and scientific prediction, and this discovery of a rhetoric by which language could assert two mutually contradictory propositions in the same phrase would be a staple of all Thomas's subsequent poetry. While it is a critical commonplace to mention Thomas's taste for paradox, its source in cosmology has hardly even been remarked.

Within the apocalyptic scope of the poetry, then, birth and death (equally of humans, of stars and of the universe), often with a mythic or Christian dimension, are common. They reflect the Anglo-Welsh outsider's fear of silencing, and his attempts to engineer his origin. Thomas's instinct is to do so within a cosmic frame; the origin-poem 'In the beginning was the three-pointed star' melds Big Bang Theory *avant la lettre* with Genesis by way of John's Gospel, while 'A Refusal to Mourn', with its 'all humbling darkness / Tell[ing] with silence the last light breaking', evokes the entropic heat-death of the universe at the close of its existence.[29] Speculations on the fate of the universe were commonplace at the time; the 1920s was the decade of Edwin Hubble's discovery that the universe was expanding, and of the steady-state theory advanced to explain it in 1928 by the other great populariser of science, with Whitehead and Eddington, James Jeans.[30] Crucially for any reimagining of the concept of microcosm in contemporary scientific terms, it was also confirmed in the mid-1920s that human beings are made of 'star-stuff', the debris of heavy elements produced by exploding stars. As Eddington later put it, famously, in an interview of 1932, 'we are all bits of stellar matter that got cold by accident, bits of a star gone wrong.'[31] 'I dreamed my genesis' alludes directly to this, the flesh of its speaker said to have 'filed / Through all the irons in the grass, metal / Of suns in the man-melting light'.[32] 'All flesh is grass', as *The Book of Common Prayer* has it, but, also, our bodies are composed of elements forged in the stellar furnaces, and will return to them.[33]

Thomas was characteristically flippant about such matters. Writing to Johnson on 15 April 1934, he grumbled about the way 'the atomed tides of light break and make no sound, how the God of our image, gloved, hatted, & white, sits no longer playing with his stars but curving his Infinite length to the limit of a Jew's theory.'[34] The allusion is to the *General Theory of Relativity* (1915), in which Einstein refined the concept of space-time he had propounded in 1905 by claiming that the space-time continuum is warped by mass and energy, to produce a dynamically curved space-time; the universe is saddle-shaped and folds back on itself, as light itself eventually does. But the poet's flippancy is a pose; Einsteinian physics underwrote Thomas's poetics at every level, as we might expect of the perpetrator of the enjambement at line two of 'To-day, this insect', a poem which explores the relationship between the two elements it hinges:

> To-day, this insect, and the world I breathe,
> Now that my symbols have out-elbowed space,
> Time at the city spectacles [. . .][35]

In similar vein, another letter to Johnson of 25 December 1933 had noted:

> When I learn that the stars I see *there* may be but the backs of stars I see *there*, I am filled with the terror which is the beginning of love. They tell me space is endless and space curves. And I understand. [. . .] I've saddled a bright horse, and his brightness, not his body, keeps me bouncing up and down like a rubber star on his back.[36]

In 'The Holy Six', part of the projected *A Doom on the Sun*, Mr Edger recalls the timorous old parson Mr Davies protesting belief in the face of the new physics ('howling, from a religious hill of the infinite curve of matter'), while later in the same story Mr Rafe (an anagram of 'fear') asks himself, '[w]ere the faces of the west stars the backs of the east?'[37] There can be no doubt that Thomas's 'saddling' of the 'bright' Pegasus of his poetry derived from the dissemination of Einstein's ideas by Jeans and Eddington, just as the 'process' to which he alludes in 'A process in the weather of the heart' echoes the 'philosophy of process' propounded by Whitehead in *The Concept of Nature* (1920); the similarities between Whitehead's and Thomas's ideas are just too many, and too close, to be coincidental. And, as already noted, such similarities are not only a question of subject matter or governing analogies, but of style. The poems' piled-up appositive clauses, for example, mimic the simultaneity of past, future and present events in the Einsteinian universe, how our experience of them as temporal flow is an illusion, enacted by the flimsy grammar of the sentence in which the clauses are suspended (there are thirty-four in the single opening sentence of 'When, like a running grave'). Equally, Thomas described his 'generative method' of composition in terms of nuclear physics or cell biology, each poem growing from a decentred 'host' of conflicting, breeding images and words, driven by word-fission and -fusion. He may have known of the quantum discovery that energy behaves simultaneously as wave and particle – that nothing is solid, least of all solid matter – as a punning aside in a letter to Johnson of October 1934 suggests: 'Not that it matters, anyway. Life is only waves, wireless waves, & electric vibrations. Does it matter, my little radio programme from Battersea, that the high or low tension runs down?'[38]

Darwinian bodies I: heredity, genetics, sex

If subatomic and cosmic bodies demarcate the frame Thomas's poetry inhabits, as it were, the implications of science are most vividly detailed at the intermediate level of the human body. In this sense, his work's insistent corporeality is only in part a reaction against the cerebralism of the Audenesque poets. Incarnating the new physics in verbal form required that, as he put it, 'the description of any thought or action – however abstruse it may be' should be 'beaten home by bringing it onto a physical level. Every idea, intuitive or intellectual, can be imaged or translated in terms of the body, its flesh, skin, blood, sinews, veins, glands, organs, cells or senses.'[39] Poetry itself is defined by the body: while Thomas could dismiss his work as 'anatomic slap-stick', he also opined that 'My latest definition of poetry is "The expression of the unchanging spirit in the changing flesh."'[40] As I argue elsewhere, the emergence of biomorphic, body-centred styles in some 1930s art reflected a fear of intensified regimes of state control and of the looming world war, and the threat these posed to our one inalienable and irreducible possession, our bodies.[41] Thomas's response was informed by a knowledge of Darwinian biology, and contemporary debates around genetics and heredity made themselves felt in many of the poems and short stories of the mid-1930s. 'Life', he asserts in good Darwinian fashion in 'In the beginning', 'rose and spouted from the rolling sea', and the sea is the origin of life which he asks to be de-evolved into if he cannot overcome writer's block in 'On no work of words': 'Ancient woods of my blood, dash down to the nut of the seas / If I take to burn or return this world which is each man's work.'[42] Since seawater is the source of the blood of all animals according to evolutionary theory, Thomas plumps for 'nut', or, as he explained to Desmond Hawkins:

> The sense of the last two lines is: Well, to hell and to death with me, may my old blood go back to the bloody sea it came from if I accept this world only to bugger it up or return it. The ibelin [*sic*] came out of the acorn; the woods of my blood came out of the nut of the sea, the tide-concealing, blood-red kernel.[43]

Evolution is driven by survival and ruthless sexual selection, and in the poems of 1933–35 the carnal body is equally a charnel one. The poems' two basic sexual scenarios are sex as a form of deprivation – enforced virginity, masturbation, morbid sexual fantasy generated by religious repression – and sex haunted by the fear of entrapment through pregnancy and supersession by one's offspring. A letter of 9 May 1934 to Johnson informed her that

> [t]he chromosomes, the colour bodies that build toward the cells of these walking bodies, have a god in them that doesn't care a damn for the howls of our brains. He's a wise organic god, moving in a seasonable cycle in the flesh, always setting and putting right what our howls at the astrologers' stars and the destiny of the sun leads us on to.[44]

We are compelled into sex, even as we know it leads to new life, and that, from the first mitosis, the embryo is busy elbowing its parents into the grave. To have children is to release a 'plague', to make oneself disposable, to admit time and hasten decay and death, and Eros and Thanatos are inextricably entwined in such a vision. Yet if its priorities appear male-centred, the poems themselves never quite lapse into mere misogyny. Not only is the threat of conception viewed as a shared catastrophe, but in acknowledging the greater incursion on female freedom, Thomas begins to show signs of what will eventually become a feminised poetic, in which female nurture, endurance and fecundity are the chief virtues.

The gravely elegiac, post-coital lyric 'A grief ago', of late 1934, is a good example. It traces what it means in biological and psychosexual terms when the 'country-handed grave' 'boxe[s]' us 'into love', uniting the two 'countries', or ancestral groups, of a couple in the sexual act.

The lovers are forced ('boxed' as punched) into congress by the grave (to 'box' is also to put into a coffin), which, by a bitter paradox, can only be overcome by producing the offspring who will supplant them.[45] As Ralph Maud puts it, 'lovers [. . .] make of themselves the conduit whereby ancestors become progeny', and the poem is 'about DNA [. . .] The past is being dragged into the present by the sexual act and conception, whereby hereditary characteristics ['ropes of heritage'] are acquired by the zygote'. The lines, 'The people's sea drives on her, / Drives out the father from the caesared camp [of the womb]', Maud reads thus: '[t]he girl is [. . .] a representative of her ancestors and the male seems only the means whereby her history is transmitted to the future. The impregnated woman is defined only by her "people" at that moment. And the man is nowhere.'[46] But though this is true enough, 'caesared' points to the political dimension of the poem's fear at having progeny – the Europe of the dictators – while Maud's claim of male resentment at exclusion seems excessive:

> Let her inhale her dead, through seed and solid
> Draw in their seas,
> So cross her hand with their grave gipsy eyes,
> And close her fist.[47]

In these closing lines, it seems to me, the shrugging acceptance of 'let' outweighs the sense of monitory exhortation it might contain; 'she' will inevitably reincarnate ('in-hale', make alive) and possess the joint genetic inheritance, and the speaker will without bitterness 'cross her hand' with the ancestral 'eyes', or 'I's (these imagined as coins paid, through the transposed epithet, to a gipsy fortune-teller; the lurking cliché is 'cross my palm with silver'). The woman is one with the biological juggernaut as the man cannot be after the act is completed, and this is an ungainsayable reality. It is presented as tragedy and in an unadorned way. Yet the poem's grudging tenderness towards the 'she' anticipates the way in which, from the mid-1930s, an acceptance of female primacy would resist and supplant any hints of the sexist model of male–female relationships usually derived from Darwinism. 'A saint about to fall', of September 1938, begins with a father's ejaculation, but modulates at its mid-point into the voice of the mother bearing their child, suffering her labour pangs ('the horrid / Woe drip[s] from the dishrag hands and the pressed sponge of the forehead') in a form of poetic *couvade*; while '"If my head hurt a hair's foot"', written four months later, after the birth of the Thomases' first child, cuts out the father completely to offer an extraordinarily empathetic colloquy between the embryo and its mother.[48]

Darwinian bodies II: 'You need glands ...'

Critics have dismissed the bodily insistences of Thomas's work in various ways; 'visceral' is the favourite epithet, with 'glandular' a close second. Both, however, are perfectly appropriate if taken to signify a natural interest in what contemporary science had to say about the organs which drive and control bodies, the glands.[49] *18 Poems*, in particular, might be described as a primer for a new poetic genre, the Darwinian love lyric, when viewed in the light of interwar research into glands and the hormones they produce. Although such research had begun nearly a century earlier, it became serious science only in the 1900s; the first hormone to be identified and named was secretin, in 1902, and the word 'hormone' (from the Greek *hormo*, 'I arouse to activity') was first used in 1905 by the English physiologist Ernest Starling (1866–1927).[50] The two decades following the First World War were the golden age of gland and hormone discovery; they witnessed the extraction of insulin and its first use to treat diabetes in human beings (1926), the isolation of the first sex hormone, oestrone (1929), followed by theelin, oestradiol and oestriol; the discovery of the male and female hormones androsterone (1931) and progesterone (1934); and identification of testosterone (1935). Parallel work on the glands themselves led to the discovery that the pituitary gland regulated the entire endocrine glandular system.

Thomas's first gland turned up in a notebook poem of 23 April 1933, in which a man was ironically advised to 'regain [his] fire. / Graft a monkey gland, old man, at fools' advice', an allusion to the surgical procedures which built on gland research to alter and revitalise hormonal function.[51] This was the age of hormonal and gland implants, pioneered by the Russian Serge Voronoff and popularised in America by John 'Goat Gland' Brinkley, a Kansas quack; a related popular procedure was the 'Steinach operation', submitted to by W. B. Yeats in 1931.[52] As with the new physics, these discoveries and procedures were staples of the press, which was as exercised by their sexual implications as much as today's media is by Viagra, HRT, surrogate motherhood and the like. In the years around 1930, Chandak Sengoopta argues, hormone and gland science amounted to a 'new physiology'; it would have been impossible for Thomas to have been unaware of it, even if it had not suddenly and terrifyingly made itself known to him in 1933 in the shape of his father's cancer of the mouth.[53] On 10 September 1933, D. J. Thomas's treatment began with the insertion of radium-tipped needles into the tumour, followed by surgery. As his son told Johnson in December, 'my father is going up to hospital in London in the first days of January [1934] to have, as far as I know, several very necessary glands removed.'[54] If critical sneering has marked Thomas down as a 'glandular' poet in a purely negative sense, he actually had very good reasons for being one.

And, as such critics have failed to notice, Thomas explored the subject, rather than merely succumbing to it, in a series of poems which can be seen as staging posts in the development of the process poetic, written between September 1933 and April 1934. In each, gland and hormone function are represented, albeit indirectly, from the point at which gender is decided ('Shall it be male or female? Say the cells'), through the 'tided cord' of the umbilicus, hidden in the 'brawned womb's weather', to the 'galactic sea' of the breast and '[t]he child that sucketh long' and 'shoot[s] up', and the adolescents who, like Thomas himself, have the 'hallowed gland' of the testes to send them 'daft with the drug that's smoking in a girl'.[55] Penises and vaginas lubricated with 'the maiden's slime' infuse the 'chemic blood' with 'urchin hungers' which girl and boy are forced, because of 'medieval' levels of social repression, to 'rehearse' as 'heat' on a 'raw-edged nerve'.[56] Among the short stories, in which the 'inner weather' of the poetry is externalised, the gland-science theme appears even more plainly. 'The Map of Love' finds Beth Rib and Reuben exhorted to 'return to thy father's laboratory [. . .] and the fatted calf in the test-tube'; and 'The School for Witches' alludes to testosterone injections given for penile erections ('the lust of man, like a dead horse, stood up to his injected mixtures').[57] 'The Lemon', the most striking example, opens in the laboratory of the sinister Doctor Manza:

> Early one morning, under the arc of a lamp, carefully, silently, in smock and rubber gloves, the doctor grafted a cat's head on to a chicken's trunk. The cat-headed creature, in a house of glass, swayed on its legs; though it stared through the slits of its eyes it saw nothing; there was the flutter of a strange pulse under its fur and feathers; and, lifting its foot to the right of the glass wall, it rocked to the left. Change the sex of a dog: it cries like a bitch in a high heat, and sniffs, bewildered, over the blind litter. Such a strange dog, with a grafted ovary, howled in its cage. The doctor put his ear to the glass, hoping for a new sound [. . .] Tomorrow there were to be new mastoids for the ferret by the window, but today it leapt in the sun.[58]

Writing under the anti-vivisectionist influence of the Powys brothers, two favourite authors, Thomas presents Manza as a stock type: the callous mad scientist. But the protagonist of the story is Manza's son, Nant, a split self, who at certain points in the narrative identifies with his father. It is a reminder that stereotypes in Thomas are almost invariably more than they seem, and that while miscegenations like the 'tigron' of 'Unluckily for a death' may be negative and death-dealing, his work more often celebrates bodily shape-shiftings and mutations, as in 'How shall my animal', with its metamorphoses of its 'beast' as snail, octopus, stallion, turtle, crab, fish and bird.[59] If he concedes that '"[i]n the groin's endless coil a man is tangled"', his aim is to enact the complex interaction between free will and biological drive, nature and nurture, in order to find ways to overcome fatality and determinism.

The discursive contexts of these struggles are important. Mechanical Darwinism and Social Darwinism dominated interpretations of the human implications of the new biological sciences in the 1920s and 1930s. Its most influential figures, Jacques Loeb (1859–1924) and Ivan Pavlov (1849–1936), proposed a mechanistic, materialistic conception of life and scientific control over it. Pavlov's main work, *Conditioned Reflexes*, translated into English in 1927, shaped all later physiological-behaviourist psychological theories, including those of the most influential behaviourist of the twentieth century, B. F. Skinner (1904–90), an advocate of mass conditioning as a means of social control. Belief in biological determinism, if not conditioning, was also matched by widespread support for eugenics, a support shared by leading writers of the day, including a Thomas favourite, Aldous Huxley.

Like Thomas in his early stories, Huxley is a good example of how issues relating to biology, heredity and genetics were often worked out in so-called 'marginal' literary genres, such as fable, gothic and science fiction. Indeed, in his early work, Thomas might be said to be engaged in a debate with *Brave New World* (1932). The parallels are clear enough, as 'The Lemon' shows, and Thomas could claim to 'think in cells', like Huxley '[whose] god is cellular'.[60] Even so, the difference between them on the question of eugenics was profound. Eugenics is so repugnant to us today that *Brave New World* is usually taken to be an attack on it. However, as Donald J. Childs notes, Huxley intended only a satire on its excesses. In an article Huxley published soon after the novel appeared, he observed: 'So far as our knowledge goes, negative eugenics – or the sterilization of the unfit – might already be practised with tolerable safety [. . .] we know enough [. . .] to foresee the rapid deterioration, unless we take remedial measures, of the whole West European stock.'[61] But for Thomas's generation, eugenics meant the Nazis, one of whose first acts after seizing power was the passing of the Nuremberg Laws on racial purity and legislation to eliminate the 'feeble-minded' and physically impaired. Thomas was aware of the discourses surrounding eugenics – he dismissively name-checks one of its most vociferous public exponents, W. R. Inge, the Dean of St Paul's, in his correspondence – but never countenanced it in anything he wrote.[62] On the contrary, his work views life as sacrosanct, and cherishes that which society deems grotesque or 'unfit', albeit with a sometimes morbid relish.

It may be no coincidence that the main opposition among physiologists to Pavlovian behaviourism came from researchers in embryology, a subject which is all-pervasive in Thomas's poetry. Like that of the behaviourists, but drawing opposed conclusions, the work of the embryologists was also rooted in research on glands and hormones. Again, Thomas is likely to have been aware of the popularisers of these holistic conceptions of the human organism, such as Walter Cannon (1871–1942) and Lawrence J. Henderson (1878–1942), particularly the former's *The Wisdom of the Body* (1932). Both argued for the homeostasis of all organisms; that is, their self-regulation, governed by feedback mechanisms, in a constantly changing adaptation to altering environmental or internal challenges. The obvious analogies with stable democratic societies led Cannon to offer homoeostasis as a social model. Rather than finding in Darwin a sanction for pitiless competition, it suggested that cooperation, social regulation (rather than control) and equilibrium were the natural order of things. If this sounds like the 1930s debate between the dictatorships and the democracies, it is no coincidence. Arguably, Thomas used biological perspectives to frame what he considered to be the limited, external representations of historical determinism of the Audenesque poets ('History to the defeated / may say alas, but cannot help nor pardon'), in which the commandeering of bodies by glands and their agents mimic the diktats and secret police of a world sliding towards war.[63] But his holism was not that of the liberal status quo and was never completely passive. The second and final appearance of 'gland' in the published poetry, in 'All all and all', is part of a visionary fusion of sexual liberation and people's uprising – 'the glanded morrow', the Marxist revolution as social gland-grafting.[64]

'In Country Heaven': the material-spiritual sublime.

In recent years there has been a surge of critical interest in the relationship between modernist writers and science. Very little has yet been written, however, about the attitudes to science of the writers who came of age in the 1930s, in the wake of high modernism, although we know that they were substantially different to those of their immediate predecessors.[65] Eliot disliked the very notion of 'popular' science, Pound was repelled by the 'formlessness' with which the Einsteinian universe threatened the masculine hardness of the image, while Wyndham Lewis wrote *Time and Western Man* (1927) to inveigh against ideas derived from Einstein's insights into space-time. None was happy with the messy, sexual body, although several felt that eugenic selection based on neo-Darwinian principles was legitimate, even desirable. Thomas's position was almost the opposite of these. Even when he most resembles a modernist, as, for example, in his Lawrentian vitalism and archetypal blood and soil imagery, it is striking that his usages do not have a reactionary cast. The chief reason for this is that his scientific world-view precludes the older writer's essentialism; Thomas's use of the 'mythic method' resembles Joyce's in this respect. Like Blake, Thomas attacked hyper-rationalist excess, and the later poems throw up mildly ironic epithets aimed at those who feel mechanical materialism has the measure of things: 'the discovered skies', 'interpreted evening', 'known dark', 'managed storm', for example.[66] But he was fundamentally a demystifier who felt that reverence for the universe was enhanced by scientific discovery, not – unlike the essentialist Lawrence – that it entailed an antagonism towards science.

Predictably enough, perhaps, Thomas's populist modernism meant that his work evolved from a negative interpretation of the fatalism engendered by popular science to a more benign and positive one. From 1937 onwards, redemptive sexual love would be celebrated unqualifiedly, in 'the full assemblage in flower / Of the living flesh', as his poetry strove for a harmonising of self, body and cosmos.[67] This trend intensified after 1944–45, as his poems ('Poem in October', for example) aspired not so much to embody process as to be the perfected artefact which, if still registering mutability, focused on a local, if stylised, natural world. Biographical reasons are usually cited for this mellowing – marriage (1937) and parenthood (1939) – but it also had to do with the onset of the war and (given that his style changed most radically in 1944–45) the shock of the degradation of the human body in the Nazi death camps and the unleashing of the annihilatory power of the new physics in the atom bomb. (The 'outcry of the ruled sun', which ends 'In Country Sleep', is that of the sun's nuclear furnace subordinated to the 'rule' of man, abuser of the sun / Son's power.)[68] These horrific events of the war's final year, both directed against civilian populations, impelled Thomas's later work towards a paradoxical Cold War pastoral. Hence these poems' mourning of the death of the very notion of childhood, as in 'Fern Hill', and their fear of another world war, as articulated in 'Poem on his Birthday''s 'rocketing wind', even as they praise, in Rabelaisian fashion, the 'dead and deathless [. . .] Love forever meridian through the courters' trees' of 'In the White Giant's Thigh'.[69]

Against such fears, Thomas in his later years ranged between a precariously ecological, holistic vision of the green world and the sense of a spiritual principle implicit in the material universe. His final project, the *In Country Heaven* sequence, for which several of the later poems were written, envisaged its 'heaven' as a palpable 'star', populated by Earth's former inhabitants who would memorialise news of its passing in a nuclear apocalypse by telling tales to each other of their lives there. The hybrid combination of pastoral, sci-fi and tangible afterlife is Thomas's most elaborate framing of spirit by a material, science-based universe, and reminds us that, like many contemporaries, he held that while science could increasingly approach the final truths of the universe, it would never conclusively reach and exhaust them. This, together with the inevitability and unknowability of death, involved the continuation of the metaphysical dimension of human existence, and the need to register it in his poetry. 'God', as 'Poem on his Birthday' puts it, is accordingly 'fabulous', both astonishing (and believed-in) and mere fable, non-existent.[70] This is a more elaborate version of the rhetorical doubleness of 'And death shall have no dominion', where the process vision and its poetic first came in, and the frame explains why Thomas's Christian imagery never coheres as a solid religious position; it is, rather, as it has been all along, a means for understanding the persistence of belief, a way of exploring its mechanisms. In this it echoes the way '[p]opular science writers have always been tempted to interpret scientific ideas in religious terms', with Eddington, Jeans and Whitehead all cases in point.[71] Respectively, a Quaker, an idealist who held that the universe was 'nearer to a great thought than to a great machine', and a mystic who had a conversion experience in 1927, their public appeal was in part due to the fact that they argued for a harmony between scientific discovery and religion. Far from the new physics threatening faith, in their very indeterminacy they removed the attacks on faith by reductionist Victorian science. Thomas's own lyric harmony is weirder and more appealing than the scientist-popularisers, and points to the paradoxes of their positions more richly and knowingly than they ever could; but it is deeply indebted to and shaped by them, nevertheless.

Notes

1. Leslie Fiedler, 'The Latest Dylan Thomas', *Western Review* 11.2 (Winter 1947), 103–6 (p. 105).
2. Paul Ferris, *Dylan Thomas* (Harmondsworth: Penguin, 1978), p. 2.
3. Ezra Pound, *ABC of Reading* (New York: New Directions, 1960 [1934]), p. 29.
4. *CP14*, pp. 116, 106, 42, 54, 69, 46, 47.
5. Thomas to Henry Treece, 6 or 7 July [1938], *CL*, p. 359.
6. Thomas to Pamela Hansford Johnson, [early November 1933], Ibid. p. 64.

7. Ivan Phillips, 'I sing the bard electric', *Times Literary Supplement*, 19 September 2003, 14–15 (p. 14).
8. Ibid. 14.
9. Michael Whitworth, *Einstein's Wake: Relativity, Metaphor, and Modernist Literature* (Oxford: Oxford University Press, 2004), pp. 32–3, 41–3.
10. Although I only deal with the 'hard' sciences in what follows, Freud could, of course, be added to Darwin and Einstein to make up the triumvirate of the most influential scientific minds of the early twentieth century.
11. Daniel Jones, *My Friend Dylan Thomas* (London: Dent, 1977), p. 57.
12. *CP14*, pp. 46, 52, 57, 61, 63, 68, 71, 72, 74.
13. Ibid. p. 71.
14. Ibid. p. 23. Thomas's tendency, in the late 1930s, to rewrite his earlier modernistic concerns in self-mocking vein is apparent in this exchange on the same subject in the short story 'Where Tawe Flows':

    'The mass-age produces the mass-man. The machine produces the robot.'
    'As its slave,' Mr Humphries articulated clearly, 'not, mark you, as its master.'
    'There you have it. There it is. Tyrannic dominance by a sparking plug, Mr Humphries, and it's flesh and blood that always pays.' (*CS*, p. 189)

15. *CP14*, p. 66.
16. Ibid. p. 61.
17. Ibid. p. 39.
18. Thomas to Johnson, [week of 11 November 1933], *CL*, p. 73.
19. *CP14*, p. 40.
20. Ibid. p. 64.
21. Thomas to Trevor Hughes, [early January 1934], *CL*, p. 108.
22. *CP14*, p. 46.
23. David N. Thomas (ed.), *Dylan Remembered: Vol 1. 1914–1934* (Bridgend: Seren Books, 2003), p. 141. Alfred North Whitehead (1861–1947) was a philosopher and mathematician who published extensively on logic, algebra, the philosophy of science, physics and education. Ideas of his echoed by Thomas include: nature as perpetual process; the interconnectedness of subatomic and cosmic events; simultaneity and perpetual potentiality; the impossibility of language as complete communication.
24. Thomas to Johnson, [25 December 1933], *CL*, p. 100.
25. *CP14*, p. 52.
26. Ibid. p. 24.
27. Thomas to Johnson, 9–13 May 1934, *CL*, pp. 155, 160.
28. Arthur Stanley Eddington (1882–1944) was an astrophysicist who explored the nature of stars; he discovered the relationship between their luminosity and their mass, calculated their temperature and density, and categorised different stellar types and life-cycles. His work following the experiment to determine the effect of gravity on light during the solar eclipse of 29 May 1919, the first to give observational proof of the correctness of Einstein's theories, made him a household name between the wars. His other works of popular science included *Science and the Unseen World* (1929) and *Why I Believe in God: Science and Religion, as a Scientist Sees It* (1930).
29. *CP14*, p. 172.
30. James Hopwood Jeans (1877–1945) authored *The Mysterious Universe*

(1930), *The Stars in their Courses* (1931) and *The Universe around Us* (1934).

31. Waldemar Kaempffert, 'Eddington Expounds a Mystical Cosmos', *The New York Times Magazine*, 9 October 1932, 9, 16 (p. 9).
32. *CP14*, p. 61.
33. 'Saint John Baptist's Day', in *The Book of Common Prayer*, intro. James Wood (London: Penguin, 2012), p. 241.
34. Thomas to Johnson, 15 April [1934], *CL*, p. 135.
35. *CP14*, pp. 88–9.
36. Thomas to Johnson, [25 December 1933], *CL*, p. 98. (Italics in original.) Thomas seems to be echoing Eddington's point in *Space, Time and Gravitation* (1920) that, in a finite but unbounded universe, light rays from a star could travel around the universe and converge again at their starting point: '[t]he ghost of a star appears at the spot where the star was a certain number of million years ago.' See Whitworth, *Einstein's Wake*, p. 175.
37. *CS*, pp. 102, 103. I am indebted to Adrian Osbourne for drawing my attention to these two reworkings of the letter by Thomas.
38. Thomas to Johnson, [late October 1934], *CL*, p. 195. Ferris's insightful footnote tells us that '[e]arly in October [1934] a six-day international physics conference in London and Cambridge had prompted newspaper articles about the mysteries of the atom, including (to quote the *Times*) the fact that sub-atomic matter could 'behave both as particles or as waves.'
39. Thomas to Johnson, [early November 1933], *CL*, p. 57.
40. Thomas to Glyn Jones, [mid-April 1934], *CL*, p. 141; Thomas to Johnson, c. 21 March 1934, *CL*, p. 127.
41. John Goodby, *The Poetry of Dylan Thomas: Under the Spelling Wall* (Liverpool: Liverpool University Press, 2013), pp. 194–7.
42. *CP14*, pp. 58, 104.
43. Thomas to Desmond Hawkins, 14 August 1939, *CL*, p. 448.
44. Thomas to Johnson, 9 May 1934, *CL*, p. 155.
45. *CP14*, p. 81.
46. Ralph Maud, *Where Have the Old Words Got Me? Explications of Dylan Thomas's Collected Poems, 1934–1953* (Cardiff: University of Wales Press, 2003), p. 10.
47. *CP14*, p. 81.
48. *CP14*, pp. 107, 109–10.
49. Thus Geoffrey Grigson claimed: 'The self in Mr Thomas's poetry seems inhuman and glandular', and '[Dylan] was [. . .] cartilaginous, out of humanity, the Disembodied Gland.' (Geoffrey Grigson, 'How Much Me Now Your Acrobatics Amaze', in *Dylan Thomas: The Legend and the Poet*, ed. E. W. Tedlock (London: Heinemann, 1963), p. 160.) In the tradition of Arnoldian Celticism, 'glandular' is code for a nexus of cultural, class, gender and ethnic prejudice; it is implied that, with a sufficiently stiff upper lip, one can conquer this weakness; surrender to it, and you become less than human, nothing *but* gland. See Goodby, *The Poetry of Dylan Thomas*, pp. 186–7.
50. As early as 1849, Arnold Berthold had made testicular grafts in roosters and hens, and on 1 June 1889, in front of the Société de biologie in Paris,

Charles-Édouard Brown-Séquard became the first person to inject himself with 'testicular juice, got from the male genital glands'.

51. *NP*, p. 154.
52. Better known as vasectomy, the deviser of this procedure, Eugen Steinach, claimed that severing the sperm ducts increased male hormone production, and the operation became popular for these, rather than contraceptive reasons. Yeats's operation led to his being dubbed by Dublin wits 'the Gland Old Man of Irish Letters'.
53. See Chandak Sengoopta, *The Most Secret Quintessence of Life: Sex, Glands, and Hormones, 1850–1950* (Chicago: University of Chicago Press, 2006).
54. Thomas to Johnson, [21 December 1933], *CL*, p. 82.
55. *CP14*, pp. 59, 55, 57, 52, 82, 44, 60.
56. Ibid. pp. 69, 68, 60, 60; Thomas to Johnson, [early December 1933], *CL*, p. 76.
57. *CS*, pp. 112, 67.
58. Ibid. p. 57.
59. *CP14*, pp. 176, 100–1.
60. Thomas to Johnson, [25 and c. 21 December 1933], *CL*, pp. 99, 87.
61. Cited in Donald J. Childs, *Modernism and Eugenics: Woolf, Eliot, Yeats, and the Culture of Degeneration* (Cambridge: Cambridge University Press, 2001), pp. 10–11, 18.
62. Thomas to Trevor Hughes, 8 February 1933, *CL*, p. 29.
63. W. H. Auden, 'Foreword', in *Collected Shorter Poems: 1927–1957* (London: Faber, 1977), p. 15.
64. *CP14*, p. 63.
65. See Whitworth, *Einstein's Wake*, pp. 26–57.
66. *CP14*, pp. 100, 159, 110.
67. Ibid. p. 176.
68. Ibid. p. 184.
69. Ibid. pp. 199, 197.
70. *CP14*, pp. 199.
71. Whitworth, *Einstein's Wake*, p. 169.

Chapter 6

Dylan Thomas on the BBC Eastern Service

Edward Allen

Shuttling between the sleepy town of Berwick-upon-Tweed in 1980 and the Malay Peninsula in the early 1940s, *The Railway Man* (2013) recounts the secret history of one Eric Lomax, a signals officer in the 5th Field Regiment of the Royal Artillery.[1] Lomax was dispatched, following his commissioning in December 1940, to the main island of Singapore; he was there for its bombardment by Axis forces in December 1941; and he was there to supervise the regiment's clean-up operation when Fort Canning fell into Japanese hands on 15 February 1942. One early flash-back in his biopic reveals Lomax ensconced in the 'Battlebox' among his fellow telegraphists and wireless operators, straining once more to parse a stream of distress signals, before dismantling his equipment and squirreling away a glass receiving tube. 'It might come in handy,' he tells his commanding officer. The kit Lomax manages to salvage, we soon learn, proves instrumental in establishing a connection with the Allied world when the company is taken captive. Lomax and his fellow service-men are transported to a PoW camp in Thailand, where they furtively set about constructing a makeshift radio in between their engineering duties on the new Thailand–Burma Railway. In a film brimming with long looks and tortuous reunions, an odd moment of relief comes when Lomax and his friend Finlay finally get their act together and find a way to power their equipment. Crouched in the back of an army jeep, the men dampen the static crackle just long enough to make out a distant strain, first a smattering of dance music, and then a familiar, sturdy voice: 'This is the BBC Home and Forces Programme ...'

A good deal has been written about eavesdropping in recent years, so much so that one might detect a tantalising kind of irony in its becoming a topic of open and sustained debate. Covert, precarious, breathtakingly evanescent – the very matter of tapping into remote performances of voice resists trim critical description, and this has come home strongly to those who claim that the long imaginative history of eavesdropping reached its highest pitch in the heat of the Second World War.[2] 'Careless talk costs lives', 'Tittle tattle lost the battle', 'Be like Dad; keep Mum'.[3] The watchwords of Allied propaganda live on in cultural parlance in the manner of quaint cautionary tales, but they do so at the risk of obscuring another species of wartime chatter, which is the mode of shortwave broadcasting, a no less chancy kind of information distribution that encouraged the likes of Lomax and Finlay to spend their darkest hour fumbling across time zones. Following a series of tests and trial schedules, the BBC launched the Forces Programme in February 1940, chiefly to provide an 'alternative' to its domestic channel, the Home Service, as well as to cater more specifically for those who'd begun to wonder what sort of a phoney war they'd embarked upon.[4] In this way, with the support of external bodies such as the Ministry of Information, the BBC sought to boost morale on the expanding Western Front, and thus to respond to questions raised by the Foreign Office regarding 'our old friend "the background listener"'.[5] Although there's plenty of evidence to suggest that the BBC has never taken kindly to being forced one way or the other on the issue of accommodating a particular kind of consumer – least of all the inattentive sort – the corporation appears in 1940 to have adapted quickly to the wonts and whims of just such a figure, first by imagining in the *Radio Times* what 'active-service listening' might entail, and then by including items in the Forces Programme 'that [would] not suffer unduly by interruption, either by conversation or by the call of duty'.[6] At the same time, by plugging material that might be considered 'tentative and experimental', the BBC also hoped to push some boundaries, and in pushing boundaries allure further-flung listeners, whose eavesdropping might now extend to current affairs, features, quizzes, music, comedy and – for the interests of this chapter – poetry.[7]

That the outbreak of war brought with it new sensory encounters – even poetic ones – will strike most media and cultural historians as yesterday's news.[8] Yet there remain aspects of public broadcasting, particularly in South Asia, that may only assume discernable form if we continue to puzzle over the ways in which the BBC hoped to engage a widening pool of listeners in these years, and so to scrutinise and complicate the distinctions enshrined in its own mission 'to inform, educate and entertain'.[9] Potent as these 'Reithian principles' had come to sound by the early 1930s, the corporation's approach in the interwar period to doing any of these things to or for the empire's many colonies and dominions had been frustrated, not by a poverty of ambition, but by a lack of equipment. The cost of procuring a radio set, to say nothing of connecting it to a power supply, had put an end in 1930 to the short-lived Indian Broadcasting Company; and when, in 1932, the BBC had launched its shortwave Empire Service – with a view to touching parts of the world other networks couldn't reach – it had done so with an air of caution:

> Don't expect too much in the early days; for some time we shall transmit comparatively simple programmes, to give the best chance of intelligible reception and provide evidence as to the type of material most suitable for the service in each zone. The programmes will neither be very interesting nor very good.[10]

Never mind the drive to inform, educate and entertain, Reith was swift in December 1932 to assure his target audience that an effective, integrated service was still the stuff of fantasy. There is something laudable, if laughable, about his disconsolate turn as a media-age Eeyore – resisting the urge to talk up the 'comparatively simple programmes' – yet his guardedness in the public domain hardly tallies with the tone or substance of the message he hoped to send percolating through the ranks of the BBC itself. As Simon Potter has shown, Reith's private writings and internal memoranda evince a curious blend of 'Christian idealism' and imperialist self-possession, principles that encouraged him to believe that broadcasting would 'play its part in the establishment of world unity', and could in this sense begin to allay the obvious failings of 'the printed word'.[11] One of the things I wish to do in this chapter, by way of focusing on the years following Reith's departure from the BBC in 1938, is to observe how diligently the corporation's overseas outfit went about reconciling these two Reithian visions – one that proposed to cater, as it were, for the lowest common denominator, but which would take 'each zone' on its own terms, and one that revelled in the notion of collapsing 'frontiers' and 'saving civilization' in the process.[12] As we'll see, the bid to reconcile these visions only served to point up the phenomenological discrepancies of a medium that longed still to have it both ways, to appeal to individual listeners, and yet to capitalise, as Gillian Beer puts it, on the fact that early broadcasting had 'produced a new idea of the public, one far more intermixed, promiscuous and democratic than the book could cater for'.[13] In these terms, it must be clear, the impression that one might be alone in contriving the means to tap into a network in the back of a jeep – safe from prying enemy ears – is both erroneous and enabling.

Dylan Thomas occupies a curious rank in the history of the BBC. Hovering somewhere on the radio spectrum between Reith's split personalities – Eeyore and imperial prophet – the poet appears to have found plenty to complain and rejoice about in his time at the corporation, which commenced with a short poetry reading on the Regional Programme in April 1937, six months or so after the publication of

Twenty-five Poems.[14] Critics have wondered how best to account for this first assignment in the grand scheme of the poet's media career. It may be a stretch to argue, as Ralph Maud has, that Thomas 'was already an experienced broadcaster' by the time he came to perform in the spring of 1937, but it's certainly true to say that Thomas's enthusiasm in the late 1920s for a kind of ham radio – egged on by his friend in Swansea, Daniel Jones – had done something to prepare him for the trials of engaging a home crowd.[15] For Maud, then, as for Aneirin Talfan Davies, it stands to reason that Thomas was to find his niche on the Home Service, and that he would return to the Welsh Region as and when chance permitted.[16]

Yet it is easy to imagine the ways in which his early brush with the microphone may have served in fact not to sate but amplify these ambitions. According to this line of thought, Thomas was always bound to outgrow the fifteen-minute format that was apportioned at this time to so many jobbing poets, one of whom – Louis MacNeice – encouraged him to feel his way into other styles of presentation, and to use his voice 'for all sorts of strange purposes'.[17] While his proposal to champion the 'development of Anglo-Welsh poetry' did a little to endear him to his first wave of producers, Thomas appears to have got on at the BBC precisely because he was willing 'to have a try' at writing for different types of audiences, even if this meant immersing himself in alternative 'dramatic' genres, 'like a man shouting under the sea'.[18] In time, indeed, by composing 'imaginative full-length things for the radio', Thomas succeeded in inveigling his way into the highfalutin Third Programme, the flagship of a brave new BBC, which many expected to function as 'the prime re-educative agency of the post-war world'.[19] The posthumous transmission of *Under Milk Wood* in January 1954 did much to convince the public and press alike that Thomas had not only come to see the Third Programme as the ideal venue for 'techniques which are peculiar to sound radio', but had – in doing so – strayed some way from his core demographic.[20] Rather than capitulating to the idea that his work had somehow become the 'Welsh Region's "property"', Thomas looked in his 'play for voices' to fabricate a 'never-never Wales' – 'a Welsh town that never was' – and to dramatise in the process his various connections to home as a fanciful and thoroughly mediated set of relations.[21]

Important though it was to the formation of British literary culture at mid-century, the Third Programme has fostered a sort of selective hearing among its many critics and champions. In the case of *Under Milk Wood*, at least, it is not quite right to think of its author as the pin-up boy of the new domestic regime, not least because Thomas had long since discovered a fan-base far from home. In moving beyond the shadow of Llareggub Hill, what I want to do in this chapter is shed some light on a lesser-known portrait of the artist, one for whom the business of engaging listeners at the outer reaches of the British Empire was to prove a long-lasting and lucrative challenge in the post-war years. Reith's Empire Service had been expanded and rebranded in 1939 as the Overseas Service, owing to the proliferation of Axis propaganda, and it was under the auspices of a subdivision, the Eastern Service, that Thomas accepted something close to regular employment, first as a voice artist, and later as a writer. In doing so, he not only contrived a way to disseminate his 'passionate voice' and to ease his 'hermetic' inclinations – brought on by the outbreak of war, so he said – but also found himself implicated in a debate about the BBC's political responsibilities, which had now moved on some way since Reith's talk about 'simple' programming.[22] In fact, as critics have observed in recent years, the overseas networks of the corporation had struggled from the very beginning to reconcile two critical interests – 'British government priorities', on the one hand, 'and BBC editorial independence', on the other.[23] Nowhere was this friction felt more keenly than in the literary circle for which the Eastern Service provided a home in the 1940s, a circle by no means united in its approach to press regulation, or indeed confident of its own remit in the media ecology of another world war. In thinking particularly about the part the Eastern Service hoped to play in smoothing the way for an independent India, I want in the following pages to assess Thomas's purchase on the decolonisation debate, and to notice some of the ways in which he sought in his media work to contravene the neutralising effects of public broadcasting.

* * * *

When Lomax and Finlay tuned in to the BBC in 1942, any number of voices may have come their way. John Snagge's, Alvar Lidell's, Wilfred Pickles's – voices that had once been expected to remain unidentified on-air were permitted a new degree of attention in the Second World War, owing to a widespread belief that anonymity had had its day. The erstwhile policy of seeming to keep announcers' names under wraps was abandoned in the summer of 1940, principally because it was believed that members of the public would be more likely to notice an invasion of the corporation by enemy forces if they'd grown used to listening for names as well as news.[24] Snagge, Lidell and Pickles became names to conjure with in this apprehensive climate, though no name accrued quite the same kind of prestige as that of Bruce Belfrage, whose self-styling we finally hear erupting across the airwaves in *The Railway Man*, and whose name had become a byword for blitz spirit in October 1940, when the bombing of Broadcasting House had failed to stop the announcer introducing his evening bulletin.[25] Reading the news under fire was one way to make a name for yourself on the home front, but the beauty of a network like the Eastern Service, to which Belfrage and others contributed, had to do with a strange, cultural equilibrium, whereby news flashes and verse lyrics would regularly follow one after the other, often with precious little intervention on the part of a mediating voice.

Among those to learn how to tailor content whilst courting anonymity was employee 9889, and at the end of 1943 this employee reflected on the matter of splicing intellectual content for the benefit of listeners overseas:

> It is announced that in a few minutes' time such and such a poem will be broadcast; then the music plays for perhaps a minute, then fades out into the poem, which follows without any title or announcement, then the music is faded in again and plays up for another minute or two – the whole thing taking perhaps five minutes. It is necessary to choose appropriate music, but needless to say, the real purpose of the music is to insulate the poem from the rest of the programme. By this method you can have, say, a Shakespeare sonnet within three minutes of a news bulletin without, at any rate to my ear, any gross incongruity.[26]

Employee 9889, or Eric Blair, or George Orwell – for he was known by each of these monikers in his short time at the BBC – has come to represent an important source of information for critics of the institution. We are still getting to grips with the complexity of Orwell's contribution to the war effort as a talks producer at the BBC, yet we have known for some time that his sojourn in the Eastern Service's Indian Section ended in disaffection because he longed, where others did not, for boundaries, definition and transparency.[27] His private writings are everywhere enflamed by the impression that the 'propaganda front' has descended into 'chaos' at the hands of the Foreign Office, and though for Orwell such chaos may have signalled an opportunity in 1942 to get his own message across, his frustrations appear to have been aggravated by his employer's 'ill-defined' policy: 'the fear and hatred of intelligence are so all-pervading', he recorded one day in June 1942, 'that one cannot plan any sort of wireless campaign.'[28] One way to remedy the corporation's 'continuous dithering', it seemed to him, was to feign a more than usually structuralist attitude to programming. This was not to pretend for a moment that arts broadcasting didn't have a way of evolving at the planning stage to produce 'somewhat shapeless' content; rather, Orwell sought to mitigate the amorphous quality of literary discussion by encouraging colleagues and visiting contributors to think carefully about the ways one might use the wireless medium to 'give a poem a context'.[29] Sometimes this merely involved tethering a programme to 'a single central theme'; on other occasions, as we hear in 'Poetry and the Microphone', the work of constructing a programme entailed exercising a strict sense of discretion, whereby producers would aim to 'insulate' various bits of content – in this case, by 'set[ting] a poem in music' – so as to leave listeners in no doubt that the context for such a poem is *not* the latest 'news bulletin', but something else entirely. To segue too smoothly between a press release and a sonnet might, after all, be to risk a sort of 'gross incongruity', whereas to separate your Shakespeare from the sounds of bombardment, or from the recent news from Singapore – this might be to give your reader of poetry on the 'aether-waves' a fighting chance of persuading an audience to take verse on its own terms. 'It is a question', Orwell believed, 'of getting people to listen instead of uttering a mechanical raspberry.'[30]

Though evidently introduced with the best of intentions, the policy of 'insulat[ing]' literary material with musical interludes is unlikely to have convinced listeners that the BBC had suddenly found a way 'to make [poetry] seem *normal*'.[31] On the contrary, such an elaborate policy of appearing to segregate poetry may well have served to reinforce the popular perceptions to which Orwell alludes gloomily in his essay – that poetry embodies 'intellectual pretentiousness and a general feeling of Sunday-on-a-weekday' – as well as substantiating his own conviction that reading poetry on the Eastern Service would amount to nothing more than 'a small and remote outflanking movement in the radio war'.[32] As it is, there were a number of writers in this movement who thought otherwise, chief among them Louis MacNeice, who'd sought employment at the BBC in late 1940 not only because he needed the cash, but also because he wished to resist the idea that literature might be treated as a special case. '[W]hoso tries to save his art – by insulating it – shall lose it', MacNeice had informed his sweetheart, Eleanor Clark, upon returning to Europe in October 1940, and though he too came to see the BBC as a 'deplorable' place to work on occasion, he was also gracious enough to admit that the institution 'does leave some loophole for intelligence & individual decisions'.[33]

Like it or not, Orwell was required more and more to share the airwaves with those who hoped to draw the attention of listeners to the fact that literary expression had already found ways to absorb the shock effects of news and war bulletins.

Among those Killed in the Dawn Raid was a Man Aged a Hundred

When the morning was waking over the war
He put on his clothes and stepped out and he died,

The locks yawned loose and a blast blew them wide,
He dropped where he loved on the burst pavement stone
And the funeral grains of the slaughtered floor.
Tell his street on its back he stopped a sun
And the craters of his eyes grew springshoots and fire
When all the keys shot from the locks, and rang.
Dig no more for the chains of his grey-haired heart.
The heavenly ambulance drawn by a wound
Assembling waits for the spade's ring on the cage.
O keep his bones away from that common cart,
The morning is flying on the wings of his age
And a hundred storks perch on the sun's right hand.[34]

Made in its extravagant way to sound like just another newspaper report, 'Among those Killed in the Dawn Raid was a Man Aged a Hundred' signals both a point of departure and return for Dylan Thomas. It is the first of several wartime lyrics to recycle headline material and so, in John Goodby's words, to 'announce [its] public status'; yet the poem bursts too, here and there, with the sorts of verbal *jouissance* we find erupting in Thomas's early collections.[35] There is punning, and there is polysemy, as well as pockets of semantic density that reveal the poet working against the grain of the journalist's craft. In the seventh line of the sonnet, for instance, the eyewitness's paratactic method appears for a moment to come unstuck, when an 'and' serves to confuse rather than coordinate the city's war-stricken ecology. In cultivating this curious collocation – 'springshoots and fire' – Thomas asks us to imagine a bombed-out skull that has been turned somehow into a garden feature, a macabre vision that reminds us that the surrealist in Thomas is very much alive and kicking.

As Leo Mellor has said, there is a 'rhetorical intensity' about this writing that is part and parcel of wartime elegy, and such flashes of intensity can be glimpsed in those moments when Thomas slides from a sort of hypersensitivity into the sensational mode of hypallage.[36] Having come, by the sixteenth century, 'to be restricted to instances of "exchange" in a phrase or sentence', the figure of hypallage – or the transferred epithet – has long occupied a subversive place in the English language, whose analytic texture consists in strict determinations of syntax.[37] Often, then, the effect of hypallactic displacement is to send an otherwise orderly passage spiralling into the enchanting or bizarre, as when Keats remembers in 'The Eve of St Agnes' how 'silent was the flock in woolly fold', divesting the sheep of their fleeces when they can least afford to lose them in favour of padding out his wintry landscape.[38] Yet the figure of hypallage can and has been used for more sobering purposes, and Thomas is not the first to have conscripted the figure in a state of national emergency. Think of Wilfred Owen's note of alarm in 'Dulce et Decorum Est' – 'Gas! GAS! Quick, boys!' – which diffuses all too quickly into '[a]n ecstasy of fumbling, / Fitting the clumsy helmets just in time'.[39] The substance of a transferred epithet – here, 'the clumsy helmets' – has to do so often with a fumbling of agency, and with imagining what it might mean for an inanimate object to assume the mood or aspect of an animate one. Thomas may well have learned this ontological sleight of hand from Owen, though he makes the trick his own in 'Among those Killed' by drawing out its absurd potential, pausing first to survey 'the slaughtered floor', and then turning his centenarian into a grotesque, replete with 'grey-haired heart'. In the manner of magnetised particles, these displacements of syntax appear to gather and spark with the sort of linguistic energy one associates with compounds, coinages and kennings, but it is hard, beyond the pleasures of internal lyric play, to see what Thomas's endgame may be in marshalling such rhetorical figures. There is no doubt that the blitzes in Swansea and London required a range of creative as well as descriptive responses, but it remains to be seen whether Thomas was sufficiently attentive to the efficacy of that distinction, or indeed to the effects of a poetry that mixes freely the grammars of surrealist and war correspondent.

Whatever quality of attention he hoped to garner in 1941, Thomas was well aware of how much a poem could fetch in a war economy:

> We should very much like to broadcast in a programme of Welsh poetry on Monday next, 8th February [1943], your poem 'Among Those Killed in the Dawn Raid', (14 lines).
>   We shall be glad to know whether you can authorise this subject to the payment of a fee of two guineas.[40]

The BBC Written Archives are chock-a-block with letters, memos and receipts of this kind, and Thomas appears in most cases to have replied without delay. He was rarely allowed to name his price, and though on some occasions he managed to claim expenses before travelling to undertake a recording, often in the early years of the war he was merely expected to grant the likes of the actor John Laurie permission to do the job in his absence. Still, with guineas trickling in, Thomas came to see this piecemeal work as a vital source of income, such that he fell to wondering whether a permanent position at the corporation might be secured. 'I want a job very badly, because I haven't a penny', he wrote to Vernon Watkins in August 1940. 'I've applied for a BBC job, but I think my lack of university will spoil it. It wd be a very well paid job, but boring: making preces [sic] (I mean summaries) of the world's news for Empire bulletins.'[41] A contracted post at the BBC continued to elude Thomas, but his mention in this letter to Watkins of 'Empire bulletins' was to prove unusually prescient. While dispatching the news to the Indian subcontinent remained the job of Belfrage and others, the author of 'Among those Killed' found himself enlisted in 1945 in a project that would render his voice among the flashiest of literary assets at the Eastern Service.

Over a sixteen-year period, beginning in 1937, Thomas averaged a little over one broadcast a month for the BBC, ranging from extended commissions and script adaptations to bit parts and recitations. His was a growing presence, then, particularly in Orwell's Indian Section, which played host to a reading and discussion of the Welshman's poetry in August 1942 in the first programme of a series entitled *Voice*. 'All it needs is a little electrical power and half a dozen voices', Orwell advised the first 'readers' of his wireless publication, before going on to explain that the programme's primary function would be to disseminate the work of poets 'who have been handicapped by the paper shortage'.[42] The novelty of this 'magazine' format was palpable to anyone who longed to 'choose [his] own cover design', but Orwell hoped to do something more by way of appealing to listeners 'whose English is not necessarily perfect'.[43] In doing so, Orwell's monthly programme made room in the ether for a variety of like-minded projects, which sought to make a virtue of material rationing, and which liked to think of themselves as outreach ventures. By far the most frequent of Thomas's radio stints was a slot on just such a programme, the Eastern Service's *Book of Verse* series, which was first touted in September 1944. Edward Sackville-West had produced the programme in its first quarter, and upon his resignation the reins passed to John Arlott, a radio personality better remembered these days for his cricket commentary than for his exacting poetic standards.[44] An internal review of 1948 reveals why Arlott was the man for the job:

> The under-lying purpose of 'Book of Verse' was to present an anthology of popular, easily understandable programmes in a manner which brought home to the ordinary listener that poetry was <u>not</u> something remote from everyday life spoken in an unnatural voice by earnest young men and women. For this reason, John Arlott was assigned the task of compiling a personal anthology with his own comments. He is himself a poet, and, previous to this programme, was very well-known to Light Programme's listeners as a cricket and football commentator. It was thought that his reputation in this field would reassure listeners that they were not going to be inflicted with anything recondite and long-haired. The readers too were chosen with very great care to sound as normal and human as possible.[45]

Truth be told, 'the ordinary listener' had always been a fiction – the figment of a quaint, homogenising imagination – and one which had

been firmly displaced when the war came to an end, as networks diversi-
fied, and listeners' needs were subject to scrutiny rather than dictation.
If a few at the BBC had clung too long to the idea of a radiophonic
Everyman, it may be because the corporation had been reluctant to
seek out public opinion. Reith had observed pointedly in 1931 that
'"ordinary listeners"' in Britain 'are not encouraged or invited to com-
municate' with the corporation, for – as he saw it, and as he'd put it so
testily before – 'it is occasionally indicated to us that we are apparently
setting out to give the public what we think they need – and not what
they want, but few know what they want, and very few what they
need.'[46] Not until 1936, with the founding of the Listener Research
Department, had a systematic attempt been made to understand the
public's changing habits of reception and taste, and only then, perhaps,
had administrators begun to come to terms with the difficulty of justify-
ing the BBC's 'educational ballyhoo'.[47]

For the new-fangled problem of a programme like *Book of Verse*
would have to do with fine-tuning its pedagogical agenda, while aiming
also to satisfy its very distinct corps of listeners from whom the BBC
could now expect to receive some feedback. Although pretending to
cater for the Lomaxes and Finlays who may have tuned in when the
programme went live in 1944, *Book of Verse* was always intended for
school and university communities. Zulfiqar Ali Bokhari, the Indian
Programme Organiser, had done much to engage this layer of the popu-
lation since his arrival at the BBC in 1940, drawing on his experience
at the Delhi Broadcasting Station, and giving particular thought to
varieties of language and dialect in grass-roots programming. Together
with the support of Laurence Brander, who was dispatched to India in
April 1942 to scout out the prospect of establishing a listener research
service, Bokhari moulded the Indian Section's educational provision so
as to 'catch the young Indian intellectual', and to cultivate connections
between the BBC and leading universities in Andhra, Calcutta, and
Bombay.[48] Building on Brander's suggestion that 'honest intellectualism
can be perfectly good entertainment for a minority audience' – as well
as for 'the eavesdropping Englishman' – programmes like *Book of Verse*
were not only designed to satisfy the requirements of distance learning,
but also to showcase British literary talent, partly on the assumption –
again, at Brander's behest – that 'Indians do not want to hear Indians
from London speaking on intellectual subjects'.[49] The data samples from
which such claims were extrapolated appear to have been quite small,
but whether or not the Indian Section was right to allow Brander's
report to determine its policy, the further proviso that 'Indians have no
use for the English man or woman who has had a career in India' was

to prove instrumental in persuading producers to seek and retain the services of tenderfoots such as Dylan Thomas, who'd never set eyes on the Subcontinent.

In the spirit of meeting the corporation's aim to spare Indian listeners 'anything recondite and long-haired', Arlott granted Thomas a spot on *Book of Verse* on the understanding that his main task would be to elaborate upon other poets' work rather than his own. This was in keeping with the programme's broader scholastic ethos, and with its producers' attempts to endorse and gesture beyond the syllabi of British universities. In 1946, under Thomas's guidance, listeners were treated to poems by Dekker, Cowley, Traherne, Yeats, Graves and Abercrombie, and in 1947 a string of Renaissance specials followed. '[A]ll my job', he complained to Vernon Watkins, 'is the selection of the poems for profes-sional readers to (badly, usually) read, and the interpolation of four-line comments between each.'[50] That he put up with this hackwork tells us something about the scale of his financial problems at the time – the most undemanding programme for Arlott would bring in as much as 7 guineas – yet his staying power must also have had something to do with the longer scripts he was prevailed upon to write, which were not only more profitable, but also more capacious for the sort of writer who wished, as it were, to spread out, pressing at the limits of his bandwidth. In doing, Thomas sought to reflect more deeply on what it might mean to be 'a border case', whether in Swansea, London, Bombay or 'a resting place between places' – the territory of broadcast voices – disembodied, apparently without origin.[51] His piece on 'Welsh Poetry' in January 1946 took up precisely this idea – we might call it a habit – of playing fast and loose with known coordinates. Thomas begins the script in contrary mood:

> This is not a programme of Welsh poetry, because Welsh poetry is written in the Welsh language, which few of us, including myself, can understand. The position – if poets must have positions, other than upright – of the poet born in Wales, or of Welsh parentage and writing his poems in English is, today, made by many people unnecessarily, and trivially, difficult.[52]

If poets must have positions, other than upright. That parenthetical aside is meant to do some serious work here, as jokes often do in this poet's writing. Thomas means of course to build his fellow poets up – right up, indeed, to 'upright' – though with Thomas you always know that asides of this sort have a dirty underbelly, and that 'upright' quivers with a sense of sexual prowess too, as it does in a poem like 'Vision and Prayer' (1945), in which 'upright Adam' is supposed to be at once unfallen and ready for some action.[53] Only Thomas, perhaps – or an adolescent reader of Thomas (we were all adolescents once) – could mistake moral rectitude for erective possibility, yet the gag is more complicated than its seediness implies, for Thomas also feigns to disclose a shakier truth about his subject, which has to do with its contested place in the social imaginary, and the extent to which an ideological position may or may not have taken root in the mother tongue.[54] This problem of pinpointing the spoken self has been noticed before, most recently by John Goodby, who has attributed the oscillatory quality of Thomas's writing in part to the hyphenated condition of an Anglo-Welsh poetics: 'the result is a series of overdetermined, intersecting borders and liminal zones, which traverse and constitute the subject.'[55] Such 'liminal inbetweenness' – whether it has to do with national identity or bending over backwards to please a readership – has its implications for larger social structures, as Goodby goes on to say, and those implications manifest themselves particularly vividly on air, where jokes about being in one place at one time are wont to dissolve in the instants of their articulation. Later in his broadcast, for example, Thomas muses on the poetry of John Dyer, an eighteenth-century shepherd-poet, and proceeds to recommend his blank-verse epic, *The Fleece*, which describes 'the tending of sheep, of shearing and weaving, and of trade in woollen manufactures. We must read it together one day.'[56] It's a peculiar thing to say, this – 'we must read it together one day' – like imparting an audible wink to an audience he'll never meet, but one that may yet forgive him the indulgence. For this vision of a collective reading experience is not so much a trespass or a trick as a sign of the poet's immersion in a medium that appears to know no bounds. *We must read it together one day.*

One could be forgiven for hearing Thomas's manoeuvre as a goodwill gesture, and a timely antidote to the sorts of scepticism that had begun to circulate in wireless culture. Ezra Pound had long since come to regard the radio, or 'devil box', as a mixed blessing, a 'God damn destructive and dispersive devil of an invention'.[57] In a slightly different vein, Wallace Stevens was widely applauded in the early 1940s for his indictment of the medium for precisely the reasons Thomas appears to have loved it: 'We are close together in every way', Stevens lamented in 1941: 'We lie in bed and listen to a broadcast from Cairo, and so on. There is no distance. We are intimate with people we have never seen and, unhappily, they are intimate with us.'[58] Whatever the drift of public debate, Thomas seems to have entertained no scruples about getting cosy on air, or of talking his way further into territory he had recently been employed to document. As well as his peripatetic work at the BBC, Thomas had spent a considerable part of the war writing documentary scripts, first for Donald Taylor's Strand Films, and then for its offshoot company, Gryphon Films. Less than two weeks after Neville Chamberlain's critical broadcast to the nation, Thomas had belittled 'all the shysters in London [who] are grovelling about the Ministry of Information', yet he'd done so knowing full well that a job at one of the Ministry's affiliated companies would not only suit him nicely, but also provide an opportunity to broaden his imaginative horizons.[59] Where, in lighter moods, he would speak of India on the radio as a place of 'wonder', 'bright with oranges and loud with lions', his work at Strand Films bespeaks a different, though no less colourful, quality of attention.[60] In one film of 1945, *A Soldier Comes Home*, we see a returning serviceman, Jack, chewing over his time in north-east India, first remembering his way around the bazaars of Calcutta – 'Aye, what a place. Goats and dogs and sacred cows, and chaps chewing betel' – before settling down with his son, Jim, and a well-thumbed *Popular Atlas of the World*.[61] Jim knows all there is to know about Burma, we learn in due course; he's been borrowing books from the library, and has compiled a scrapbook of newspaper clippings. Nothing can beat a proper eyewitness, of course, and in an oddly touching scene we see the father audibly retracing his footsteps, guiding his son all the way from Manipur to Mandalay. 'We had never seen a jungle', he recalls, gently waving his cigarette over the map. 'It is like living in a big steam laundry, full of enormous asparagus.'[62] It is possible to think of more recent schools of poetry that operate in this perspective-shifting manner, rendering the unknown familiar and the familiar alien; the line about 'enormous asparagus' is just the kind of thing Craig Raine might say if he were lost in a jungle. But, unlike Raine's Martian excursions, Thomas's homespun vignette speaks in finer ways to the problems of naturalising a distant theatre of war. Even now, with a child's atlas before him, the soldier must go on, struggling with the idea that he has been, in *his* words, 'very far away', and will continue to be in some sense so long as he longs to be 'out on a patrol'.[63] To do so, as a serviceman not yet demobilised, is to feel distinctly embattled, even in the comfort of his own living room.

Thomas had reconnoitred this terrain a few years before in a documentary called *Battle for Freedom* (1942). Of all his contributions to the Ministry of Information, *Battle for Freedom* has done little to persuade critics that Thomas was motivated at this time by anything like a higher purpose. Spoken in the form of an elegy to imperial order, the film weighs up the 'raw materials of the British Empire', and so appears to value and reap the fruits of 'fullest collaboration' at the expense of those who'd sooner see 'the Commonwealth of New Nations' continue to expand.[64] The political message of the film is desperate and conflicted, muddling as it does the priorities of 'freedom and independence' that might pertain to the colonies and dominions, yet the commentary is alive to such muddles. Though Thomas seems in most respects to have toed the line so neatly demarcated by the Ministry of Information – there's no whiff of asparagus here – the details suggest a familiarity on his part with the latest developments in foreign policy:

> Despite their refusal of the Cripps proposals, the people of India are, more than ever before, determined to withstand and throw back Japanese aggression. For well they know that a successful Japanese invasion would mean slavery – would mean that the certainty of the British promise of India's independence would vanish like smoke.[65]

In March 1942, following the loss of Burma, Malaya and Singapore, one of Winston Churchill's ministers, Stafford Cripps, had travelled to New Delhi to negotiate a draft declaration regarding India's self-determination – a deal policymakers in London were willing to strike with Congress in exchange for its continued support on the Far Eastern Front. Cripps hoped to persuade Mohandas Karamchand Gandhi and Muhammad Ali Jinnah to rally their respective parties, Hindu and Muslim, and so to defer for a moment the claims of separatist pressure groups on the understanding that a revised system of provincial government after the war would give rise to a new constitution, which might itself prepare the way for an independent Pakistan.[66] The mission was a disaster. Gandhi is reported to have likened Cripps's proposal to a 'post-dated cheque drawing on a crashing bank', and though the spokesman of the pending Quit India Movement was quick to disavow the soundbite, he paused before dispensing entirely with the analogy, and spoke sadly of the way the proposal had floundered. '"Sir Stafford has come and gone"', he declared. '"How nice it would have been if he had not come with the dismal mission. [. . .] I made suggestions but all to no avail."'[67] Cripps returned home to find himself, on the one hand, celebrated by his Labour colleagues as the architect of a new age in subcontinental politics, and pitied, on the other, by those who could see that the minister had never stood a chance in persuading Congress to accept a package that had evidently originated on the other side of the House. One of these was Orwell, who helped to broadcast Cripps's parting speech in April 1942, only to detect between the lines a distinctly Conservative cadence:

> It is a curious fact that in the more exalted passages in his speeches Cripps seems to have caught certain inflexions of voice from Churchill. This may point to the fact – which would explain his having undertaken this mission when only having such bad terms to offer – that he is at present much under Churchill's personal influence.[68]

Orwell was not the only one to foster a conspiracy theory, or to see that Cripps's rhetoric had 'caused a lot of offence' in India; and by the autumn of 1942 there were plenty of readers, listeners and cinemagoers who were unwilling to believe the official line – peddled by the BBC – that 'only the supporters of Fascism' had taken joy in Cripps's 'failure'.[69] On the contrary, the listener research department's weekly report from India tells a very different story, which is that a small but vocal minority had found Cripps's radio talks in the spring 'trite and platitudinous', and had come to see the minister's contributions to a post-war settlement as 'positively mischievous'.[70] In spite, or more probably because, of such findings, the BBC appears to have talked down Gandhi's policy of nonviolent resistance as best it could, electing instead to shift focus and to suggest that only Axis troublemakers had interpreted the breakdown of Cripps's mission 'as a refusal on the part of India to defend herself'.[71] Which raises the tantalising question – was Dylan Thomas merely stating the facts when he mentioned the bungled plan in *Battle for Freedom*, or was he himself making mischief? Did he know, in plumping for that apparently innocuous word – 'refusal' – that he was departing from script?

It is impossible to say for sure, and to resolve questions of this sort one way or the other would be to divine ideological motivations that Thomas was in any case expected to repress. What we can say more certainly is that by the time Thomas arrived at *Book of Verse* in 1945, the problem of *mediating* the India question had become for him part and parcel of being a vocal public figure on the Eastern Service. This may or may not be what endeared Thomas to John Arlott, the programme's producer, whose own work in this area would include an hour-long memorial documentary in the wake of Gandhi's assassination in January 1948. At any rate, Thomas's programme on 'Welsh Poetry' went down well with Arlott, and it paved the way for another single-author feature, 'Wilfred Owen', which went out in July 1946, not quite a year since the formal conclusion of hostilities in the eastern theatre. In both cases, Thomas experiments with a style of literary criticism that relies on a particularly fluid kind of prosopopoeia. In neither piece, in other words, is Thomas quite speaking for himself; he speaks *through* borrowed phrases and patterns of speech, allowing him to impersonate and personify, and so to replace direct political assertion with masked forms of expression – implication and suggestion:

> At this time, when, in the words of an American critic, the audiences of the earth, witnessing what well may be the last act of their own tragedy, insist upon chief actors who are senseless enough to perform a cataclysm, the voice of the poetry of Wilfred Owen speaks to us, down the revolving stages of

thirty years, with terrible new significance and strength. We had not forgotten his poetry, but perhaps we had allowed ourselves to think of it as the voice of one particular time, one place, one war.[72]

The nuclear threat was no less pressing in the summer of 1946 than it had been a year before, and Thomas strains in this script to achieve a sense of control by stage-managing the prospect of apocalypse.[73] With a grand, theatrical gesture he casts the world's politicians as 'actors' and their tinkering as a 'senseless' sort of performance; he declines, of course, to imagine the ways this 'last act' should play out, though knows 'there may be no historians' to do the work of historiography in the '"atomic age"', so prefers to look back, and not forward, to a 'prodigious' voice of reason. Owen's has not been forgotten, we're told, but the process of reclaiming it – of repurposing it for mid-century ears – has somehow set free a 'new significance and strength'. It has taken thirty years and another war for us to really get to grips with Owen, Thomas seems to say, not only to understand 'the trench and shellhole and hospital', but also to grasp 'the collapsed and apprehensive calm of sick-leave'.[74] Only historical distance, in the end, can produce such forms of knowledge; that, and the conducting element of a radio set.

Thomas plays throughout the programme with this question of belated affect, and particularly with the idea of naturalising a voice that has been delayed or displaced through time. One of the reasons the broadcast has not shown up on the critical radar, I suspect, is because its real achievement consists in the things Thomas *doesn't* say, or rather in the things Thomas allows *Owen* to say, as in this passage from the soldier's lyric, 'Exposure':

> Watching, we hear the mad gusts tugging on the wire,
> Like twitching agonies of men among its brambles.
> Northward, incessantly, the flickering gunnery rumbles,
> Far off, like a dull rumour of some other war.
>   What are we doing here?
>
> The poignant misery of dawn begins to grow ...
> We only know war lasts, rain soaks, and clouds sag stormy.
> Dawn massing in the east her melancholy army
> Attacks once more in ranks on shivering ranks of grey,
>   But nothing happens.[75]

We hear in these uneven lines a voice entrenched, grasping wildly at a few known truths, and little comforted by the thought that 'know[ing] war lasts' must count, under the circumstances, as its own kind of epistemological victory. In some respects, it's an unremarkable frontline poem – overblown in places, as Owen's poems sometimes are – but how must it have sounded in the mid-1940s, liberated from its first combative origins, unleashed afresh in the wake of the latest ceasefire? It is not, I think, that listeners would have garbled the poem exactly, or have made it their own in any deliberate sense – only that they may have tuned into 'Exposure' and found, as Owen puts it earlier in the poem, 'our memory of the salient' illuminated and 'confuse[d]'.[76] 'Far off, like a dull rumour of some other war' must have carried with it a double resonance in the summer of 1946 – the echo of an echo, almost, or the sign of a mind playing tricks on itself – such that an Indian listener might have grimaced to think that history had not merely repeated itself, but that 'some other war' had materialised in his backyard, far beyond the earshot of a French trench. For what would listeners in the Subcontinent have made of this poem's stark polarities? '*Northward*, incessantly, the flickering gunnery rumbles' – 'Dawn massing in the *east* her melancholy army'. Where, for Owen – stuck on the Western Front – these compass bearings had signalled rumour and change, for devotees of the *Eastern* Service, these apprehensions must have sounded almost comically belated in 1946, witnessing as they had a thorough crumpling of the Empire's map. To hear the poem rebounding in these ways – pulling in new directions – might have been to learn something about the distance a poem can travel, and so apparently to confirm the substance of Thomas's remark that 'we can see, re-reading Owen, that he is a poet of all times, all places, and all wars.' Yet it is foolish to imagine that any amount of 'Exposure' in July 1946 would have done much to comfort listeners, or to allay their fears that something much worse than a 'flickering gunnery' had come to occupy the horizon. As Thomas observes, Owen had weathered an 'infernal winter' in 1917; thirty years on, the prospect of a nuclear one had begun to determine the forecast.[77]

I have been looking in this chapter for a way to elucidate a point about reception. It is a delicate and speculative business, historicising scripts that were always intended for real voices and real ears. '[I]s it possible to understand a historically embedded and embodied act of listening?' wonders Ian Whittington in one recent essay, before reflecting that '[e]ven the thickest description of a particular historical moment risks reducing a diversity of embodied listening experiences into a single one.'[78] If Owen's poetry managed to speak in unexpected ways to the survivors and veterans of another war, it is important to recognise the provisional quality of that experience – a strange meeting of minds – which may be the condition of good public broadcasting. Even so, but for the effects of such teasing speculation, there *are* concrete things we can say in the case of 'Wilfred Owen' that may help to shore up the impression that

Thomas's script was felt by some to appeal too sharply to political sensibilities. The script available to most readers now is the text printed in Ralph Maud's edition of *The Broadcasts* (1991), which states that the programme was recorded on 19 June 1946. A little digging in the archive suggests otherwise (Figure 6.1).[79] Apparently unbeknownst to

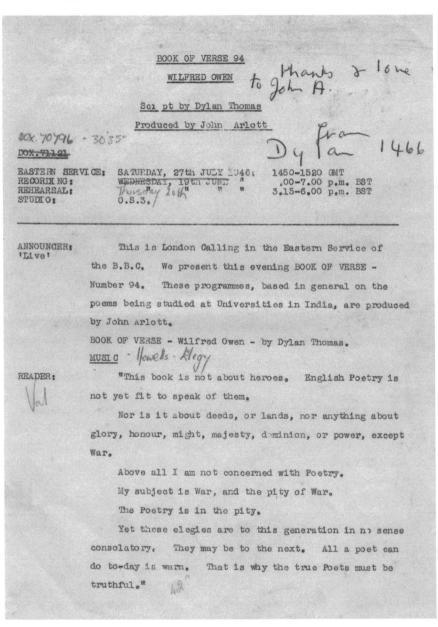

Figure 6.1   'Wilfred Owen', *Book of Verse*, 27 July 1946, p. 1.

Ralph Maud, the script held at the Harry Ransom Center reveals some last-minute tinkering. A dedication to John Arlott can be seen in the right-hand corner, scribbled (and dated) in Thomas's mischievous hand; and the recording timetable has been altered too, not by 'Dylan 1466', but probably by Arlott himself, the producer, whose pencil markings riddle the script. What a revision of this sort underlines, of course, is that five weeks went by between recording and transmission – five weeks in which almost anything could happen to jeopardise or inflect the content of a script, and in which certain types of editing would have to be undertaken in order to prime the talk for life beyond the studio.

Of all the intervals in all the world, those five weeks in the summer of 1946 were especially turbulent for Eastern Service listeners, for whom the news of nuclear testing in the Pacific is unlikely to have eclipsed a story much closer to home. A new British delegation had been sent to India in March by Clement Attlee – it was dubbed the 'Cabinet Mission' – with a view to kindling discussion between the Indian National Congress and the All-India Muslim League. 'The precise road towards the final structure of India's independence is not yet clear', Frederick Pethick-Lawrence had confessed upon the Mission's arrival in Karachi, yet for all the Secretary of State's tentative overtures, no one at the negotiating table could doubt that the Mission had set out to secure Britain's strategic interests in India as a matter of priority.[80] The wish to establish an administration that would share assets and resources with its Commonwealth partners was by no means incompatible with the short-term aims of either interested party, Congress or League; the rub, rather, had to do with reconciling one side's interest in centralising power (particularly economic power) with the other's dream of a sovereign Pakistan, whose grouped provinces would be entitled to equal representation in a union government. In May, following a conference in Simla, a proposal by the Mission of a three-tier federation appeared to herald a third way of sorts, but in order to proceed, both the Congress and League were obliged to sign up to an interim government. The composition of such a government was to prove an irresolvable point of contention. By 29 June – a little over a week since Thomas had recorded his talk – negotiations had collapsed and the Mission had flown, only to leave in suspension the matter of forming a caretaker government. The month of July witnessed further resistance and agitation on both sides, and in August, following the League's call for 'direct action', violence swept across the Punjab and Bengal. In Calcutta alone, between 16 and 20 August, over four thousand people were killed.[81]

It would be difficult to overstate the fragility of Hindu–Muslim relations in the summer of 1946. Difficult, too, to imagine the pressure exerted on a media institution like the BBC, whose responsibility in such a moment (you might think) would be to remind itself that the business of *media* – of playing the intermediary, of occupying the middle ground – is never clear-cut. Cutting is what the BBC tends to do in these situations, and its archive reveals that a cut would ordinarily be made to pre-recorded broadcasts at this time for one of three reasons: length, quality or content. On 27 July 1946, only one cut was made to *Book of Verse* (Figure 6.2). Timings jotted in the margin of the script indicate

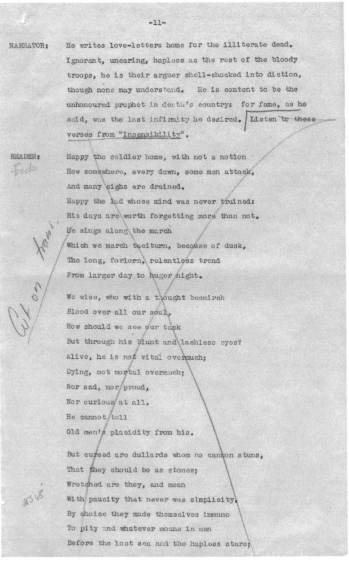

Figure 6.2   'Wilfred Owen', *Book of Verse*, 27 July 1946, p. 11.

that the programme was just about spot on in length – indeed, Thomas had mastered by now the skill of compiling 30-minute scripts – so we've got to wonder why these lines by Owen were scrubbed in the event of transmission. Striking a balance between verse and commentary was always tricky, and perhaps Arlott felt it was one poem too many on this occasion; or perhaps this bit of the recording was simply too grainy to use. Either way, the cut must also have appeared diplomatic – politic, even – given the public mood at this time. 'Insensibility', from which these lines are taken, is an ode to various forms of 'strange arithmetic' – to the kind that seems to have deserted those who 'keep no check on armies' decimation', and to the kind that occupies lyric poets, for whom the drift of pronominal identity is very often a numbers game.[82] Not until line 37 of the complete poem is Owen's speaker minded or emboldened to count himself a member of the group ('*we* march taciturn'), with the effect that 'the lad' who pops up at that moment appears to do so in blithe defiance of the poem's gathering choric momentum. 'Happy the lad whose mind was never trained'. Had that line made it onto the airwaves, it would have resonated in two ways among Thomas's listeners: first, no doubt, as a playful nod to the pedagogical function of the programme (*Book of Verse* was all about training supple minds, after all); but second, and more pertinently, as a short, sharp blow to imperial uniformity. How easy it would be – or would have been – to trace the all-too-familiar dividing line between the 'we's, 'he's and 'they's of these closing stanzas, between the 'wise' who know they have a 'task' to accomplish, and the 'dullards' who merely traipse on, insensitive and 'immune' to a higher calling. These were evidently subject positions the BBC was unwilling to countenance in the wake of recent political upheaval, and one suspects the corporation's in-house regulators were especially relieved to see the last lines of the poem crossed through:

> By choice they made themselves immune
> To pity and whatever moans in man
> Before the last sea and the hapless stars;
> Whatever mourns when many leave these shores;
> Whatever shares
> The eternal reciprocity of tears.[83]

Whatever mourns when many leave these shores. The striking truth in July 1946 – as the sun finally began to set on British India – was that few would indulge in any such act of grief when the time came to bid farewell to the Raj.

In sickness and in health, Dylan Thomas remained a faithful contributor to *Book of Verse*. He plainly found ways to deal with the occasional cut and editorial intervention, though one wonders what he made of the corporation's decision in 1947 to commission another poet to report on Indian partition, given his steadfast commitment to the Eastern Service. As so often before, the BBC picked Louis MacNeice instead, who promptly flew out to Karachi in August 1947 with the Features Department, only to discover groups of young Indian students expecting to clap eyes on Thomas.[84] It's nice to suppose that these students had warmed to the Welshman on air, had perhaps even encountered there a kindred spirit, whose aim in voicing and compiling anthology pieces for *Book of Verse* had always been to keep his listeners guessing, and to persuade them that the shape of literary history is worth puzzling over precisely because 'the course of poetry is dictated by accidents'.[85] It is a sadness to think that such a conviction may finally have counted against Thomas at the BBC, prompting the likes of Arlott to offer his accident-prone friend work that was unlikely to raise alarm or to be mistaken for political meddling. Indeed, Arlott may have felt that he was acting kindly towards Thomas in 1947 by sending him a series of Shakespeare readings to get his teeth into, for these – to Arlott's mind – were just the sorts of readings that could not be mangled or misconstrued on *Book of Verse*:

> It has had more favourable press notices in English magazines than any other literary programme. Under two Service Heads – each of whom had been BBC representative at New Delhi – it worked under a strict briefing to aim at the Indian intellectual audience without the slightest condesension [*sic*] or angling [. . .].
>
> Parallel with this it fed Indian schools and universities with high standard English literary instruction, again without giving a particularly Indian angle – which is, in fact, impossible so far as a Shakespearean play or anything similar is concerned.[86]

Most of the scripts and recordings have not survived, so we will never know whether Thomas's takes on Shakespeare were as anodyne as Arlott intimates in this memo. I like to imagine him acting up as Richard III and Titus in January 1947, delighting listeners, no doubt, but also prompting them to ponder anew the trappings of leadership, villain or viceroy. In any case, one would be hard pressed to assent to Arlott's idea that contributors to the Eastern Service had given up so easily on the impulse to 'angle' material for Indian listeners. As we've seen, the nature of Thomas's employment in the mid-1940s bespeaks a definite attempt to repurpose the verse of others, and so to think of the recording studio as a kind of reception area, soundproofed but not at all impervious to the latest in foreign affairs. Try as editors might to keep him on message, Dylan Thomas always liked to think outside the box.

Notes

My thanks to the following individuals for their advice and assistance at various moments in the research for this chapter: Lauren Barr, Christopher Potts, David Reynolds and, above all, John Goodby.

1. *The Railway Man*, directed by Jonathan Teplitzky, screenplay by Frank Cottrell Boyce and Andy Paterson, book by Eric Lomax.
2. See Victoria Stewart, *The Second World War in Contemporary British Fiction: Secret Histories* (Edinburgh: Edinburgh University Press, 2011), pp. 9–12, 109–13; and Ann Gaylin, *Eavesdropping in the Novel from Austen to Proust* (Cambridge: Cambridge University Press, 2002).
3. The illustrator responsible for many of the Ministry of Information's anti-gossip posters – Cyril Kenneth Bird, or 'Fougasse' – is the subject of James Taylor's book, *Careless Talk Costs Lives: Fougasse and the Art of Public Information* (London: Conway, 2010).
4. Asa Briggs gives a full account of the corporation's restructuring in *The History of Broadcasting: The War of Words*, vol. 3, revised edn (Oxford: Oxford University press, 1995 [1970]), pp. 118–28. Notwithstanding their evolving remits, the Home Service and Forces Programme frequently over-lapped in content. It is not unusual, then, as in the case of *The Railway Man*, to hear the two conflated. For another example, see the story archived on the BBC's website *WW2 – People's War*, which tells of a family in Hastings, whose custody of a neighbour's budgerigar (Samson) almost ended in dis-aster: 'One morning, a doodlebug (V1 flying bomb) was shot down by two Spitfires trying to catch it before it could reach London and the blast from the explosion when it fell in Alexandra Park blew out the windows in our hall [. . .]. In the middle of the floor lay Samson's cage which had been blown off the window sill, with him cheerfully perched in his depleted home, calling out stoically "BBC Home and Forces Programme".' <http://www.bbc.co.uk/history/ww2peopleswar/stories/84/a4385784.shtml> (last accessed 12 March 2017).
5. See A. P. Ryan's field survey, 'Listening by the BEF [British Expeditionary Force]', 23 January 1940, repr. in David Cardiff and Paddy Scannell, 'Radio in World War II', in *Radio: Critical Concepts in Media and Cultural Studies*, vol. II, 'History and Institutions', ed. Andrew Crisell (London: Routledge, 2009), pp. 170–204 (pp. 182–4).
6. [Editorial], *Radio Times* (16 February 1940), p. 3.
7. Ibid. p. 3.
8. See, for example, Friedrich A. Kittler, 'Gramophone', in *Gramophone, Film, Typewriter*, trans. Geoffrey Winthrop-Young and Michael Wutz (Stanford: Stanford University Press, 1999 [1986]), esp. pp. 99–114; Carolyn Birdsall, *Nazi Soundscapes: Sound, Technology and Urban Space in Germany, 1933–1945* (Amsterdam: Amsterdam University Press, 2012); and Sam Halliday, *Sonic Modernity: Representing Sound in Literature, Culture and the Arts* (Edinburgh: Edinburgh University Press, 2013), p. 159.
9. The influence of John Reith, the corporation's first Director General (1927–38), can still be felt today. See, for instance, the section written by

the Select Committee on Communications that pertains to 'The "Reithian Principles": Inform, Educate and Entertain', in *BBC Charter Review: Reith Not Revolution (HL Paper 96)* (London: The Stationery Office, 2016), pp. 18–19.

10. John Reith, 'Inaugural Address: BBC Empire Service', 19 December 1932, transcribed from an audio recording featured on the BBC World Service's 75th Anniversary website, and now available on AudioBoom: <https://audioboom.com/posts/660533-bbc-empire-service-1932> (last accessed 12 March 2017).

11. John Reith, 'Memorandum of Information', cited in Simon J. Potter, *Broadcasting Empire: The BBC and the British World, 1922–1970* (Oxford: Oxford University Press, 2012), p. 35. For more on Reith's 'evangelical fervor', see Todd Avery, *Radio Modernism: Literature, Ethics, and the BBC, 1922–1938* (New York: Routledge, 2016 [2006]), pp. 11–32.

12. Potter, *Broadcasting Empire*, p. 35.

13. '"Wireless": Popular Physics, Radio and Modernism', in *Cultural Babbage: Technology, Time and Invention*, ed. Francis Spufford and Jenny Uglow (London: Faber, 1996), pp. 149–66 (p. 150).

14. 'Dylan Thomas will read some of his own poems', 21 April 1937 (West and Wales), 9.45–10pm. For a comprehensive list of Thomas's BBC engagements, see *TB*, pp. 283–305.

15. Ralph Maud, 'Introduction', in *TB*, pp. ix–xviii (p. ix). Daniel Jones tells the story of his and Thomas's stint at the 'Warmley Broadcasting Corporation' in *My Friend Dylan Thomas* (London: Dent, 1977), pp. 32–3.

16. See, for instance, Aneirin Talfan Davies, 'Preface', in *QEOM*, pp. vii–x.

17. Louis MacNeice, 'I Remember Dylan Thomas', *Ingot* (December 1954), repr. in *Selected Literary Criticism*, ed. Alan Heuser (Oxford: Clarendon Press, 1987), pp. 194–9 (p. 196). MacNeice's influence on Thomas, as a writer and producer at the BBC, has been well documented. See Barbara Coulton, *Louis MacNeice in the BBC* (London: Faber, 1980), pp. 87–8.

18. Thomas to T. Rowland Hughes, 3 November 1938, *CL*, p. 385.

19. Thomas to Douglas Cleverdon, 23 August 1952, *CL*, p. 931; Robert Reid's reference to the 'post-war world' comes from an internal report, written in 1942, which is quoted by Kate Whitehead, *The Third Programme: A Literary History* (Oxford: Clarendon Press, 1989), p. 10.

20. Julian Symons, 'Dylan Thomas's Last Work', *The Times Literary Supplement* (5 March 1954), 148.

21. Whitehead, *The Third Programme*, p. 133; Thomas to A. G. Prys-Jones, 21 November 1952, *CL*, p. 946; and Thomas to David Higham, 6 July 1953, Ibid. p. 1007.

22. Thomas to Kenneth Patchen, 27 November 1939, *CL*, p. 491.

23. Annabelle Sreberny and Massoumeh Torfeh, *Persian Service: The BBC and British Interests in Iran* (London: I. B. Tauris, 2014), p. 12.

24. See '1940/1941: War Prompts Naming and Campaigning', *The History of BBC News*: <http://news.bbc.co.uk/1/shared/spl/hi/newswatch/history/noflash/html/1940s.stm> (last accessed 12 March 2017).

25. Helen Jones, *British Civilians in the Front Line: Air Raids, Productivity and Wartime Culture, 1939–45* (Manchester and New York: Manchester University Press, 2006), pp. 59–60.

26. George Orwell, 'Poetry and the Microphone' (1943), first publ. *New Saxon Pamphlet* 3 (March 1945), repr. in *The Complete Works of George Orwell: I Belong to the Left: 1945*, ed. Peter Davison, Ian Angus and Sheila Davison (London: Secker & Warburg, 2001), pp. 74–80 (p. 76).

27. Among those to assess Orwell's employment at the BBC, which commenced in August 1941 and ended in November 1943, is Douglas Kerr, 'Orwell's BBC Broadcasts: Colonial Discourse and the Rhetoric of Propaganda', *Textual Practice* 16.3 (2002), 473–90.

28. George Orwell, 'War-time Diary', 22 March 1942, *The Complete Works of George Orwell: All Propaganda is Lies: 1941–1942*, ed. Peter Davison, Ian Angus and Sheila Davison (London: Secker & Warburg, 2001), p. 239; 'War-time Diary', 21 June 1942, Ibid. p. 366.

29. 'War-time Diary', 21 June 1942, Ibid. p. 367; 'Poetry and the Microphone', *I Belong to the Left*, pp. 75–6.

30. Ibid. pp. 76–8.

31. Ibid. p. 78.

32. Ibid. pp. 79 and 75.

33. Louis MacNeice to Eleanor Clark, [10 October 1940], *Letters of Louis MacNeice*, ed. Jonathan Allison (London: Faber, 2010), p. 411; MacNeice to Clark, 20 April [1941], Ibid. p. 429.

34. *CP14*, p. 140.

35. John Goodby, *The Poetry of Dylan Thomas: Under the Spelling Wall* (Liverpool: Liverpool University Press, 2013), p. 346. As Goodby explains, the poem's title can be traced back to a newspaper article that Thomas read in the company of Charles de Lautour, which reported the death of a centenarian in an air-raid on Hull: *Discovering Dylan Thomas: A Companion to the 'Collected Poems' and Notebook Poems* (Cardiff: University of Wales Press, 2017), pp. 182–3. Among the other poems to reveal this sort of borrowing are 'A Refusal to Mourn the Death, by Fire, of a Child in London' and 'Ceremony after a Fire Raid', whose second section once bore the headline-like subtitle 'Among Those Burned To Death Was A Child Aged A Few Hours' (*CP14*, p. 381).

36. Leo Mellor, *Reading the Ruins: Modernism, Bombsites and British Culture* (Cambridge: Cambridge University Press, 2011), p. 76.

37. Andrew Zurcher, 'Milton on Tragedy: Law, Hypallage, and Participation', in *Young Milton: The Emerging Author, 1620–1642*, ed. Edward Jones (Oxford: Oxford University Press, 2013), pp. 182–205 (p. 186).

38. Ibid. p. 186; John Keats, 'The Eve of St Agnes', *Poetical Works*, ed. H. W. Garrod (London: Oxford University Press, 1973), pp. 195–206 (p. 195).

39. Wilfred Owen, 'Dulce et Decorum Est', *The Complete Poems and Fragments: Volume I: The Poems*, ed. Jon Stallworthy (London: Chatto & Windus, 2013), p. 140.

40. S. McGrath to Dylan Thomas, 4 February 1943, Dylan Marlais Thomas, File 1 (1937–46), BBC Written Archives Centre, Caversham (hereafter, BBC WAC).

41. Thomas to Vernon Watkins, 8 August [1940], *CL*, p. 522.

42. '"Voice," 1: A Magazine Programme', 11 August 1942, repr. in *All Propaganda is Lies*, pp. 459–69 (p. 459).

43. Orwell to Henry Treece, 25 July 1942, Ibid. p. 432.

44. See, however, his account of these literary years in *Basingstoke Boy: The Autobiography* (London: Willow Books, 1990), pp. 107–10, 156–7.
45. T. W. Chalmers, 'Committee of Enquiry: Poetry Programmes', 20 December 1948, '*Book of Verse*' (1944–50), BBC WAC.
46. 'Radio Differs across the Sea', *New York Times*, 31 May 1931, XX9; John Reith, *Broadcast over Britain* (London: Hodder and Stoughton, 1924), p. 34.
47. John Reith quoted in 'Radio Differs across the Sea', XX9. A vast swathe of the LRD's early research can be viewed in the British Online Archives: 'BBC Listener Research Department, 1937–c.1950', <https://microform.digital/boa/collections/16/bbc-listener-research-department-reports-1937-c1950> (last accessed 12 March 2017).
48. 'Laurence Brander's Report on Indian Programmes', 11 January 1943, repr. in *The Complete Works of George Orwell: Two Wasted Years: 1943*, ed. Peter Davison, Ian Angus and Sheila Davison (London: Secker & Warburg, 2001), pp. 343–56.
49. 'Laurence Brander's Report on Indian Programmes', pp. 346–7.
50. Thomas to Vernon Watkins, 27 April 1946, *CL*, p. 658.
51. Thomas, 'Address to the Scottish Society of Writers in Edinburgh' (1948), Miron Grindea (ed.), *Adam: International Review*, 238 (1953), 68; Thomas to A. E. [Bert] Trick, [summer 1935], *CL*, p. 218.
52. 'Welsh Poetry', *Book of Verse*, 5 January 1946 (Eastern), repr. in *TB*, pp. 31–49 (p. 31).
53. William Tindall notes that 'upright Adam' appears at once to be 'Jesus and phallus' in 'Vision and Prayer': *A Reader's Guide to Dylan Thomas* (Syracuse, NY: Syracuse University Press, 1996 [1962]), p. 244.
54. It's worth noting that Thomas would return to the terms of this debate in a later broadcast, in conversation with Vernon Watkins, Alfred Janes and John Prichard: 'Swansea and the Arts', 24 October 1949 (Welsh), repr. in *TB*, pp. 218–22.
55. Goodby, *The Poetry of Dylan Thomas*, p. 239.
56. 'Welsh Poetry', p. 35.
57. Ezra Pound to Ronald Duncan, 31 March 1940, *The Selected Letters of Ezra Pound: 1907–1941*, ed. D. D. Paige (New York: New Directions, 1971), pp. 342–3.
58. Wallace Stevens, 'The Noble Rider and the Sound of Words' (1941), repr. in *Collected Poetry and Prose*, ed. Frank Kermode and Joan Richardson (New York: Library of America, 1997), pp. 643–65 (p. 653).
59. Thomas to John Davenport, 14 September 1939, *CL*, p. 464.
60. 'Reminiscences of Childhood', 21 March 1945 (Welsh), rebroadcast on 6 May 1953, repr. in *TB*, pp. 16–20: 16. The films at issue in this chapter have been collected and reissued: *Dylan Thomas: A War Films Anthology*, DVD (London: Imperial War Museum, 2006).
61. *A Soldier Comes Home*, in *TCSP*, pp. 97–101 (p. 97).
62. Ibid. p. 98.
63. Ibid. p. 101.
64. *Battle for Freedom*, in *TCSP*, pp. 33–7 (p. 34).
65. Ibid. p. 35.
66. For one particularly influential account of 'the Cripps offer', see R. J.

Moore, *Churchill, Cripps, and India* (Oxford: Oxford University Press, 1979).

67. Sankar Ghose, *Mahatma Gandhi* (New Delhi: Allied Publishers, 1991), p. 286.

68. Orwell, 'War-time Diary', 11 April 1942, *All Propaganda is Lies*, p. 270.

69. Orwell, 'War-time Diary', 18 April 1942, Ibid. p. 276; 'News Review, 18', 18 April 1942, ibid. pp. 272–5 (p. 273).

70. 'Sunday Night Postscript: Sir Stafford Cripps', January–December 1942, ref. R9/1/2, BBC WAC.

71. 'News Review, 18', 18 April 1942, *All Propaganda is Lies*, pp. 272–5 (p. 273).

72. 'Wilfred Owen', *Book of Verse*, 27 July 1946 (Eastern), in *TB*, pp. 94–101 (p. 95).

73. According to Ralph Maud's edition, the programme was recorded in the third week of June 1946, less than a fortnight before the first of two nuclear weapon tests was conducted publically on Bikini Atoll by the United States. By the time 'Wilfred Owen' aired at the end of July, listeners would have known the extent of the devastation wreaked by *Able* (on 1 July) and *Baker* (25 July). For more on the testing, see Jonathan M. Weisgall, *Operation Crossroads: The Atomic Tests at Bikini Atoll* (Annapolis, MD: Naval Institute Press, 1994).

74. 'Wilfred Owen', p. 94.

75. Ibid. p. 96.

76. Ibid. p. 95.

77. Ibid. p. 97.

78. Ian Whittington, 'Archaeologies of Sound: Reconstructing Louis MacNeice's Wartime Radio Publics', *Modernist Cultures*, 10.1 (2015), 44–61 (p. 46).

79. 'Wilfred Owen', Dylan Thomas Collection, Box 2, Folder 6, Harry Ransom Center, University of Texas at Austin.

80. Frederick Pethick-Lawrence, ['Press statement'], 23 March 1946, in *Constitutional Relations between Britain and India: The Transfer of Power, 1942–47: Volume VII: The Cabinet Mission, 23 March – 29 June 1946*, ed. N. Mansergh and Penderel Moon (London: HMSO, 1977), p. 1.

81. For more on this tense period, see Barbara D. Metcalf and Thomas R. Metcalf, *A Concise History of Modern India*, 3rd edn (Cambridge: Cambridge University Press, 2012), pp. 212–18.

82. 'Insensibility', *The Poems*, pp. 145–6 (p. 145).

83. 'Wilfred Owen', Dylan Thomas Collection, pp. 11–12.

84. So Coulton reports in *Louis MacNeice in the BBC*, pp. 99–100.

85. 'Wilfred Owen', p. 100.

86. John Arlott to H. East. S., '*Book of Verse* Programmes', 18 October 1949, '*Book of Verse*' (1944–50), BBC WAC. Thomas was booked to perform selections from *Richard III*, *Titus Andronicus* and *Henry IV* in early 1947. See *TB*, pp. 291–2.

Chapter 7

Film, Gramophones and the Noise of Landscape in Dylan Thomas and Lynette Roberts

Zoë Skoulding

In Dylan Thomas's 1935 poem 'I, in my intricate image', the coastal landscape is presented as 'the grooved land rotating' under the 'stylus of lightning'.[1] The emphasis on sound and light links the motif not only to recorded sound but also to film. A further reason for considering this poem in relation to film is its reference to 'splitting the long eye open', which, as John Ackerman and John Goodby have noted, evokes the image in Salvador Dalí and Luis Buñuel's surrealist film *Un chien andalou* (1928), a link borne out by the reference to medical instruments and, later on, the 'slash of vision'.[2] While William Tindall's 1962 reading of the poem is emphatic in interpreting the 'ghost in metal' as lyric's impression in the metal of printers' type, there is also a possible reference to the silver screen.[3] This surrealist cinematic legacy is remote from Thomas's actual engagement with film during the Second World War, during which his 'war work' from 1941 involved the scripting and production of wartime propaganda at Strand Films.[4] However, Thomas's early passion for cinema informed the imagery of his poems long before his own films for the Ministry of Information.[5] The expansive scope of Thomas's poem and its densely detailed coastal imagery is echoed in the work of his contemporary Lynette Roberts, who, though less well known than Thomas, wrote in the same landscape with a similar attentiveness to the possibilities of film. Charles Mundye has explored the friendship between the two writers, particularly from the time of Roberts's marriage to Keidrych Rhys in 1939, at which Thomas was best man.[6] By discussing her work alongside Thomas's, I aim to offer a broadened context for Thomas's poem and its prefiguring of his interests in film, recorded sound and representation that would intensify in the subsequent wartime years.

During the war years Roberts wrote her modernist epic *Gods with Stainless Ears: A Heroic Poem* in Llanybri, just across the estuary from Laugharne.[7] In Part II of this work, a gramophone washed up on the

South Wales seashore alerts the reader to the sound of the landscape, since the silent machine is juxtaposed with 'the tidal lapping of the water'.[8] Roberts's gramophone does not play songs but is surrounded by the sound of water and songs of birds as a cinematic motif. As we are told in the introductory Argument, it 'remains as the only symbol of a lost airman'.[9] A machine for playing recorded sound, poignantly misplaced and useless on the beach, therefore comes to stand for death, though its relationship to the airman does not emerge through any obvious narrative logic. The poem as a whole, while it engages with the voices and traditions of a rural landscape, responds to the sounds of modernity and war without nostalgia, looking forward to a post-war Wales.

Like Thomas, Roberts writes in response to Welsh rural environments at a time when the perception of environmental sound was being changed by the influence of recorded sound in film; both poets demonstrate alertness to the possible relation of film to their practice as poets. Roberts herself highlighted her practice of drawing on film, which took on a particular importance in the Second World War, as newsreel photography made military action seem immediate and all-pervasive. In the preface to *Gods with Stainless Ears*, she explains: 'when I wrote this poem, the scenes and visions ran before me like a newsreel.'[10] In an account of tea with the Sitwells, she describes a conversation about the future of poetry readings, in which she imagines poems accompanying films as 'unseen voice'.[11] However, rather than presenting poetry and film as potentially complementary elements, *Gods* evokes filmic techniques through its juxtapositions and awareness of environmental sound.

Changed sensibilities in relation to the rise of film as a medium in the first half of the twentieth century are as much to do with the aural as the visual. According to John Cage, film had created a new awareness of noise:

> Wherever we are, what we hear is mostly noise. When we ignore it, it disturbs us. When we listen to it, we find it fascinating. The sound of a truck at fifty miles an hour. Static between the stations. Rain. We want to capture and contain these sounds, to use them not as sound effects but as musical instruments. Every film studio has a library of 'sound effects' recorded on film. With a film phonograph it is now possible to control the amplitude and frequency of any one of these sounds and to give to it rhythms within and beyond the reach of the imagination. Given four film phonographs, we can compose and perform a quartet for explosive motor, wind heartbeat and landslide. [...] WHEREAS, IN THE PAST, THE POINT OF DISAGREEMENT HAS BEEN BETWEEN DISSONANCE AND CONSONANCE, IT WILL BE, IN THE IMMEDIATE FUTURE, BETWEEN NOISE AND SO-CALLED MUSICAL SOUNDS.[12]

While Roberts registers the way in which 'unseen voice' might make an acousmatic separation between speaker, location and listener, every other sound on film is likewise cut from its source and newly available for manipulation. The attention to environmental sound in her poems reveals this new sense of sonic potential, one that disturbs the figure–ground relation between a voice and its surroundings. Her surroundings were those of rural Welsh-speaking Wales in wartime, but locality in her poems is shot through with news from elsewhere coming through the radio and the sound of planes. Wales, as we hear it in her work, is noisy in the sense that it is hybrid, full of mixed messages and interrupted signals, and cannot be reduced to a pure form of nationhood or belonging. Human voices in both languages are experienced along with other environmental sounds such as birds and machines, forming a palette of sonic references that resonate through a poetics in which sound is foregrounded.

In considering the landscape of both writers as mediated through twentieth-century technology, I refer to 'soundscape', a term established in the work of the Canadian composer R. Murray Schafer, whose World Soundscape Project has focused attention since 1969 on listening as a means of understanding social and aesthetic relationships.[13] However, his view of sound ecology, which critiques the effects of industrialisation on rural and historical contexts, also tends to be conservative and nostalgic. There is, by contrast, an embrace of the modern in both poets, particularly Roberts, who deliberately explores, through what she describes as 'ugly grating words', the 'discords' of modern life.[14] While she is attentive to the local rhythms and the strangenesses of English language in Carmarthenshire, and to the traditions of Welsh-language poetry, these are always inflected by the modernity that is fundamental to her vision of Wales and cannot be excluded from it. Like Thomas in his propaganda films, she looks ahead with ambiguous optimism to a post-war future, though there are differing attitudes in the two poets' work towards the kind of Wales that will emerge from the post-war rubble. In what follows, I suggest that for both poets landscape is mediated by a sense of film's possibilities, and in particular by the approach to environmental sound that film enables. Film's sensory simultaneity provides a model for locating the lyric and narrative energies of the poem within a rural Welsh landscape as well as the media landscape of the mid-twentieth century. Furthermore, it allows us to listen differently to these poems by revealing the tension between music and noise in lyric expression.

The sense in which I refer to noise relies neither on its common-sense meaning of aural discomfort, nor on its information technology definition as interruption to a message. Greg Hainge argues that noise must be viewed as a 'relational ontology', its capacity to resist similar to the resistance found in electrical circuits, where

> any expression, which is to say any material entering into expressive relations (which is to say, of course, everything) necessarily enters into a systemic process with its own material ontology (read medium). This medium *resists* the transmission of the expression at the same time as the expression is entirely dependent on the system at the most fundamental level of base materiality, for its expressive potential can only be actualised in a material assemblage formed between the system and the expression that reconfigures both of them.[15]

Hainge follows Michel Serres in seeing noise as 'primordial and foundational', and refers back to Deleuze's reading of Spinoza in order to make the case for ontology as inseparable from a conception of the world in which everything is 'expressive, arising out of the movement or force of differentiation through which all being expresses itself in existence'.[16] Since all matter vibrates, emitting waves that may or may not be audible to the human ear, we might also consider sound, following Frances Dyson, in terms of 'a flow or process rather than a thing, a mode of being in a constant state of flux, and a polymorphous subjectivity'.[17] Hainge stresses that noise is not necessarily acoustic, and although it may draw attention to its medium, he is not describing a viewpoint similar to Marshall McLuhan's where 'the medium is the message'.[18] Rather, noise arises from an event or process within an 'expressive assemblage' that includes the person perceiving it.[19] In considering the poem as taking place within an expressive assemblage, I am interested in listening to it alongside the changed perception of recorded sound that comes from film, and also in the poem's relationship to the soundscape it evokes.

Thomas's wartime film scripts, although they work in a literal and instrumentalist vein, provide some insights into his thinking by placing noise in a specifically Welsh context. One of his earlier scripts, *Wales – Green Mountain, Black Mountain* (1942), works to the model of film accompanying the 'unseen voice' that Roberts imagines, rather than through dialogue.[20] Its declamatory, oratorical style evokes the performative space of the chapel and the musical structure of the sermon. Juxtaposed with this is the industrial noise that the speaker describes:

> In the furnaces of Llanelly, in the roaring cauldrons of the Swansea Valley, in the stamp and clatter and glare of the black and red works where the fires never go out they fight with blinding, blasting rods and pistons, rams, they fight to the rhythm of iron forests thrusting between flames, they fight with the white hot muscles and arms of steel.

> In the docks of the South they fight with ropes and crane and hoists, they
> load the ships to slide into the mined and death-sprung waters, and all the
> quays are alive, loud with war.[21]

The fire and brimstone connotations of the rhetoric, with its furnaces
and roaring cauldrons, are put to a very particular use, which is not to
condemn industry as hellish, as might at first appear, but to celebrate
the industrial opportunities offered by war. The heroic, futuristic metal-
limbed workers are, in the narrative of the script, rescued from the
destitution and unemployment of the 1930s by the wartime economy,
and the industrial din they create is to be welcomed as a time of new
possibility. Despite the political force of the script, with its reminder of
Wales's struggle against the English and of its economic suffering, the
effort to present a unified vision of Wales veers into clichéd evocation
of a romanticised past: 'Here the bards and minstrels meet, as they met
in the Middle Ages, though the lovely valleys of the south where they
played on harps and sang are barnacled with smoking chimneys, and
clustered with bad streets.'[22] The idea of Wales as 'a musical nation',
however, is juxtaposed with the reality of industrial landscapes, and is
no less ironically framed here than in the Reverend Eli Jenkins's famous
exclamation in *Under Milk Wood*.[23] Like Roberts, Thomas looks ahead
to the post-war future, where the 'procession of old-young men' recalled
from the Depression 'must not happen again'.[24] Against the background
of decay and poverty, the forward-looking attempt to boost morale
presents the wartime soundscape as ambiguously and troublingly positive, since 'all the quays are alive', but this is because they are 'loud with
war'.[25]

Some of the odd disjunctiveness of the script comes from the pressures of the propagandist medium, and from what feels like a search
for the appropriate register. 'To listen to the poetry and oratory of the
preacher,' Thomas writes, young and old will 'come down miles of
mountain, or climb up from the sooted valley towns'; at the same time,
he positions himself through his speech patterns as the very unifying
preacher figure to which he nods.[26] This produces a tension with the
progress that the film ostensibly celebrates, as the attempt to incorporate
scientific discovery into preacherly oration results in bathos:

> It is not only the miner and the farmer, the steel-worker and the shepherd,
> who fight for peace among their mountains. In Aberystwyth, at the University
> Department of Agriculture, Professor Stapledon has succeeded in breeding
> new and more luscious kinds of grass.[27]

While agricultural scientists ought to have the same heroic stature
as Thomas's archetypical worker figures, grass, however luscious, is

difficult to fit into the symbolic frame of technological progress. As writer of the parodic script for the unreleased (and now lost) film *Is Your Ernie Really Necessary?*, it is clear that Thomas was fully aware of the jarring effects produced by the exigencies of the medium.[28] His sensitivity to the inherent ironies of propaganda becomes a creative tool in his 1943 script *These are the Men*, which undercuts Nazi propaganda by repurposing Leni Riefenstahl's film of the 1934 Nuremberg Rally *Triumph des Willens* [*Triumph of the Will*] as backdrop to a script that puts confessions into the mouths of Nazi leaders, with Hitler admitting: 'I took up art. / I gave up art because I was incompetent.'[29] While this film is made with brilliantly calculated satirical intent, it reveals the vulnerability of all propaganda to unintended interpretation. The more forcefully singular the message, the less able it is to accommodate noisy proliferation of meaning.

The rhetorical instability of Thomas's film reflects his own reluctance to subscribe wholeheartedly to a singular Welsh nationalist vision, or to anyone's vision other than his own, even as he fully inhabited a complex and hybrid Welsh identity. This is in contrast to Roberts, who, like many of the writers published in *Wales*, edited by her husband, Keidrych Rhys, was committed to the idea of Wales as an independent nation. Although not a fluent Welsh speaker, she notes of *Gods with Stainless Ears*, 'I have intentionally used Welsh quotations as this helps to give the conscious compact and culture of another nation.'[30] That is, the presence of Welsh in her work is a noisy but deliberate resistance, in Hainge's terms, within a cultural system dominated by English. Thomas's much-discussed disavowal of the Welsh language acknowledges the same tension from a different point of view:

> There is a number of young Welshmen writing poems in English who, insisting passionately that they are Welshmen, should, by rights, be writing in Welsh, but who, unable to write in Welsh or reluctant to do so because of the uncommercial nature of the language, often give the impression that their writing in English is only a condescension to the influence and ubiquity of a tyrannous foreign tongue. I do not belong to that number.[31]

What is interesting here is the 'should by rights', coming from a first-generation English speaker whose lofty distancing from linguistic identification belies a far more complex relationship to Welshness. His insistence on English should be read in the context of a hybridity that, as John Goodby notes (following Homi Bhabha), should be understood in terms of '"identity" as an "effect" created through subversive mimicry, parody and the deployment of stereotypes'.[32]

In searching for the signifiers of 'Wales' that will be effective in the

mass medium of film, Thomas draws on the soundscape of the past
– harps, minstrels, preachers – and the contrast between this and the
industrial development of the Valleys in the nineteenth century. His later
script for *The Three Weird Sisters* (1948) voices the irony of this perspective through the character of Owen Morgan-Vaughan, who exclaims:

> I've been driving for hours and hours, slag heaps and pit heads and vile black
> hills. Huh! How vile was my valley! I'm sick of all this Celtic claptrap about
> Wales. My Wales! (*mockingly*) Land of my Fathers! As far as I'm concerned,
> my fathers can keep it.[33]

Both Thomas and Roberts were deeply sceptical about Celtic romantici-
sation of Wales, though they responded to it in different ways. *Wales –
Green Mountain, Black Mountain* is meant to offer an optimistic view of
life after the war, but hope is only offered in negative terms: what 'must
not happen again' is not war but pre-war industrial decline. Efforts to
support the Valleys did continue after the war with the 1947 nationali-
sation of British coal mines, but ultimately the sounds of heroic heavy
industry evoked by Thomas were already becoming history. This was
the sound of Wales that would be heard and understood by a wartime
public in this particular medium, but it is replayed in Thomas's language
with a noisy and ironic over-identification. While Roberts's more futuristic and technological language might have been better equipped to deal
with scientific discovery as part of Wales's future, this very aspect of her
work would have prevented her from being commissioned to write a
script like Thomas's.

A more direct parallel to Roberts's interest in film as an experimental
creative medium rather than one of mass communication emerges in the
discussion between the film-maker Maya Deren and Dylan Thomas at
City College, New York City, in 1953 at a symposium on poetry and
film.[34] David Annwn has drawn attention to the sudden and unexpected
clash between the two artists, who had apparently been on friendly
terms beforehand, noting that 'the charges of mere sexism on Thomas's
part and intellectualism on Deren's have obscured one of the most
important confrontations in Modernist and Romantic Post-Modernist
intermedial discourse.'[35] Deren's contribution to the debate focuses on
her definition of poetry as a structure of thought in a particular moment.
Probing the nature of lyric as opposed to narrative, she argues that 'a
poem [...] creates visible or auditory forms for something which is invisible, which is the feeling, or the emotion, or the metaphysical content of
the movement', distinguishing between the 'vertical' movement of lyric
as opposed to the 'horizontal' unfolding of narrative.[36] In comments
similar to Roberts's in her preface to *Gods with Stainless Ears*, Deren

also explores the possibility of the film poem as offering an expanded relationship between lyric and narrative energies. While Deren's notion of verticality and depth refers overtly to metaphysical intent, or expression of underlying psychological truths, the context of her talk implies that such depth is in fact achieved within the embodied perception and through the possibilities for montage in film as a material medium:

> the way the words are used in films mostly derives from the theatrical tradition in which what you see makes the sound you hear. And so, in that sense, they would be redundant in film if they were used as a further projection from the image. However, if they were brought in on a different level, not issuing from the image which should be complete in itself, but as another dimension relating to it, then it is the two things together that make the poem. It's almost as if you were standing at a window and looking out into the street and there are children playing hopscotch. Well, that's your visual experience. Behind you in the room are women discussing hats or something, and that's your auditory experience. You stand at the place where these two come together by virtue of your presence. What relates these two moments is your position in relation to the two of them.[37]

We might therefore read what Deren calls the 'vertical attack' of the poem as one that juxtaposes sensory elements in unexpected ways through the body's location, or the ways in which location is implied through an expressive medium, whether film or poem. While the cinema screen creates virtual space, the disjunction between auditory and visual experience in Deren's example paradoxically foregrounds embodied location. Lyric attention is made visible and audible through a multi-sensory experience that is inherently disjunctive. To 'stand at the place' where different sense perceptions seem to collide or clash is also what Roberts's poem invites us to do. Deren explains her theory from a practitioner's perspective, in terms of a logic produced by 'the feeling, or the emotion, or the metaphysical content of the moment' – a subjectivity to which language cannot give us access. It sounds close, at first, to familiar ideas about lyric as poetry that expresses emotion – but the process of making visible or making audible might be better understood in terms of Hainge's 'expressive assemblage', where the cinematic means of expression offers its own form of resistance to embodied perception.

Thomas was famously sceptical of Deren's theorisations, saying that he found the poetic aspects of film within narrative, and dismissing the idea that the two forms might give rise to a hybrid. In his view, the poetic aspect of a silent film might involve 'somebody coming down some murderous dark, dark, silent street, apart from the piano playing. Or it might have been a little moment when Laurel and Hardy were failing to get a piano up or down a flight of stairs.' In a non-silent film, on the other hand, 'in the best of those moments, the words seemed to fit. They were really the right words, even though the right word might only be a grunt.'[38] Yet this apparent straightforwardness does not do justice to the complexity of Thomas's most interesting poems, and while he may have been resistant to the idea of poetic film, his use of sound in 'I, in my intricate image' clearly asserts the potential of the filmic poem. Our attention in this poem is drawn to sound spreading over a death-haunted landscape. The simultaneity is underlined by the interconnection of sound, particularly the repeated cluster at the end of lines – *al/ le/ail/il/el/all* – as the chime passes through the represented environment of seaweed and sea spray. It is also enacted in the suspended syntax that connects a series of geographical and mythological dislocations, resolving on 'tongues of burial' that are both the tongues of a diving bell and the tongue of the poet:

> As they drown, the chime travels,
> Sweetly the diver's bell in the steeple of spindrift
> Rings out the Dead Sea scale;
> And, clapped in water till the triton dangles,
> Strung by the flaxen whale-weed, from the hangman's raft,
> Hear they the salt glass breakers and the tongues of burial.[39]

The poem foregrounds its own articulation within the soundscape. In line with the poem's emphasis on the natural world as mediated by representation, the following stanza in parenthesis introduces the landscape itself as gramophone:

> (Turn the sea-spindle lateral,
> The grooved land rotating, that the stylus of lightning
> Dazzle this face of voices on the moon-turned table,
> Let the wax disk babble
> Shames and the damp dishonours, the relic scraping.
> These are your years' recorders. The circular world stands still.)[40]

The synaesthetic effect of a visually perceived landscape expressed in terms of sound ('Dazzle this face of voices') is reminiscent of Roberts's work. As in her poems, speech, and by implication the poem itself, is part of a larger environment formed from interactions between sound and light, and between animate and inanimate matter. The 'grooved land' holds captured sound. As Ann Mayer points out, 'implied in the imperative mood is the artist's ability to manipulate the record physically', yet the poem as a whole, troubled by the artist's reflexive relationship with the images he creates, makes the question of control problematic.[41] Furthermore, we might hear 'your years' recorders' as 'your *ears*' recorders', and thereby the suggestion that recording, in

shifting hearing from passive reception to a more active mode of remembering, mediates between immediate embodied experience and control
of time. The image here is not dissimilar to the wholly unproven but
attractive hypothesis that sound could be released from ancient pottery,
which might in the process of being turned have picked up the sound
waves of its environment.[42] The intriguing promise of captured sound
depends on re-embodying it in the elements of a place – in that case the
earth as clay used to make the pot. Here, a more contemporary image
of recorded sound situates the poem within a noisy plurality of voices in
an expressive assemblage that encompasses technological and 'natural'
soundscapes.

Despite Thomas's protestation in the New York colloquium, a poem
such as this can be read productively alongside Deren's notion of 'vertical attack', and alongside film that is seen less as a narrative (Laurel and
Hardy with a piano) than as a troubling of its own medium. The poem
presents the lyric self as 'intricate image', not just inflected by its print or
screen medium as metallic ghost, but formed in a process of articulation
and reflection between cultural and natural contexts. Following the
title, the 'I' of the poem is stressed at the beginning of lines, three times
followed by a comma, isolated in such a way that the pronoun becomes
like an object, even when it functions technically as a subject. This
impression is intensified in the fifth stanza, when the first person in 'I
with the wooden insect in the tree of nettles' lacks an active verb and thus
seems integrated with its surrounding environment.[43] The term 'man' is
repeated so often that rather than standing for a powerful masculine
universality it begins to disintegrate, for example becoming 'a man of
leaves and the bronze root, mortal, unmortal'. 'Natural', repeated three
times in the fourth stanza, is a term that is equally thrown into question
by paranoid foregrounding. Despite the poem's concern with dispersal
of self into a mediated environment and its construction in language,
the sound and syntax of the poem offer an embodied perspective within
a landscape that is expressive to an extent that disrupts the lyric self.
There is a noisiness within lyric expression, the 'face of voices' which is
resisted by its own medium, which is inseparable from mediatised and
geographical environments, and which cannot be reduced to singular
clarity.[44]

In Roberts's writing the embodied positioning within a landscape
results in some similar effects as the poem is located through juxtaposition. This process becomes evident when we look at Part II of
Gods with Stainless Ears, where unexpected pairings of adjectives and
nouns, forced together by sound patterning, create a strong awareness
of physical presence:

Bring plimsole plover to the tensile sand
And with cuprite crest and petulant feet
Distil our notes into febrile weeds
Crisply starched at the water-rail of tides:
On gault and green stone a gramophone stands,

In zebeline stripes strike out the pilotless
Age: from saxophone towns brass out the dead:
Disinter futility that we entombing men
Might cure our runaway hearts. –
On tamarisk; on seafield pools shivering

With water-cats, ring out the square slate notes
Shape the birdbox trees with neumes, wind sound
Singular into cool and simple corners
Round pale bittern grass and all unseen
Unknown places of sheltered rubble

Where whimbrels, redshanks, sandpipers ripple
For the wing of living. [. . .][45]

The wrong-footing of sense impressions is part of what causes the linguistic density here. For example, 'tensile' is applied to sand, whereas it seems more obvious to apply it to the muscles of the birds' feet in the next line. Feathers take on a mineral weight in 'cuprite crest'. 'Our notes' – birdsong and human lament together – are distilled into the heat sensation of 'febrile weeds'.

As a man-made object in the natural landscape, the gramophone is a strangely unresolved detail like so many in Roberts's work. Rather than drawing together the poem's sonic imagery, as Thomas's gramophone does, it directs us to a way of thinking about sound as part of a system in the landscape so that the lyric sounding of the poem is heard in relation to the other references to sound sources, such as the songs that might have played on the gramophone, birdsong, slate and brass bands. The section begins with the call 'We must uprise O my people', which sounds psalm-like and therefore musical, but there is a dissonance throughout the poem in the tension between music and noise. The line 'Shape the birdbox trees with neumes, wind sound' refers simultaneously to the musical notation of plainsong, the noise of breath that accompanies its performance, and the sound of wind in inanimate (though possibly inhabited) 'birdbox trees'.[46]

As a call to 'uprise', the soundscape is politicised in the sense described by Jacques Attali, for whom noise is a challenge to political authority, and who, like Roberts, sees parallels between bird cries and human sound in defining territory:

More than colours and forms, it is sounds and their arrangements that fashion societies. With noise is born disorder and its opposite: the world. With music is born power and its opposite: subversion. [...] Among birds a tool for marking territorial boundaries, noise is inscribed from the start with the panoply of power. Equivalent to the articulation of space, it indicates the limits of a territory and the way to make oneself heard within it, how to survive by drawing one's sustenance from it. And since noise is the source of power, power has always listened to it with fascination.[47]

In the sense that music, in this case the fractured musicality of modernist poetry, is both a precursor and an indicator of opposition, Roberts's poetry may usefully be viewed in these terms. However, in Attali's work, the tension between noise and power is played out dialectically as new forms of music challenge the status quo but then become absorbed by it. In the continuous process of development that he describes, noise is one step ahead; it is what we have not yet learned to listen to, but when we do, it loses its capacity for subversion. Because Roberts's political and territorial subversion is attuned to complex particularities of place, and to hybridised Welsh and Welsh-speaking identities, Hainge's view of noise as process explains why it has not been tamed or neutralised. It may also go some way to explain why her voice, having been critically obscured for many years, is a less familiar one than Thomas's. Those who have championed her work in Wales have included Tony Conran and Patrick McGuinness, who have valued her modernism respectively as a 'primitive' or 'naïve' refusal of literary norms that also implies a friction with the English national identity on which those norms might often be predicated.[48] A slightly different approach, which emphasises the significance of Roberts's contribution to a broader Welsh modernist tradition, is taken by Leo Mellor, and in a chapter by John Goodby and Chris Wigginton that places her alongside Dylan Thomas and David Jones as a means of arguing for 'a more radically inclusive and protean sense of Britishness'.[49] In either case, her work can be seen as a form of resistance within the expressive assemblage of nationhood.

The dissonance in Roberts's work can be understood in relation to her aim as discussed with her editor, T. S. Eliot, in 1948:

[T]hat of returning to the elemental words and simple voices of living – i.e. basic rural structures, earth rhythms ... what we will be forced back to if that atom war arises. A cleansing purity and rebirth of sound, recreation refolding of the world such as we had the refolding of the various strata, Icelandic stone and bronze age etc. And ... hitting against that view which is one of isolation, severe pruning. The whole discordant universe, the cutting of teeth, one rhythm grating against another, the metallic convergence of words, heavy, colourful, rich and unexplored.[50]

While Attali's view of time is linear and progressive, Roberts places noise in a cyclical process that links nature, technology and language. Because these elements are interdependent, their noisy friction cannot be absorbed into a simple model of progress. The prospect of atomic apocalypse devalues neither the 'metallic convergence' of linguistic discovery nor the soundscape of village life with its social rhythms of the kind that R. Murray Schafer seeks to preserve. Her relation to the future of Wales is productively conflicted; unlike Thomas, who was working from a central position within his culture that led to a degree of detachment and irony, Roberts's Australian–Argentinian outsider status means that speech patterns, the sounds of her surroundings, the sounds of Welsh, are all relished as part of a distinct environment, one from which, as her diaries show, she frequently feels estranged, as much as she is passionately committed to participation in it.

The different languages that collide in Part II of *Gods with Stainless Ears* include Welsh and English – the opening poems by Dafydd ap Gwilym address summer and a swan, respectively. Within her English, too, there is exploration of clashing registers in the listing of plant names, echoing the lists in Roberts's diary, a taxonomy relished for its strangeness: 'Foetid Hawk's-beard, Black Horehound, Bloody-veined / Dock, Blue Broomrape, and Bastard Toadflax'.[51] The sensory evocations of these names and their *b/d* sound patterning intensify the relationship of the poem to its rural surroundings. In a contrasting register, 'XEBO 7011' was Roberts's wartime identity number, to which she also refers in one of the stories in *Village Dialect* (1944). Towards the end of the section we switch to a set of instructions with local references – 'Take thou my lover 4 pints from the "Farmers' Arms" / Or, if flat, 6 glass tankards from Jones / "Black Horse".'[52] The noisiness of Roberts's work stems from a view of soundscape that advances and develops that of R. Murray Schafer, one in which the poem is opened as intensely as possible to the physical positioning implied by plural sound relationships in a specific environment.

The modern post-war vision that emerges in Part V of *Gods with Stainless Ears*, where 'magnates out of prefabricated / Glass, may build Chromium Cenotaphs – work and pay for all!', points to the regeneration of urban spaces that depends on global relationships and 'Contract aerodromes / To lift planes where ships once crawled'.[53] As Roberts imagines aircraft flying on 'red competitive lines: chasing / Chinese blocks of uranium', she listens to a future where instead of the noise of war, the sky is filled with the noise of trade. The 'steel escalator' on which the protagonist and her lover rise suggests the large-scale, modern urban environment to which post-war planners would aspire.[54] It was this loss of local scale to which the World Soundscape Project responded, but Lisa Robertson writes of the global paradox in its position:

> The WSP's acoustic ecology sought to return to and preserve what they sensibly theorised as a more livable and human-scaled soundscape. For them, the record and preservation of clear figure / ground sonic relationships would contribute to a continuity of tradition-based human meaning, and by extension, individual psychological health. But the concept of acoustic ecology was a direct expression of late capitalism's division not only of labour but of labourer from consumer. The din and racket of resource extraction and manufacture was sent out to an anarchically polluted and polluting productive beyond – Mexico, China, the oil-rich sub-Arctic of Canada – while the freely circulating consumer of the North American or European city was to enjoy a healthful, hi-fidelity, noise-free, symbolically authentic soundscape.[55]

By acknowledging the presence of noise as a constitutive element of the future she imagines, Roberts provides an alternative version of the soundscape that defines the local without excluding its networks of global interdependence. Her vision of a future Wales is not one that marginalises everyday rural life and localised experience, but reveals the ways in which these are inflected by war and trade.

A consideration of soundscape in relation to Thomas reveals a complex set of relationships to nature, technology and national identity. While he might appear less interested than Roberts in making a case for Wales's distinct nationhood, or articulating a rural landscape shaped by modern technology, his revoicings through irony or repetition introduce a degree of noise and resistance that becomes more evident in comparison with her work. The image of the phonograph in connection with Thomas brings to mind from our perspective an association that would not have been present when the poems discussed here were written, which is that of his Caedmon recordings of the 1950s. It is difficult to separate Thomas's poems now from the sound of his recorded voice reading them, a voice technologically separated in time and space from the environment in which it originated. That distance, which is also the distance explored in 'I, in my intricate image', is a site of resistance in which the naturalness of belonging to place is thrown into question. Recording the landscape into itself, the voice can only record its failure to do so, as the landscape disappears into manufactured sound. Neither *Gods with Stainless Ears* nor 'I, in my intricate image' has become less noisy with the passing of time, each poem using sound to link natural, technological and poetic landscapes in a process that is both continuous and conflicted.

Notes

1. *CP14*, p. 73.
2. John Ackerman, 'Introduction', *TCSP*, p. ix; John Goodby, *The Poetry of Dylan Thomas: Under the Spelling Wall* (Liverpool: Liverpool University Press, 2013), p. 273.
3. William Tindall, *A Reader's Guide to Dylan Thomas* (Syracuse, NY: Syracuse University Press, 1996 [1962]), p. 79.
4. Qtd. in Ackerman, 'Introduction', *TCSP*, p. xii.
5. Ackerman, 'Introduction', *TCSP*, pp. xi–xviii; some of Thomas's work in the cinematic medium can be viewed on *Dylan Thomas: A War Films Anthology*, DVD (London: Imperial War Museum, 2006).
6. Charles Mundye, 'Lynette Roberts and Dylan Thomas: Background to a Friendship', *PN Review*, 220, 41.2 (November–December 2014), 20–3.
7. Lynette Roberts, *Collected Poems*, ed. Patrick McGuinness (Manchester: Carcanet, 2005), pp. 52–3.
8. Ibid. p. 52.
9. Ibid. p. 52.
10. Roberts, *Collected Poems*, p. 43.
11. Ibid. p. xxviii.
12. John Cage, 'The Future of Music: Credo', first delivered as a lecture in 1937, repr. in Christoph Cox and Daniel Warner (eds), *Audio Culture: Readings in Modern Music* (New York and London: Continuum, 2004), pp. 25–6.
13. R. Murray Schafer, *Our Sonic Environment and the Soundscape: The Tuning of the World* (Rochester, VT: Destiny Books, 1977).
14. Roberts, *Collected Poems*, p. xxxiii.
15. Greg Hainge, *Noise Matters: Towards an Ontology of Noise* (London: Bloomsbury, 2013), p. 17.
16. Ibid. p. 14.
17. Ibid. p. 12.
18. Marshall McLuhan, *Understanding Media: The Extensions of Man* (London: Routledge and Kegan Paul, 1964), p. 15.
19. Hainge, *Noise Matters*, p. 58.
20. *TCSP*, pp. 26–31.
21. Ibid. p. 28.
22. Ibid. p. 30.
23.   POLLY GARTER:
      [. . .]
      Oh Tom Dick and Harry were three fine men
      And I'll never have such loving again
      But little Willy Wee who took me on his knee
      Little Willy Weazel is the man for me.
         REV ELI JENKINS:
      Praise the Lord! We are a musical nation. (*UMW*, p. 41.)
24. *TCSP*, p. 31.
25. Ibid. p. 28.
26. Ibid. p. 30.

27. Ibid. p. 29.
28. Constantine FitzGibbon, *The Life of Dylan Thomas* (London: Dent, 1965), p. 281.
29. *TCSP*, p. 41.
30. Roberts, *Collected Poems*, p. 76.
31. 'Welsh Poetry' (1946), *TB*, p. 31.
32. Goodby, *Under the Spelling Wall*, p. 29.
33. *TCSP*, p. 299.
34. This was a symposium held in two sessions at Cinema 16 in New York City on 28 October 1953 with Maya Deren, Parker Tyler, Dylan Thomas and Arthur Miller as speakers, chaired by Willard Maas. A transcription of the symposium was printed in 'Poetry and the Film: A Symposium', *Film Culture*, 29 (Summer 1963), repr. in *Film Culture Reader*, ed. P. Adams Sitney (New York: Praeger, 1970), pp. 171–86.
35. David Annwn, 'Opening the Ellipse: Dylan Thomas and Maya Deren in America', *Poetry Wales*, 44.3 (Winter 2008), 17–20; 'The Vectors of Vertical Attack: Dylan Thomas and Maya Deren', Annwn's abstract for *Dylan Unchained: The Dylan Thomas Centenary Conference, 1914–2014*, is available at <http://www.swansea.ac.uk/dylanthomas/programme/panel-themes-&-abstracts/> (last accessed 12 February 2016).
36. 'Poetry and the Film: A Symposium', p. 174.
37. Ibid. p. 179.
38. Ibid. pp. 175–6. As Thomas's early essay 'The Films' makes clear, he had a longstanding and informed admiration for silent film, but also understood the possibilities introduced by the coming of sound: 'There is no way of treating the motion picture with sound and without sound: they are far too differentiated.' (Dylan Thomas, 'The Films', *Swansea Grammar School Magazine*, 27.2 (July 1930), 54–6; repr. in *EPW*, pp. 87–9 (p. 89).)
39. *CP14*, p. 73.
40. Ibid. p. 73.
41. Ann Elizabeth Mayer, *Artists in Dylan Thomas's Prose Works: Adam Naming and Aesop Fabling* (Montreal: McGill-Queen's University Press, 1996), p. 83.
42. Richard Woodbridge, 'Acoustic Recordings from Antiquity', *Proceedings of the IEEE*, 57.8 (1969), 1465–6.
43. *CP14*, pp. 71–2.
44. Ibid. p. 73.
45. Roberts, *Collected Poems*, p. 53.
46. Ibid. p. 53.
47. Cox and Warner (ed.), *Audio Culture*, pp. 7–8.
48. Patrick McGuiness, 'Introduction', in Roberts, *Collected Poems*, p. xxxiv.
49. Leo Mellor, *Reading the Ruins: Modernism, Bombsites and British Culture* (Cambridge: Cambridge University Press, 2011), pp. 109–15; John Goodby and Chris Wigginton, 'Welsh Modernist Poetry: Dylan Thomas, David Jones, and Lynette Roberts', in *Regional Modernisms*, ed. Neal Alexander and James Moran (Edinburgh: Edinburgh University Press, 2013), pp. 160–83 (p. 180).
50. Roberts, *Diaries, Letters and Recollections*, ed. Patrick McGuinness (Manchester: Carcanet, 2008), p. 150.

51. Roberts, *Collected Poems*, p. 54.
52. Ibid. p. 55.
53. Ibid. p. 65.
54. Ibid. p. 65.
55. Lisa Robertson, *Nilling: Prose Essays on Noise, Pornography, the Codex, Melancholy, Lucretius, Folds, Cities and Related Aporia* (Montreal: Bookthug, 2012), p. 68.

III. Confluences and Influences

Chapter 8

Trouble at the Explosive Plant: Ceri Richards and Dylan Thomas

Leo Mellor

In the late summer of 1940 Dylan Thomas travelled from Laugharne to London – and was caught in one of the first major bombing attacks from the Luftwaffe. He reported the experience, and the psychic shock-waves it sent out, in a letter to his friend Vernon Watkins:

> I had to go up to London last week to see about a BBC job, & left at the beginning of the big Saturday raid. The Hyde Park guns were booming. Guns on the top of Selfridges. A 'plane brought down in Tottenham Court Road. White-faced taxis still trembling through the streets, though, & buses going, & even people being shaved. Are you frightened these nights? When I wake out of burning birdman dreams – they were frying aviators one night in a huge frying pan: it sounds whimsical now, it was appalling then – and hear the sound of bombs & gunfire only a little way away, I'm so relieved I could laugh or cry. [. . .] But I haven't settled down to a poem for a long time. I want to, & will soon, but it mustn't be nightmarish.[1]

This is an initial and partial report from a city undergoing bombing – but also a self-examination of the fears that bombing brought in the 1940s. It combines touches of popular surrealism (the animated taxis with fearful faces) with real faces being shaved (signs of apparent normality). Moreover, it marks the start of Thomas's engagement with the war as brute actuality rather than a dreaded future, and the difficulties inherent in thus writing *of* and *from* such destruction. He did 'settle down' to writing poems again before too long. They were, in their different ways, both 'nightmarish' and yet replete with possibilities of how lyric poetry could engage with the specifics of industrialised warfare. This chapter situates these Second World War works in a comparative context, reading them alongside the art of one of Thomas's contemporaries. Such a move shows the multiple analogies between both aesthetic fields, but also reveals that a different model of understanding this specific visual and literary relationship might be possible.

The artist Ceri Geraldus Richards was born in Dunvant, a small

village on the Gower Peninsula 5 miles west of Swansea, in 1903. He
grew up in a working-class bilingual family, one in which cultural
nationalism and the rituals of the Eisteddfod and the Nonconformist
chapel played a formative part. Despite being apprenticed to a firm of
electricians, Richards enrolled in Swansea College of Art in 1920, and in
1924 won a major scholarship to the Royal College of Art in London.
His work, initially consisting of figurative paintings and reliefs, became
more abstracted throughout the 1930s – and his works were exhibited in
both the 1936 and 1937 Surrealist Exhibitions.[2] He was also a member
of the London Group. Richards spent the Second World War in Cardiff
and, in 1943–4, began to produce works inspired by Thomas's poems.
The two men met once, briefly, in Laugharne in 1953.[3] After Thomas's
death in 1953 Richards again worked extensively on paintings that
responded to Thomas's works, and which acted to memorialise him.
These paintings include the mythopoetic *Homage to Dylan Thomas*
series of 1953–6. He also designed the drop-cloth and décor for the
memorial evening of music and readings which took place at the Globe
Theatre in London on 24 January 1954. In the following years this
engagement and memorialisation continued, culminating in the stark
black-and-white *Twelve Lithographs for Six Poems by Dylan Thomas*
(1965). Up until his own death in 1971, Richards continued to work on
both paintings and sculptures which either depicted parts of Thomas's
poems or took inspiration from them, whether through a line or a
single word. Understanding this profound and extensive engagement
in terms of homage and memorialisation is important – and it has
been analysed and dexterously tracked.[4] Yet to perceive the relationship
between Richards's work and Thomas's as *only* one of inspiration and
commemoration is to elide what is perhaps the most important aspect of
the interaction: the reasons why such a connection was possible. These
reasons pertain, I believe, to the fundamentally parallel development of
both the poet and the artist during the Second World War itself.

These parallels are significant, for both Richards and Thomas combined a highly geographically specific and a precisely historically contingent set of influences. A list of these would include: their Swansea
lineages; their multiple European aesthetic influences; their significant
creative periods spent living both in and outside Wales; and, most
importantly, their compulsive if horrified fascination with beauty-in-
destruction in the years 1939–45. Vitally, the wartime works of both
Richards and Thomas repeatedly return to representations of the organic
as a way both of capturing these moments of intense violence, and of
drawing meaning from them. But from this process results a paradox
which affects both Richards's paintings and Thomas's poems: for if

these works aim to capture the incendiary horrors and transformative energy of the moment when all is in violent flux, how can they do this using the organic? How can they do so, indeed, if the organic problematically naturalises destruction and, temporally, offers a momentary image which is nonetheless replete with signs of past growth and the promise of future fecundity? If a ferocious moment is knowable through a version of the natural world, how then is destruction itself changed? What other kinds of temporalities are imported into such a 'timeless second' – to use William Sansom's phrase from 'The Wall' (1941), his short story of transfixed blitz-time?[5] And, concomitantly, how is the idea of nature and the natural changed if it is being used to portray blast and terror? The final stanza of 'Deaths and Entrances' (1941) allows some of Thomas's ambitions for a war poetry to become clear – but it also provides a starting point for comparisons with Richards, and for understanding why their use of the organic was both potent and problematic:

> On almost the incendiary eve
> Of deaths and entrances,
> When near and strange wounded on London's waves
> Have sought your single grave,
> One enemy, of many, who knows well
> Your heart is luminous
> In the watched dark, quivering through locks and caves,
> Will pull the thunderbolts
> To shut the sun, plunge, mount your darkened keys
> And sear just riders back,
> Until that one loved least
> Looms the last Samson of your zodiac.[6]

This is a poem which lays traps for anyone attempting an easy understanding either of its temporality or of the cast of individuals implicated or invoked. Indeed, critical attempts at explication end up rendering down the power of the poem into a series of torturous reversals – or, after failure, simply decrying the form (in the words of a notorious critique by Geoffrey Grigson) as a 'meaningless hot sprawl of mud'.[7] Such an approach, especially prevalent in earlier attempts to contextualise Thomas's war poetry within the genre (or rather to guard and gate-keep the genre against Thomas), comes from prejudice rather than sustained engagement. A better approach beckons. For firstly, this poem dramatises both the potential *and* the terrors of comprehending conflict in a corporeal manner – that is, by understanding it throughout the body and not just in the mind – in ways which seem to echo the sentiments of Thomas's letter to Watkins in 1940. The poem has a polyvalenced apprehension – of fear *and* recognition – of death, one which is felt throughout the newly shuddering and (over)sensitised body. Such a body locates itself through the second-person pronoun, implicitly in the flesh of the reader. This corporeality as intimacy is an extension of the inchoate bodily knowledge that preoccupied Thomas from the earliest Notebook poems – such as 'Find meat on bones' and 'Before I knocked' – but now it operates as a way of acknowledging violence from aerial attack. The poem does this through offering an anatomy of parts, of meaning only emerging from a kind-of *sparagmos*, the ripping apart of the body and the rendering of it into a system of signs.

Secondly, it is poem which is shaped by the creation of rituals. These rituals, while not overtly deity-led, move through time and space, and through stages of fear and hope. Such repeated movements (typified by the in-and-out, or rather out-and-in, formulation of 'Deaths and Entrances', which opens each stanza) are a way of comprehending violent shards of chaotic experience according to a hitherto undisclosed pattern, a 'Zodiac' of sorts, where chaos does cohere into beauty and significant form. Thirdly, beyond corporeality or ritual, the poem starts to put Thomas's biomorphic tendencies – his way of seeing organic landscapes in bodies and also bodies in landscapes – at the service of an *urban*, supremely violent, experience of warfare. For it takes a symbolic ecosystem of water and thunderbolts, the sun and the sea, and turns them into a way of writing about collapsing buildings, bombed airbases, and terrified humans. Such a way of understanding Thomas's Second World War poetry has gained credence in recent years, notably with John Goodby's readings.[8]

Thus 'Deaths and Entrances', so densely strange and rewarding, offers aspects of each of the three key elements I want to track simultaneously in Thomas's war writing and in the art of Richards. Namely: transfigured-corporeality (and its status as a form of knowing); the use of nature-as-ritual, a way that art (in whatever form) could matter spiritually as well as rhetorically, and thus shape the experience of time itself; and finally the biomorphic, including the particular way in which the biomorphic (traumatised, mutilated, fecund) could offer a mode of depicting not some abstract idea of nature, but rather the immediacy of wartime experience. Together, these elements add up into a repeated return to the organic as talismanic for creative desires. But now the organic is also revealed in the poem as containing multitudes; it is inherently and enticingly branching, twisted and rhizomic, and thus able to send forces (organic, libidinous, galvanic) both out to obvious blossoms and down into hidden root-systems. In doing so, the nature of the organic is itself changed. These categories listed above are not meant to be an exhaustive taxonomy, but they represent *collectively* a way of writing about a new kind of war, and of mourning a new kind of victim – the civilian enduring, or killed by, bombs. When taken together, these aspects also offer lines of continuity from Thomas's 1930s writings into his wartime poetry; but, most importantly for this chapter, they are where comparative work can be done. To understand wartime Thomas, we must situate him in relation to the works of his contemporaries – not only poets, but also artists and film-makers, the most suggestive of whom is Richards. Various critics have, since Thomas's death, drawn connections between them – most notably in Richard Burns's heavily Jungian study of archetypes, and Iain Sinclair's ruminative and investigative travelogue.[9] But both these volumes, and several other studies and essays, have focused on modes of influence, and especially on how Richards, in the years after Thomas's death in 1953, took his poems as inspiration and challenge – whether, palimpsestically, by drawing over the texts themselves in a *Collected Poems*, or by designing backcloths, engravings, and painting pictures of homage.[10] What this chapter wishes to do, through a tracking of tropes, is to analyse Thomas and Richards in *parallel* across the years 1940–5, seeing how both a writer and an artist created works from – and of – destruction.

Corporeality and vulnerability

'Deaths and Entrances' remains one of Thomas's most significant experiments in writing the traumatised body – a mode of checking corporeal knowledge against external, and aerial, threat. Such a way of working, in relation to war, was developed by a poetics – produced by Thomas and others – which dwelt upon the way fear felt and could be conveyed through the human frame. 'Deaths and Entrances' offers a vision of the fragmented subject, each part suffering and yielding meaning, which is then reunified temporarily – in the form of a poem – into a moment of testimony. The 'lips and keys' of speech, the 'organs of the counted dust', and the 'near and strange wounded' all have a part to play. This dispersal of meaning throughout the body is, of course, consistent with the preoccupations of Thomas's 1930s works, as we see, for instance, in 'How shall my animal' and 'O make me a mask', which picture the flesh splitting into a blazon of meanings.[11] Yet a wartime focus on the body as holding corporeal meanings, ones which are only disclosed in fragmentation and momentary flashes of mythic reintegration, places Thomas in another context of Second World War literature, alongside the writers of the loose grouping known as the New

Apocalyptics. The key figure is J. F. Hendry, the central theorist and force behind this movement. In thinking along these lines, I'm indebted to recent scholarship, especially that of James Keery, which has shown the New Apocalyptics as probably the most persuasive cultural context for reading Thomas and his changing forms in the late 1930s and early 1940s.[12] For the Apocalyptics mixed mythic structures with a poetic technique which, while owing much to surrealism, allowed for a comprehending and organising human subject writing – and suffering – at its core. Questions surrounding Second World War writing and corporeality had, in poetry and especially Apocalyptic poetry, been developed in response to the Spanish Civil War, with human vulnerability and the apparent omnipotence of the bomber brought brutally together in numerous works.[13] The bombing of Guernica on 26 April 1937 proved talismanic in both the history of airpower and interwar culture; and the connections between the two have been well explicated.[14] Hendry's response to the bombing attempted a kind of mimesis of the violence, but also of the violence contained in the *subsequent* aesthetic representation of the attack. 'Guernica – for Picasso' (1939) builds incrementally until, finally, a first-person point of narration (and ekphrasis) emerges:

> Frozen in the fright of light chilled skull and spine
> Droop bone-shriek-splinters sharper than the Bren:
> Starve Franco stroke and stave the hooves of bulls.
> I am the arm thrust candle through the wall.[15]

The notion that a painting would induce others to physical action, a thrusting out through whatever 'wall' of inertia or physical distance separated the viewer from political action or a change in form, was not limited to Hendry. Among those who also visited the Expo 1937 in Paris to see Picasso's *Guernica*, while it was displayed there in the Spanish Government's pavilion, was Ceri Richards. His reaction to it was partly practical: he subsequently became involved in multiple artistic groupings and projects which attempted to bring attention to Spain, such as his work with Sam Haile, painting billboard murals in support of food aid for Spanish children.[16] But there was also an aesthetic shift. It was not an immediate change, but it is possible to see how Picasso offered Richards models of what it might be possible to transform corporeal shapes *into*. A starting point would be his pre-war humanoid forms, such as the relief *Two Females* (1937–8), or his paintings of strangely feathered figures of costermongers and coconut shies (1936–9). These rendered the human body in muted tones, curves and stylised details – but, after a few months of war, they were replaced by more violent and abstract attempts. Richards's key paintings from this period are then the 'target-blossoms' series, and especially *Blossoms* (1940) (Plate 1). Richards himself, over a decade later, glossed its title as emerging from another chapter of interwar airpower and its violence:

> I remember the impression made on me when I read a description (brutally factual but observant) by a well-known Italian about an air attack on Abyssinia during that unprovoked war, and the title *Target Blossoms* stems from these impressions and later ones, when air bombardment broke out here in earnest. These paintings, obscurely maybe, make flowers into explosions and vice versa, aeroplanes look like insects, [and] aggressive plants and an incendiary sun rise over the landscape.[17]

The description Richards alludes to is that by Count Galeazzo Ciano, reportedly lauding how the bodies of Abyssinian tribesmen opened up like roses when hit by high explosives. *Blossoms* animates this energetic but deathly way of thinking through organicism with two central blade-like or wing-like forms, each slashing through the painting, and slicing into any substance that attempts to resist. The human subject is dispersed and transformed; memorialisation takes place through the transformation of the human into other elements. The tension in the painting – between slow growth and swelling potentiality – with the leaves and tendrils on both sides resolving into blades, gouged furrows, and flayed sharp edges does not allow for an opposition between the organic and the forces of mechanised destruction; rather, the transformation of human forms into victims shows how the natural world in its radical otherness might be a form of representation for suffering which does not fall back into stock tropes, naive mourning or realist propaganda. This understanding of the organic as a way of directly depicting conflict prefigures the more famous paintings of the war artist Paul Nash later in the war, but – unlike Nash – makes a moment of horrific violence inescapable. For Nash's dreamscape visions would both abstract and etherealise wartime aeriality, as he elucidates in his extraordinary essay 'Aerial Flowers' (1945):

> I began to dream of other methods, new aerial adventures. It was at this point I encountered my first aerial flowers. I say encountered because they were hardly thought about in the sense of being planned, yet I regard them as a direct result of my imaginings in my almost subconscious search for flight expression. They are, I suppose, equivalents of some sort.[18]

Nash's subsequent account of his lyrical visions proposes that a 'collage' can then be made in response to an apparent 'communique'. This would state: 'Last night heavy and medium hellebores bombed the mountains of the moon.' Such a flight of fancy could appear demi-whimsical were it not for the Thanatos-inflected precision of the final pages. For such a vision of flowers, which had started from parachutes and gardens, ends with his statement: 'what I have written here is only the preliminary to my theme. Death, about which we are all thinking, death, I believe is the only solution to this problem of how to be able to fly.'[19]

Something akin to Richards's directness in trying to convey an aerial attack, but also Nash's visionary remaking of possibilities, is to be found in one of Thomas's early Second World War poems which uses the organic. 'Among those Killed in the Dawn Raid was a Man Aged a Hundred' (1941) renders what bombs do to the human form legible *and* makes it into a transformation, rather than just death, suffering and nullity. This poem was apparently inspired by a newspaper headline concerning an air-raid on Hull that Thomas cut out and saved, and it remains both redolently elusive and terrifyingly immediate:[20]

> When the morning was waking over the war
> He put on his clothes and stepped out and he died,
> The locks yawned loose and a blast blew them wide,
> He dropped where he loved on the burst pavement stone
> And the funeral grains of the slaughtered floor.
> Tell his street on its back he stopped a sun
> And the craters of his eyes grew springshoots and fire
> When all the keys shot from the locks, and rang.
> Dig no more for the chains of his grey-haired heart.
> The heavenly ambulance drawn by a wound
> Assembling waits for the spade's ring on the cage.
> O keep his bones away from that common cart,
> The morning is flying on the wings of his age
> And a hundred storks perch on the sun's right hand.[21]

This is a poem which wishes, as homage to an individual and as resistance to the meaninglessness of death, to imagine a form of corporeality that transcends physical realities – but also chronological normality: it bids farewell to a knowable progression of linear and apprehendable time. The man – nameless and a near-archetype, here – is located at the outset both temporally and spatially in the alliterative and punning lines, with age and place suborned to war – and then, at the end of the second line, to death. His body is then rendered into a sign of transformative suffering, such as the 'ambulance drawn by a wound', as the incantatory patterns move away from the materiality of stone, floor and street up towards a pantheistic heaven *outside* knowable human time. The generative potential of the seventh line – 'the craters of his eyes grew springshoots and fire' – is all the more disturbing as it makes the wounded eye, so long fetishised by surrealism, into a space from which war, or the violent riposte to war, will come. Moreover, and perhaps

Plate 1   Ceri Richards, *Blossoms* (1940). Tate Gallery, London. © Ceri Richards Estate.

Plate 2 Ceri Richards, *Cycle of Nature* (1944). National Museum and Gallery of Wales, Cardiff. © Ceri Richards Estate.

Plate 3 Ceri Richards, *The force that through the green fuse drives the flower* (1945). Front page and final page of a set of lithographs for *Poetry London 5* (1947). © Ceri Richards Estate.

Plate 4 Ceri Richards, *The force that through the green fuse drives the flower* (1945). Centrespread of a set of lithographs for *Poetry London 5* (1947). © Ceri Richards Estate.

most disturbingly, the body of this nameless victim then becomes both a symbol and originator for a moment of celestial expansiveness: 'a hundred storks perch on the sun's right hand'. A tutelary function is thus gifted to corporeality, here, by both Thomas and Richards – but is of the body sundered and so transformed. Such violence of dispersal, in both *Blossoms* and 'Among those Killed', makes the body another way of according significance – and another way of knowing time.

Different kinds of time

Richards's work *Desolate Landscape* (1941) is a vision of jostling, swelling, bulbous and semi-feathered entities, crowding around a central – and rather calmer – point of focus; it is rendered in a strange combination of ink and watercolour, partly monochrome-bleak, and partly bruise-lurid where the tints of pink and red come through. But the strangest part of all is what lies at the centre of the scene: it is a timepiece mechanism – replete with cogs, hands and springs – which seems to combine a clockwork bomb fuse. This is a reference to a contemporary object, one which embodies a visible teleology, ticking towards destruction and utter erasure; yet, when studied more closely, this central form contains parts of both a chronometer and a sundial, which together allow very different ways of measuring temporality, and non-explosive outcomes, to remain visible. For this is not a melted clock, such as we might expect of Dalí; it is rather more sharply unsettling and materially contingent than that, and yet it keeps alive the possibility that things might not end with a bang or a whimper. If it is reminiscent of anything, it is of the small assemblages Richards made in 1938–9 and exhibited, typified by his 'constructed object' *Sculpture for Terror* (1937). This was exhibited at the London Gallery's 1937 Surrealist Exhibition; here, what looks like a bomb-tail is buried, obliquely at 30 degrees right of the vertical, spearing down in folds of cloth and circular parts.[22] The influence of this pre-war work shapes *Desolate Landscape* as the vista (space) is denoted in the title; but the focus (time) dominates and orders the desolation around its gnomic but implacable centrality. It thus conceives, through what appears to be the freeze-frame moment of some ritual, not only time as a problematic subject, but also – in the conditions of total war – another way of understanding time. Yet this process might rather be trying to create another kind of time, one which might exist beyond (or above, or beneath) wartime.[23]

Thomas also understood the power of ritual within a specific wartime context – a context that had to do with reanimating language to try and carve out a space for sanctified reflection. His great work which succeeded in doing this was the poem 'Ceremony after a Fire Raid' (composed in April or May 1944). This is an ambitious, public and combative poem, developing over its three sections a philosophy of suffering, transcendence and *meaningfulness* from animated fragments. This is due partly to how much it is aware of what poetic form owes to ritual, and partly to how form can steer and shape performance. This is the opening stanza of the first section:

> Myselves
> The grievers
> Grieve
> Among the street burned to tireless death
> A child of a few hours
> With its kneading mouth
> Charred on the black breast of the grave
> The mother dug, and its arms full of fires.[24]

Here, the different formal aspects work together: the self is split ('[m]yselves'); the imperative thus generated has a line of its own; the image of the burnt baby – reaching back into Thomas's work, as well as being a singular image for suffering – is both suckled and buried; and then the terrifying fecundity of the figure of Blodeuwedd from the *Mabinogion* can be glimpsed here, though now with 'arms full of fires' instead of flowers.[25] Each stanza of this first section then follows the same pattern: incantatory, allusive and forceful without being didactic. But it is shaped – as is much of Richards's wartime work – with the broken and yet still potently tangible residues of Christianity. Here is the second half of Part II:

> I know the legend
> Of Adam and Eve is never for a second
> Silent in my service
> Over the dead infants
> Over the one
> Child who was priest and servants,
> Word, singers, and tongue
> In the cinder of the little skull,
> Who was the serpent's
> Night fall and the fruit like a sun,
> Man and woman undone,
> Beginning crumbled back to darkness
> Bare as nurseries
> Of the garden of wilderness.[26]

Here a theological frame is rearranged; the child – now only a burnt trace – is made central to a reimagining of a hierarchy with the 'priest and servants'. This then starts the process of unravelling, with the generative force of the 'sun' being 'undone', leading not only back through a human span to 'nurseries' but also to an Edenic garden that is now a 'wilderness'. A death thus becomes the point of starting backwards, of collapsing what a civilisation has wrought.

But here, through ritual drawn *from* but not *of* Christianity, another comparative point can be made. Thomas closes this section of his poem with 'wilderness' – a potent term for theologically minded readers and listeners – but also a reportage-based description of the vistas in blitzed London. It was also a word whose tensions were picked up on by Rose Macaulay in *The World My Wilderness* (1950).[27] In this novel, two teenagers – Barbary and Raoul – inhabit the overgrown bombsites of London. But these bombsites are not just zones of destruction; they are rather 'a new London jungle', one which is now 'wild' in a botanical sense – with rosebay willowherb and ragwort – and also in terms of morality. In among the ghosts of buildings as spectral presences – 'the ghosts of Noble Street and Addle Street' – one jagged and painful sorrow is the centrality and yet inadequacy of religion. In this cityscape, the ruin of St Giles Church (a burnt-out shell) becomes central for Barbary. Lyndsey Stonebridge, rightly, calls it 'a wonderful scene of early Beatnik camp' in her study of the period, and it is hard to argue with her:[28]

> Sunday Morning in St. Giles. The small portable radio (stolen by Jock and presented to Barbary) stood at the base of a pillar and played jazz. Barbary and Raoul stood before the east wall, whereon a Judgement Day painting now faintly burgeoned: God the Father, with the blessed souls smiling on his right hand, on his left the wicked damned taking off for the leap to the flames. [. . .] Looking up at it Barbary sang from a torn hymn-book in her hand:
>
> > 'With thy favoured sheep O place me,
> > Nor among the goats abase me,
> > But to thy right hand upraise me ...'
>
> Raoul meanwhile held out a black kitten before the phantom altar.[29]

Macaulay was writing in the aftermath of the war, seeing what traces could be re-awoken through rituals which both re-enact trauma and dispel it into the smothering forgetfulness of the verdant bombsites. But what kind of ceremony is then taking place in Thomas's ruins in 'Ceremony'? What can be glimpsed is the animating energy of the vision, as the movement of the poem takes you repeatedly 'over' and 'into' a symbolic cityscape:

> Into the organpipes and steeples
> Of the luminous cathedrals,

Into the weathercocks' molten mouths
Rippling in twelve-winded circles,
Into the dead clock burning the hour
Over the urn of sabbaths
Over the whirling ditch of daybreak
Over the sun's hovel and the slum of fire
And the golden pavements laid in requiems,
Into the bread in a wheatfield of flames,
Into the wine burning like brandy,
The masses of the sea
The masses of the sea under
The masses of the infant-bearing sea
Erupt, fountain, and enter to utter for ever
Glory glory glory
The sundering ultimate kingdom of genesis' thunder.[30]

Part of this panorama is the after-image of the bomber's-eye view, with the sprawling chaos of suffering outlined beneath as misshapen disorder, filled with deliriously uncontained juxtapositions and *objets trouvés* rescued from erasure. But another part is rhetorical – the incremental suggestion of movement without any idea of what is moving. The eye is following, but what is going 'over' or 'into'? It is only at the twelfth line of the final section that the reader gets 'the masses of the sea' – and then the reader has to gauge the potency of religious traces in this amniotic, amnesiac and aquatic force. Such attempts at a totalising effect, by meshing together sound, rhythm and image, and building a cumulative intensity through assonance, make for terrifying and potentially filmic works.

   As others have noticed in this volume, Thomas worked in these years for Strand Films, one of the largest providers of documentaries and propaganda to the Ministry of Information. His productions included the short *Balloon Site 568* (1942) and the more intriguing *Wales – Green Mountain, Black Mountain* (1943). But Thomas's idiosyncratic use of this medium, and a direct point of comparison with his wartime poems, is perhaps most visible in *Our Country* (1944). The plot is rudimentary: a merchant seaman (an Everyman figure with added wanderer-potential) is on shore leave, and travels around Britain, from Dover to Aberdeen, via blitzed cityscapes and harvest fields. He is not the only one who speaks; ceremony is also created through a bricolage of other voices describing their place in wartime life. Against the background of industrial Sheffield, the following lines are given to a girl from a factory, whose fears are counterpointed by the relief and a place for song:

Night after night, night after night, walking back from the factory all alone, all alone, and then the warning going, and looking up at the sky just like someone looking up to see if it's going to rain to-night, quite calm you'd think from looking at me but running home all the same because you never knew you never knew if there wouldn't be a whine and a scream and a noise like the whole town blowing up and then suddenly all the houses falling down on you and everybody you knew lying all dead in the street. [. . .]

Oh, walking through the streets in the morning would make you nearly want to sing, though there were people dead under the stones, or people not dead, sing because the world was alive again in the daytime, and I was alive, and you were alive.[31]

This creation of ritual in everyday life as both defiance and illustration of an undefinable life-force is typical of this work, and yet stands apart from Thomas's other, more measured films, which are constrained by both form and censorship. For in *Our Country*, the counterpointing of scenes and responses gives a visual corollary to the narration – which is continually hoping for, and rhetorically willing, a redemptive pattern to be found in the suffering. In this script, Thomas's phrases stutter as the camera pans outwards, with fluidity and grace, to complete the unarticulatable 'something':

And then birds flying
suddenly easily as though from another country.
And all the stones remember and sing
the cathedral of each blitzed dead body that lay or lies
in the bomber-and-dove-flown-over cemeteries
of the dumb heroic streets.
And the eyes of St Paul's move over London [. . .][32]

Roused from being dumb material, the stones 'sing' and the buildings become animated with uncanny 'eyes' – but the body (the dead body which has to be mourned) also becomes a cathedral, as the camera pans across an actual cathedral frontage. One might also think here of the city animated with comparable intensity in Humphrey Jennings's poem 'I see London', or of Mervyn Peake's personification of the capital as 'half masonry, half pain' in his brief 'London 1941', in which 'eyes' are glimpsed as 'lidless windows of smashed glass'.[33] So it is not just in Thomas's work that the urban biomorphic of the fractured body allows a kind of pantheistic ceremony – as smashed stone becomes human, and smashed humans become stones. Richards's painting *Shrine* (1941) gives his version of what might trouble the sanctification of space among the ruins. *Shrine* is a potently peculiar work: it brings together a meditative centre – the altar – with violent debris apparently from the aftermath of bombing. Recognisable shards or fragments of material are placed in a relationship that is filled with tension – they are both exploding outwards, reminiscent of a blast, but also growing inwards – animated by an organic force, or blest by the heron-monster-priest which stares fixedly from the top right corner. In Richards's own words, there is 'rolling smoke like foliage [. . .] a marvellous or delicate flower – or a demon roaring in a squall'.[34] Thus there is both a past and a future, here, as well as a terrifying present. Moreover, such contradictions of apparent time are elided, or rather submerged, beneath the resurgent organic energy that manifests itself in buds and tendrils – and under which nothing of human chronology survives.

The organic

At an auction to support refugees held in December 1938, Richards bought a small painting by Max Ernst, *La Mariée du vent* [*The Bride of the Wind*]. Dating from 1926, and previously owned by Paul Éluard, it depicts a contorted and energised apparition – part-horse, part-man – against a lowering sky. Richards himself described it, in notes for a lecture at Cardiff in 1940, as

> a fine vigorous design – dramatic colours and shapes full of vitality and movement [. . .] But there's something more important than all those qualities – it is a mysterious fantastic unfamiliar quality – an atmosphere of foreboding. We receive from it suggestions which push our imagination into a strange world.[35]

As Gooding, J. R. Webster, and others have shown, the mythological potential of Ernst's picture as resource and talisman shaped much of Richards's work in the later parts of the Second World War, culminating in paintings of archetypes such as *Bird and Beast* (1944).[36] The place where Ernst's influence came fully to the fore, and animated the idea of the organic as a way of moving beyond reportage or verisimilitude in wartime, are the paintings Richards produced in 1944–5, especially his vast and compelling canvas *Cycle of Nature* (1944) (Plate 2). This was also his first major response to Thomas's poem, 'The force that through the green fuse', which had been given to him in 1943; yet while Richards hoped to engage with the organic energy of the poem, his painting was also a chance to extrapolate from it. First exhibited as *The Green Projector* at the Redfern Gallery in Cardiff in 1946, the painting's sheer exuberant force has best been described by my father, David Mellor:

> This is a bacchanal, a biomorphic carnivalesque of grapes, leafy bodies, tendrils, galumphing Cyclops' feet and animated plants: an orgiastic motif, with a blurring of organic bodies which has analogies with De Kooning's *Attic* and *Excavation* of three or four years later: an outpouring of somatic excess.[37]

The structure of Richards's piece has something to do with reuse and reabsorption; it is replete with fruits and tendrils, wounds and streamers, feet and eyes – and all are caught in a vortex, making generative sacs and buds shudder expectantly under the counterintuitive calm of a Magritte-blue sky. There is certainly an active and engorged cycle of nature at work here; but it is one that is indifferent to human time and only aware of human form as it devours it.[38] The clumsy feet in the far-left corner are linked, through knotty and distorted connective tissue, with entrails and leaves, splayed organs and viscous folds. What Gooding rightly sees in it are 'dynamic natural processes which generate their own distinctive and recurrent combination [. . .] [making] an intensified apprehension of the world in which stark beauty and deepest meanings are to be discovered in numerous visible affinities and correspondences'.[39] But, given that the painting combines inspiration from Thomas and Ernst, it is important also to register how it encodes what Richards saw in Ernst, the 'atmosphere of foreboding'. For at the centre of this work, in a branching circle within a circle, is verdant life, a zone of energy which is oblivious – in terms of time and morality – to the human chaos around it.

Only months after Richards had finished *Cycle of Nature*, Thomas completed 'A Refusal to Mourn the Death, by Fire, of a Child in London' (first published in March 1945). This is a poem whose knottiness has been usefully untangled and re-tangled by a number of critics, but I want to locate it as being both the summation of the three aspects I've identified – the corporeal, the ritualistic use of time, and the organic – and yet also as the moment Thomas starts to change and move away from those modes. In its constant deferral of the possibility of elegy, the setting of impossibilist conditions where 'mourning' would be possible – and then the rejection of those conditions – the poem speaks of the point where the possibility of extracting meaning from conflict is overwhelmed, not by the sea with its residues or flotsam of faith, but rather by a totalising nullity. For 'Refusal to Mourn' also ends, as 'Ceremony' does, with water, but this is a very different close:

Deep with the first dead lies London's daughter,
Robed in the long friends,
The grains beyond age, the dark veins of her mother,
Secret by the unmourning water
Of the riding Thames.
After the first death, there is no other.[40]

This is the end of the possibility of individuated elegy, and an end to the trajectory which had made the elegy both potent and problematic throughout the 1930s.[41] The rhetorical term *adynaton* (where hyperbole presages impossibility) allows the scale of catastrophe to be glimpsed without permitting the action of a literary form – the elegy – to operate. As in Richards's painting, there is a refusal to inscribe human-scale meanings, or to validate human emotions, among such totalising catastrophe; yet the organic cannot function here with countervailing energy.

But what can then come next? Part of the answer might be in how an understanding of Thomas is transformed not only by what he wrote in the period from 1945 until his death, but also by how his works were read, and what changed the way in which they were read. The history of *Poetry London* has been covered by various critics, ranging from the engaged to the dismissive.[42] One of the most careful recent pieces of analysis of why the magazine, and Poetry London editions, mattered in the years 1939–51 is by A. T. Tolley.[43] He traces the editorial policy of its idiosyncratic editor, Meary James Thurairajah Tambimuttu, and offers some reasons why Tambimuttu became such an important cultural figure in the literary world of wartime London. Key to Tambimuttu's success was his policy of mixing art forms, and his commissioning of Richards in late 1943 to draw some versions of a lyrebird as a motif for the magazine was part of a wider practice, one which most famously included Graham Sutherland illustrating and counterpointing David Gascoyne's poems in the Poetry London edition from 1943. But for Richards it mattered that Tambimuttu, after being impressed by his versions of the lyrebird, sent him various Thomas poems.[44] Then, throughout 1943–4, Richards painted several works directly inspired by Thomas (including *Cycle of Nature*), and afterwards modified and reworked them into three lithographs. These lithographs, finally published as a full-colour insert in *Poetry London* in 1947, signify much beyond their apparent size, as they are neither an illustration of the poem nor an explanation. Rather, they are a reimagining of the apparently ahistorical and abstract personal mythology of the poem within a specific wartime context – one shaped by the historical fact not only of the Blitz of 1940–1, but also of the V1 rocket and V2 missile attacks.

These lithographs, collectively using 'The force that through the green fuse' as a title, comprise two single sheets and a central two-page spread printed back to back. The first single sheet (left-hand side of Plate 3) has the first line from the poem given in cursive script across a yellow and green base; then growing around and dominating the image at its centre is a branching plant, complete with stamen and buds, reminiscent of *Cycle of Nature*. But its leaves are filigree and its topmost bud becomes a metallic and technological spear – akin to Richards's pre-war *Sculpture for Terror* – piercing the flaccid and eviscerated humanoid form. The human form, absent except in broken parts from *Cycle of Nature*, is here presented as an exercise in vulnerability. Then the central two-page spread (Plate 4) gives, on the left-hand side, another vertical form, but now it's curving and spinning – a blue/green vortex. This implausible Fallopian tube or tuber leads to seeds and buds, themselves enfolding and sucking in life, but also reaching upwards to the fecundity of what initially appear to be fruit or grapes (again reminiscent of *Cycle of Nature*). Yet what hangs above is, on closer inspection, pendulously dark serried ranks, not fruits but high-explosive bombs, lambent beneath an aircraft. Set in opposition, on the right-hand side of this lithograph and taking up the majority of the A5 sheet on that side of the centrefold, is Thomas's entire poem. Apart from some swirls in the left-hand vortex, this is the only white part of the page. But the pallid background for the text of the poem is emerging from a cadaverous and flayed figure; indeed, it appears – perhaps in homage to seventeenth-century medical illustrations – to be written on the figure's own skin, which he has obligingly disrobed for such scribal purposes. The 'force' which is obviously spinning and swelling on the left-hand side has left him dismembered, flayed and staring fixedly away from the reader and towards a horizon. The final single-page lithograph (right-hand side of Plate 3) redoubles this theme: a distorted (crushed?) skull, with a dislocated jawbone and spinning eyes like whirlpools, guards the final lines of the poem – acting as a *memento mori* and showing, through the sleeping child inset below, that all generative possibilities are enfolded by fear, not to mention the blackness of the sky, the claw-like forms, and the blooded earth beneath all. Taken collectively, their relationship with Richards's *Cycle of Nature* is clear: two phantasmagorical figures in a state of metamorphosis, with much movement and flow throughout, are acting as a connective, non-human, force. Gooding calls this 'undifferentiated energy into which all sexuality dissolves', but I'm not so sure: the energy in the resilient organic forms, when set against the traumatised and wracked bodies, seems to show instead a rather more direct usurpation, and an erasure of the human as coherent subject. These images are not attempts to fix and comment upon a historical moment; rather, they instead try to make the moment of composition visible as the *outcome* of processes and 'forces'. But what did these illustrations mean – what *could* they mean – for thinking about Thomas? Among other things, they give a certain – 1945 – context to a poem of 1933. This version of the biomorphic vision then changes 'The force' as a poem when it is placed beside the 1940s versions of the post-human. The politics of 'The force', as initially written, seem intensely personal (such as 'my green age' and 'my destroyer'), and the only body under question or threat is that of the protagonist. But now, with these illustrations, and after poems such as 'Refusal to Mourn', the rhetorical weight falls on the 'dumb to tell' refrain: for this, too, is now a poem about poetic limitations and the lack or absence of a lyric escape route, one in which the enmeshing of humans and nature is realised. Thus, this is a poem less about 'the force' as comprehended by an individual, and more about the effects it brings, and what such effects mean for the potential of poetry.

Atomic coda

What are the implications for thinking about Thomas, especially as a war poet who used the biomorphic, after making this comparison with Richards, and particularly with Richards's lithographs of 1945? What aesthetic possibilities come in the post-1945 'peace'? An answer of sorts is revealed in Thomas's tantalisingly unfinished poem 'In Country Heaven'. This is a war poem for 'peacetime' – but a peace filled with the threat of atomic annihilation. In the 'Note' which Thomas appended to 'In the White Giant's Thigh' for publication in *Botteghe Oscure*, he explained how this poem would fit within the larger frame of 'In Country Heaven', and how the mood of the poem overall would be of cataclysmic ending, the destruction of the world as it 'drops dead, vanishes screaming, explodes, murders itself'.[45] What 'In Country Heaven' also shows, however, is that the transformative urge, the desire to understand the suffering of the bombs through making bodies into signs (corporeality) – or the biomorphic, or indeed the persistence of a transmuted ceremony – cannot, and will not, be adequate to depict total destruction, a destruction that spreads beyond the confines of the earth itself. The final reworking of this fragment (October 1951) is bleakest of all:

> Light and His tears dewfall together
> (O hand in hand)
> Out of the pierced eyes and the cataract sky,
> He cries his blood and the suns
> Dissolve and run down the ragged
> Gutters of his face: Heaven is blind and black.[46]

The gouged eyes, reminiscent of the punctured orbs in Richards's early-wartime work, are back again – but they now belong to a blinded God. This is not an attempt to write an elegy, or to refigure shards of material as transmuted form. The description might use aspects I've tracked in both Richards's and Thomas's earlier works, but now it is scaled up to an horrific extent: a description of a blast-shattered deity, not of (mournable) life on earth. This, then, is rather the witnessing of totalising disaster, a disaster so vast it spreads to heaven. Because of Thomas's death in 1953, we only have hints of where the poet may have gone next; one of the most tantalising is the libretto he was due to work on with Igor Stravinsky. The opera was going to be set in a cave in the aftermath of a nuclear war, and the two singers – a boy and a girl – would try to describe the pre-atomic world to each other. In Thomas's words, as recollected by one his friends: 'the boy tried to remember and explain to the girl what a tree was'.[47] Organic and cyclical recuperation can now only be preserved in language; outside, all would be ash. Yet while Thomas's works moved outwards in scale to this post-global level of destruction, Richards, after Thomas's death, was faced with another problem. For the works he made in memory of Thomas are not just mourning the poet as an individual; they are also mourning the very specific context of parallel experimentation and inspiration which occurred in those war years. Thomas found the admixture of the corporeal, the distortions of time, and the organic (allowing for biomorphic transformations) fundamentally inadequate to the actualities of the late-war and the post-war world. For Richards, this complex combination would continue to inform his painting in the 1950s – but it was also limited to memorialising Thomas, rather than depicting – or reporting upon – the actualities of a post-1953 world.

Setting poet and artist alongside each other reignites questions of how far an aesthetic in a global war might stem from a Welsh context that is specific to a time and class, to a mixture of European influences, and to a very particular register of motifs and landscapes. If, moreover, the scope of 'war poetry' and 'war art' is changed by the inclusion of Second World War works by Richards and Thomas, then an evacuation into the organic may no longer seem a bucolic retreat. For 'war culture', as a category, has then to enlarge and unravel, and it has – vitally – to include non-combatants as well as soldiers, and abstraction as well as reportage. But both Thomas's and Richards's Second World War works show the difficulties inherent in the attempts to make culture from destruction, and also the point where it becomes impossible – with questions of what might then come in the blind and blackened wake, overshadowed by aerial atomic fears which were so many orders of magnitude greater than Thomas's 'burning birdman dreams' of 1940.

Notes

1. Thomas to Vernon Watkins, [early September 1940], *CL*, p. 524.
2. For further biographical details, see Mel Gooding, *Ceri Richards* (Moffat: Cameron & Hollis, 2002).
3. For an account of their meeting in Laugharne just before Thomas left for his final US tour, see Gooding, *Ceri Richards*, pp. 116–17.
4. For example, see the account in Gooding, *Ceri Richards*, pp. 116–21. This includes the elusive hint that John Berger suggested to Richards in 1961 that he develop his drawings of 'Do not go gentle' into large-scale paintings (p. 121). Richard Burns, in *Keys to Transformation: Ceri Richards and Dylan Thomas* (London: Enitharmon, 1981), reproduces the pages of Thomas's *Collected Poems* which Richards, in the years after 1953, changed and altered with his own drawings.
5. William Sansom, *Fireman Flower, and Other Stories* (London: Hogarth Press, 1944), pp. 108–11 (p. 108).
6. *CP14*, p. 123.
7. Geoffrey Grigson, 'How Much Me Now Your Acrobatics Amaze', in *Dylan Thomas: The Legend and the Poet*, ed. E. W. Tedlock (London: Heinemann, 1963), pp. 155–67 (p. 160).
8. John Goodby, *The Poetry of Dylan Thomas: Under the Spelling Wall* (Liverpool: Liverpool University Press, 2013), pp. 302–70.
9. See Burns, *Keys to Transformation: Ceri Richards and Dylan Thomas*; and Iain Sinclair, *Black Apples of Gower* (Dorchester: Little Toller, 2015).
10. See Gooding, *Ceri Richards*, pp. 113–21.
11. *CP14*, pp. 100–1, 98.
12. See James Keery's series of articles in *P.N. Review*, especially 'The Burning Baby and the Bathwater II', 29.5 (May–June 2003), 49–54; see also Keery's chapter in this volume.
13. See Leo Mellor, *Reading the Ruins: Modernism, Bombsites and British Culture* (Cambridge: Cambridge University Press, 2011), pp. 11–46.
14. See Ian Patterson, *Guernica and Total War* (Cambridge, MA: Harvard University Press, 2007).
15. 'Guernica – For Picasso', in *The New Apocalypse*, ed. J. F. Hendry and Henry Treece (London: Fortune Press, 1939), p. 72.
16. See Gooding, *Ceri Richards*, p. 36.
17. For Richards's letter – with detail about the method and composition of his wartime work (30 November 1958), and the influence of Count Ciano's statements about war – see Gooding, *Ceri Richards*, p. 57.
18. Paul Nash, *Writings on Art*, ed. Andrew Causey (Oxford: Oxford University Press, 2000), pp. 155–61 (p. 160).
19. Ibid. p. 161.
20. Goodby, *Discovering Dylan Thomas: A Companion to the 'Collected Poems' and Notebook Poems* (Cardiff: University of Wales Press, 2017), pp. 182–3.
21. *CP14*, p. 140.

22. The sculpture was destroyed – but there is a photograph in Gooding, *Ceri Richards*, p. 41.
23. For questions of chronology and perception in the Second World War, see Beryl Pong, *For the Duration: British Literature and Culture in Blitz-Time* (forthcoming, 2018).
24. *CP14*, p. 142.
25. In the 'Fourth Branch' of the *Mabinogi,* the Welsh medieval tale, Blodeuwedd was a woman made from the flowers by the magicians Math and Gwydion. Her long influence and afterlife ranges beyond Welsh literary culture, typified by works such as Alan Garner's *The Owl Service* (1967).
26. *CP14*, p. 144.
27. For a sustained analysis of the novel, see Mellor, *Reading the Ruins*, pp. 173–88.
28. Lyndsey Stonebridge, *The Writing of Anxiety: Imagining Wartime in Mid-Century British Culture* (Basingstoke: Palgrave, 2007), p. 96.
29. Rose Macaulay, *The World My Wilderness* (London: Virago, 1983), p. 166.
30. *CP14*, pp. 144–5.
31. *Our Country, TCSP*, pp. 63–73 (p. 72).
32. Ibid. p. 68.
33. 'I see London', in *The Humphrey Jennings Film Reader*, ed. Kevin Jackson (Manchester: Carcanet, 1993), pp. 296–7; 'London 1941', in *Peake's Progress: Selected Writings and Drawings of Mervyn Peake*, ed. Maeve Gilmore (Harmondsworth: Penguin, 2000), p. 164.
34. Cited in H. S. Williamson, 'Ceri Richards', *Horizon*, 9.52 (April 1944), 277–82 (p. 278).
35. Cited in Gooding, *Ceri Richards*, p. 55.
36. Ibid. pp. 65–6; and see J. R. Webster, *Ceri Richards* (Cardiff: Welsh Committee of the Arts Council, 1961), [n.p.].
37. David Mellor, *A Paradise Lost: The Neo-Romantic Imagination in Britain, 1935–55* (London: Lund Humphries in association with the Barbican Art Gallery, 1987), p. 29.
38. Such a version of transformed figures dissolving into the resurgent organic is prefigured in the interwar work one of Richards's favourite artists, André Masson, and especially in his interwar dryads and mutilated figures in *Acéphale.*
39. Gooding, *Ceri Richards*, p. 72.
40. *CP14*, p. 173.
41. See Mellor, *Reading the Ruins*, pp. 76–81; also Patricia Rae, 'Double Sorrow: Proleptic Elegy and the End of Arcadianism in 1930s Britain', *Twentieth Century Literature*, 49.2 (Summer 2003), 246–75.
42. For an overview, see Robert Hewison, *Under Siege: Literary Life in London, 1939–45*, revised edn (London: Methuen, 1988), pp. 108–22. For extensive detail about *Poetry London* and Tambimuttu's career, and the disentangling of myth from reality, see Chris Beckett, 'Tambimuttu and the *Poetry London* Papers at the British Library: Reputation and Evidence', *The Electronic British Library Journal* (2009): <http://www.bl.uk/eblj/2009articles/article9.html> (last accessed 15 March 2017).
43. A. T. Tolley, *British Literary Periodicals of World War II & Aftermath: A Critical History* (Kemptville, ON: Golden Dog Press, 2007), pp. 116–24.

44. For the notebook sketches, 'Lyre Birds' (1943), see Gooding, *Ceri Richards*, p. 68.
45. The note is reproduced in Thomas's *Collected Poems: 1934–1953*, ed. Walford Davies and Ralph Maud (London: Dent, 1998), p. 262.
46. *CP14*, p. 405.
47. Cited by Goodby, *The Poetry of Dylan Thomas*, p. 423.

Chapter 9

'The verticals of Adam': Dylan Thomas and Apocalyptic Modernism

James Keery

[I] *have kept one criticism of that night's work*, because of the appearance in it of the quite unusual word 'apocalypse': 'At the fading of that bravely forced smile, [Queen Gertrude's] face became a very apocalypse of woe', it reads – where is Polonius, with his 'mobled queen'? Would he say, 'apocalypse is good!' or would he not?[1]

'The Apocalyptic writing of Dylan Thomas'

Although the infamous 'forties sneer' is still to be heard in the land, it is now possible to treat Dylan Thomas and the Apocalyptic movement with post-polemical respect. John Goodby documents a reception history that has tended to diminish Thomas by numerous strategies, but principally by failure to take the measure of his intelligence and gifts, permitting him only a subcategory of 'genius' so heavily taxed at source as to justify neglect.[2] Yet neglect of Thomas is ruinous to any understanding of post-war modernism. My argument, here, is that to assign him a place in the modernist canon entails a reconsideration of the canon itself.

Having resolved a number of historical disputes, research on the Apocalypse has progressed. Attempts to dissever Thomas from the movement, or to draw distinctions (whether chronological or qualitative) between the Apocalypse and neo-Romanticism, ought no longer to darken counsel. There should be no need to refute the misconception that the decade in question, or any part of it, was a poetic doldrums. Once agreed to be intrinsically malign, Thomas's enabling influence can now be seen to extend beyond the Apocalyptic poets of the 1940s to include many post-war British poets, including some of the finest poets of the Movement of the 1950s.

Recent discoveries by Peter Manson among the papers of Dorian

Cooke, from the earliest days of the Apocalyptic movement, include a draft by John Goodland of the proposal to Faber for 'an anthology of post-Auden-Isherwood prose and poetry', 'mainly concerned with "apocalyptic" writing'.[3] The proposal confirms that the original referent of the 'adjective', for the founders of the Apocalyptic movement, was Dylan Thomas: 'we think Miss Bowen uses this adjective for the first time as applied to Dylan Thomas in her introduction to "The Faber Book of Modern Stories"'. Thus, the godfather of the movement is neither D. H. Lawrence, author of *Apocalypse* (1931), nor Henry Miller, whose 'apocalyptic language' in *Tropic of Cancer* (1934) had struck a chord, but a god*mother*, Elizabeth Bowen, in 1937:[4]

> [T]he general trend of the short story has been, lately, towards inward, or, as it were, applied or functional fantasy, which does not depart from life but tempers it. Pure (as opposed to applied) fantasy has, it is true, reappeared in the apocalyptic writing of Dylan Thomas: the delirium or the dream. This may be another beginning.[5]

Prescient as she is, however, it is not Bowen who applies the word to Thomas 'for the first time'. Reviewing *Twenty-five Poems* in the *Catholic Herald* on 2 October 1936, J. Alban Evans (later Dom Illtud Evans of St David's College, Lampeter) anticipates her:

> [P]oems of frustration, of the unresolved question and the unachieved desire. Their difficulty proceeds from this sense of incompletion: an apocalyptic range of metaphor overreaches the slow stages of thought. [. . .] This slender collection [. . .] will be obscured by the work of older and noisier contemporaries. It will instead, one supposes, be hailed by the coterie and the clan. Which is a pity, for Mr Thomas has revealed, with integrity and significance of expression, the malady of a whole generation.[6]

For both critics, Thomas's poetry, with its delirious range of oneiric metaphor, represents a 'beginning' – a beginning to be 'hailed', by a young 'coterie', as excitingly different from the work of their 'older [. . .] contemporaries'. The 'significance' of the word 'Apocalyptic' is more complex. As I hope to demonstrate, a grasp of its evolution, during the lifetime of Dylan Thomas, from an ornament of arcane erudition (biblical usage always excepted) into a highly contentious item of critical nomenclature, is integral to an understanding of the modernist century, a point appreciated by two recent American critics: 'Modernists tend to be Apocalypticists.'[7]

'I John saw these things, and heard them'

In an article in *Encounter* in 1966, Frank Kermode identifies an 'essential' feature of modernism that had taken root in the 1890s: '[i]f there is a persistent world-view it is one we should have to call apocalyptic'. He distinguishes 'two phases', 'palaeo- and neo-modernism', but finds them 'equally apocalyptic', a view endorsed by a critic of Robert Lowell: '[t]he sense of the apocalypse is perceived by many as one of the crucial shaping forces behind the whole Modernist discourse'.[8] A parodist of T. S. Eliot's quatrains in *The London Mercury* in 1924 thus scores a direct hit: '*Apocalyptic chimney cowls* / Squeak at the sergeant's velvet hat / Donkeys and other paper fowls / Disgorge decretals at the cat'.[9]

'Palaeo-modernism' is Apocalyptic in its response to catastrophe and in its preoccupation with (im)mortality. However, it is also Apocalyptic in sourcing energy directly from the Book of Revelation. One of the lines deleted by Ezra Pound from the manuscript of *The Waste Land* attributes its prophetic vision, not to Tiresias, but to St John the Divine (22:8): '(I John saw these things, and heard them)'.[10] The purport of Eliot's note would thus have been specifically Apocalyptic: 'What [St John] *sees*, in fact, is the substance of the poem.'[11] In *Paris: A Poem* (1920), a putative source of *The Waste Land* but itself deleted until 2011, Hope Mirrlees anticipates Eliot's *mélange* of onomatopoeic Greek, 'demotic French', riverine allegory and the Apocalypse: 'Brekekekek *coax coax* / we are passing under the Seine / *DUBONNET* / The Scarlet Woman shouting BYRRH and deafening St John at Patmos / Vous descendez Madame?'[12] The source of Pound's war cry, 'Make it new!', is not a 'Shang dynasty' bathtub, but, again, the Book of Revelation (21:5): 'Behold, I make all things new'.[13] H.D.'s triple allusion in *Tribute to the Angels*, published in London in April 1945, is an epitome of the Apocalyptic modernism of both world wars: 'I John saw. I testify [. . .] I make all things new' (22:8; 22:18; 21:5).[14] In *The Criterion* in 1927, Wyndham Lewis also elides both conflicts, with satirical prescience: 'Oh it is a wild life that we live in the near West, between one apocalypse and another!'[15]

Lewis's sarcasm reveals a fault line between, on the one side, the ironic modernism to which criticism has devoted much attention, and, on the other, a practice that has been aptly described as 'visionary modernism'.[16] The fault line opens up in the 1920s; divides the poets of the 1930s and 1940s; and has a bearing on the usage of, and responses to, the word 'Apocalyptic' from this point on. In a 1927 review in *The New Criterion*, the Imagist poet F. S. Flint attributes to his American colleague John Gould Fletcher 'a vision that is apocalyptic in its embrace of ultimate things'.[17] Edith Sitwell's amusingly apt remark to Gertrude Stein in 1926, that 'everything in *The New Criterion* is regarded as a newer and more important Apocalypse', illustrates both strains at once.[18]

This distinction produces a more coherent alignment of the poets of the 1930s and 1940s than the more familiar distinctions, both between the decades as typified by W. H. Auden and Thomas, and between the classical and (neo-)Romantic styles. Thomas, George Barker and David Gascoyne each published a first collection in the first half of the 1930s. Considering 'new poetry from Fabers' by Auden, Stephen Spender and Louis MacNeice in August 1938, Gascoyne improvises his own manifesto of visionary modernism:

> I feel the existence of a great gap between their generation's conception of poetry and my own [. . .] Poetry is [. . .] not rhetoric, [. . .] nor is it argument or reportage [. . .] The tradition of modern English poetry is [. . .] quite different from the tradition of Hölderlin, Rimbaud, Rilke, Lorca, Jouve. – I belong to Europe before I belong to England.[19]

This is exactly the context in which this distinction was first drawn by A. T. Tolley:

> European modernism had little influence on the development of poetry in England [. . .] [I]f we characterise Surrealism and the type of writing out of which it grew as 'visionary' modernism (in contrast with the 'ironic' Anglo-American modernism) we can see the poetry of Barker, Thomas and Gascoyne as being in that stream.[20]

'The current sense of apocalypse'

As it transpires, Gascoyne would also be a key witness in the dispute over the currency of the word in the 1930s. On 29 September 1938 he responded to Neville Chamberlain's 'exhausted voice' and 'sincere horror of war', quailing at 'tremendous perspectives of horror and desolation, worthy of the biblical language of the Psalms or of Dante'.[21] A few months later, in reference at once to Munich and to Pierre Jean Jouve, he not only specifies, but italicises, an alternative source of such 'biblical language': 'I know of no-one who has so fully expressed the *apocalyptic* atmosphere of our time.'[22] In the same entry, for 23 January 1939, he notes a conversation with Spender about Thomas and Barker, and a meeting with Henry Miller, 'whom I hadn't seen for months', on return from a stay in England with Lawrence Durrell, whose nominations for the planned anthology are recorded, in Goodland's handwriting, on the only extant copy of the manifesto.[23] Gascoyne was attuned not only to Jouve's wavelength independently of the winter proceedings in England, but also to the Zeitgeist, and it seems highly likely that rumours of an Apocalyptic movement would have found him among those with 'an ear [to] hear what the Spirit saith' (Revelation 2:7).

By contrast, the two most influential chroniclers of the 1930s, Samuel Hynes and Valentine Cunningham, contrive to narrate the history of the decade as though the Apocalyptic movement had never existed; yet both manifest a near-obsession with the word, using it, between them, over fifty times. With an air of innovation, Hynes isolates an 'element' in 'the mood of the decade's end' which '*I have called* the sense of apocalypse', a term subsequently adopted by Valentine Cunningham, despite the fact that none of the principal poets uses the word in the 1930s.[24] Spender would appear to be an exception, but as deployed in 'The Uncreating Chaos (Double Portrait in a Mirror)', the word 'Apocalypse' is a revision, reflecting its prestige in the 1940s.[25] The elements of this curious complex are made obligingly explicit by John Lehmann, a partisan of 'the Auden generation':

> [T]he word 'apocalyptic' had [. . .] already been appropriated as banner and slogan by a group of poets from which most of the good poets appeared anxious to dissociate themselves. And yet this apocalyptic sense was everywhere in the poetry that was being written at this time.[26]

For these critics, then, there is nothing ridiculous about the word 'Apocalyptic' itself, rather a sense of resentment at its usurpation. Yet, as regards the poets themselves, the record suggests that it had become distinctly unfashionable, associated with bombastic verbosity. The key figure in this regard is J. L. Garvin, target of a helpful gibe by Keidrych Rhys, a friend of Thomas and the editor of *Wales*: 'And then we come to *The Apocalypse* (favourite word of J. L. Garvin), whose brain is J. F. Hendry, while Henry Treece is Chanticleer'.[27] Geoffrey Grigson makes the critical point precisely: 'For poets the Upas Tree wore out. But eventually what poets have used [. . .] sinks down into the consciousness of politicians [. . .]. I fancy its present lodging is in the mind of Mr Garvin'.[28] During the 1930s, the veteran editor of *The Observer* was warning against the 'laboratories [. . .] of death': 'Fire and poison are to be rained upon the cities according to the new Apocalypse'.[29] In 1946 Garvin was still at it, evoking horrors in Europe 'never imagined [. . .] until these last ten days of *apocalyptic* judgement'; while, as early as 1897, the same aspiring journalist had acclaimed Francis Thompson's *Sister Songs* as 'a very apocalypse of poetry'.[30] The review of her performance in *Hamlet* which amused Clara Morris, and which provided this chapter with an epigraph, is in the same devotional vein – a vein in which, during the nineteenth century, 'the quite unusual word' is most likely to have been used, if not as the alternative title of the Book of Revelation.

As for the 'politicians', the official transcript of Parliamentary Debates, *Hansard*, records only biblical invocations during the nineteenth century and, with two exceptions, for the next forty years. There is a spike of seven in 1934–5, with contributions from Stafford Cripps, Hugh Dalton and Winston Churchill, but, remarkably, a nil return throughout the Second World War. The noun disappears between 1939 and 1955, and so does the rarer adjective (recorded first in 1919, then twice in the 1920s) between 1927 and 1946.[31] Evidence for the currency of the word thus tends to support Rhys and Grigson rather than Hynes and Cunningham. However, as Spender had the grace to acknowledge as late as 1945, and as Hynes and Cunningham confirm, its validity, as a critical neologism, was self-evident:

> Surrealism has ceased to be fantasy, its 'objects' hurtle round our heads [. . .] The youngest and newest school of English poets signified this [. . .] by calling themselves 'apocalyptics'. Instead of being prophets, they were now witnesses in a world which had been taken over by prophecies.[32]

'Apocalyptic visions'

If Auden and Thomas are, in a sense, 'apocalyptic "twins"', the salient distinction, within a shared Apocalyptic modernism, is between their ironic and visionary styles.[33] The same terms may be extended to Lewis and to several other combatant poets. Wilfred Owen, in 'Uriconium: An Ode' ('Apocalyptic visions of world-wrecks'), and Isaac Rosenberg, in 'The Unicorn' ('[t]he lightning of the heavens / Lifts *an apocalypse*'), both use the word in the 'visionary modernist' sense.[34] The 'unnerving inevitability' of the 'hour of apocalypse' in David Jones's *In Parenthesis* (1937) is in the visionary vein; but the 'very latest winged-pigs, whose baleful snouts rend up no mean apocalypse' are more reminiscent of Lewis's *Blasting and Bombardiering* (1937), from which another of Jones's vignettes might also have been snipped: 'When Bomber Mulligan & Runner Meotti approach the appointed channels you can count on an apocalypse.'[35]

Owen's visionary modernism is one of the strongest strains in the poetry of Dylan Thomas, who might well have subscribed to 'the Philosophy of Many Soldiers' expressed in 'A Terre': '"Pushing up daisies" is their creed, you know. // To grain, then, go my fat, to buds my sap'.[36] A cluster of cognate images – some bearing a positive, some a negative charge – can be traced through Thomas's first two collections: 'the slant sap's tunnel'; 'the leaden bud / Shot through the leaf'; '[h]eads of the characters hammer through daisies'; 'the shades / Who periscope through flowers to the sky'; 'My second struggling from the grass'.[37] This cluster culminates in 'I dreamed my genesis', which is explicitly concerned with the outbreak of the First World War in the year Thomas was born, but also informs his signature poem, 'The force that through the green fuse'.[38] Another trope of 'pushing up daisies', the title-line of this poem is also an image of explosion, the flower exploding from the stem with the force 'that blasts the roots of trees', as in the explicitly violent rewrite: 'My fuses timed to charge his heart, / He blew like powder to the light'.[39] Alluding to the burial of hanged criminals, 'the hanging man' and 'lime' in the third stanza also recall the 'hanging face' of the soldier 'flound'ring like a man in [. . .] lime' in 'Dulce et Decorum Est'.[40] As integral to the iconography of the First World War as blasted trees, 'the fallen blood' of Thomas's poem is also the blood of 'The Fallen'; and the biblical image of 'my clay' (Job 10:9) is an implicit response to the question posed in 'Futility': 'Was it for this the clay grew tall?'[41] It is no accidental affinity that the line, '[a]t home, whispering of fields unsown', should originally have read, '[i]n *Wales*, [. . .]'.[42]

Owen's importance both to Thomas and to modernism in general is typified by the visceral involutions of 'The Show', which is the source of the recurring trope, 'death's feather': 'I reeled and shivered earthward like a feather. // And Death fell with me, like a deepening moan'.[43] Taking its decadent epigraph from Yeats, 'The Show' subjects 'the dreams [of] the ever-living' to lacerating irony.[44] Word by Parnassian word, the rapt opening line is dragged into the 'mire'; and the Dantesque companionship 'with Death', as though the speaker were *one* of the 'ever-living', results in a fastidious demonstration, to 'a manner of worm', of its crawling mortality. Yeats's 'ivory hands' and Owen's 'dithering feet' are cruelly incongruous. And what is this but modernism, in all its unnerving, utter conviction: 'I watched those agonies curl, lift and flatten'? Lewis could not be colder, Pound conciser, nor Eliot more unforgettable.

Originally entitled 'Vision', 'The Show' is closely related to Owen's literally 'Apocalyptic visions'. Jon Stallworthy footnotes a stream of allusions to Revelation, illuminating, for example, the irony of 'Mental Cases'.[45] One oversight in his exegesis is the allusion in the same poem to Revelation 22:8 – as in Eliot's draft: 'Always they must see these things and hear them'. The allusion in 'Inspection' completes the imaginative logic by which the soldiers are 'duly white-washed', but this time in *blood* (Rev. 7:14): 'they [. . .] have washed their robes, and made them white in the blood of the Lamb'; and the Sassoonian swipe at 'Field Marshal God' is given another dimension by the Apocalyptic twist of 'his own blood' (Rev. 1:5) into 'blood, his own', a characteristic identification of the soldier's sacrifice with Christ's.[46]

In a reverent BBC talk entitled 'Wilfred Owen', broadcast on 27 July 1946, Thomas presents Owen, 'in his flame-lit perspective', burying 'his smashed head with his own singed hands', in the image of St John the Divine in 'A Winter's Tale', on 'his firelit island' with 'scrolls of fire [. . .] in his heart'.[47] In defiance of a snide *TLS* review, two weeks earlier, entitled 'A Priesthood of Poets' ('poets are to take over [. . .] the responsibilities of the priesthood'), Thomas appoints Owen in this radio piece as 'the intoning priest' of 'the church of the broken body'.[48] Yet the broadcast is as topical as it is Apocalyptic, imagining 'Owen alive now, at the age of fifty-three, and half the world starving', just days after Attlee had put bread on the ration, a measure successfully avoided throughout the war: 'Germany was [. . .] facing imminent famine [. . .] Britain would have to go without in order to help.'[49] At the 1945 Labour Party Conference, Attlee had, after all, delivered his own Apocalyptic manifesto: to 'build Jerusalem / In England's green and pleasant land'.[50]

'The humble Eden of a drop of dew'

Owen may have been proud to be 'held peer by the Georgians', but the anthology in which 'his first poems in book form' appeared was edited by the modernist nemesis of Georgian verse, Edith Sitwell, the true editor, before relinquishing the manuscripts, of Owen's *Poems* (1920).[51] Sitwell found the poems 'so magnificent that it has been almost impossible to choose'; they 'should', she observed, 'overwhelm anybody who really cares about poetry'.[52] The set of seven in *Wheels: Fourth Cycle*, which is dedicated to Owen, includes 'Disabled', 'Strange Meeting', 'A Terre' and 'The Show', perhaps the finest ever small press scoop.[53]

Reviewers of *Wheels* agreed 'that its overall tone was [. . .] cynical, dark, even apocalyptic'.[54] In 'Sunrise', by Sherard Vines, night's 'black Host' is put to flight 'like the damned of apocalypse', while ironic modernism is represented in the anthology's 'third cycle' by Aldous Huxley.[55] A decade later, in *Point Counter Point* (1928), Huxley ironises the process 'creed' itself: 'the hand that wrote [. . .] the *Jupiter Symphony* [. . .] manured [. . .] a Viennese cemetery, to be transformed into grass and dandelions, which in their turn... It was all obvious, but to Lord Edward an apocalypse.'[56]

Wheels was integral to 'an *English* modern movement', encompassing its respectable cousin, *Art and Letters*, which was also committed to 'war poetry as part of the modernist experiment'.[57] There is nothing chauvinistic about Rebecca Beasley's construction, nor any obtuse antipathy to American modernism, such as that of H. J. C. Grierson and J. C. Smith in 1944: 'Eliot can scarcely be counted the pioneer of English modernism. That honour may fairly be claimed by Miss Edith Sitwell.'[58] Philip Hobsbaum's equally protectionist notion of an 'English Modernism' (1965) – comprising Owen, Rosenberg and Edward Thomas – is nonetheless compatible with the insight of David Daiches, in 1950, that Rosenberg was developing, not 'towards anything reminiscent of "Prufrock"', but 'into a poet much more like [. . .] the Apocalypse group [. . .] One can almost see in him something of Dylan Thomas.'[59] Daiches might have cited 'Significance', a vision of 'Chaos' in which '[a]ll twisted things continue to our clay'; and, indeed, he might have extended his analysis to Sitwell herself.[60] Much of her 'Metamorphosis' (1920) is chemically pure Eliot ('I, too, from ruined walls hung upside down [. . .] And knew the anguish of the skeleton'), but it is also notable for its use of half-rhyme, and for a prolepsis of 'The force that through the green fuse': 'the infinite / Wild strength the grass must have to find the light'.[61] There is, however, a more startling anticipation in 'Sylph's Song – Waltz': 'The humble Eden of a drop of dew'.[62] Sitwell's metaphor and biblical proper name inspire the first, while her cadence and syntax inform the second, of Thomas's beautiful wartime images: 'the round / Zion of the water bead / And the synagogue of the ear of corn'.[63] The genuine but exalted humility common to both texts bears little relation to the grim prudence of George Crabbe (whom Sitwell detested): 'Yet let us calmly view *our present fate*, / And make a humbler Eden of our state'.[64] In an unusual feedback loop, her later poetry shows the reciprocal influence of Thomas: 'all the deaths that Adam has endured / Since the first death'.[65]

'Throats where many rivers meet'

One tenet of the 'Philosophy' of modernism, improvised by Owen in 'A Terre' and implicitly developed by Dylan Thomas, has been succinctly defined by Harold Bloom: 'Blake, Shelley [. . .] and Nietzsche have an apocalyptic vitalism more or less in common.'[66] It is Shelley to whom Owen attributes his process 'Philosophy', resetting two lines of 'Adonaïs': 'I shall be one with nature, herb and stone'.[67] Alongside Shelley's inspired, anticipatory gloss on 'A Refusal to Mourn the Death, by Fire, of a Child in London' – 'Nature [. . .] has withdrawn his being to its own' – is another prolepsis of 'The force that through the green fuse': 'The leprous corpse [. . .] Exhales itself in flowers'.[68] As Hugh Kenner has shown, citing Ernest Fenollosa ('The forces which produce the branch-angles of an oak lay potent in the acorn'), Pound's comparable sense of 'our kinship to the vital universe, to the tree and the living rock' is one of the keys to the ideology of modernism: 'We have about us the universe of fluid force, and below us the germinal universe of wood alive, of stone alive.'[69] The sources of Pound's vitalism include Whitehead, whose process philosophy also influenced Thomas, but the 'living stone [. . .] chosen of God' (I Peter 2:4) is an image of election to immortality, as in the title of the 1941 anthology *This Living Stone*.[70] Again, according to Bloom, if 'Lawrence's apocalyptic vitalism had esoteric sources', its primary source was Revelation.[71] Like the word itself, Lawrence's *Apocalypse* (1931) was unfashionable during the 1930s, a notable omission even from an inventory by Auden of the influential works 'of that dangerous figure, D. H. Lawrence the Ideologue, author of *Phantasia on the Unconscious* [i.e. *Fantasia of the Unconscious*] and those sinister novels *Kangaroo* and *The Plumed Serpent*', despite his indebtedness to the dubiously forgotten text.[72]

As it happens, Thomas was even more in debt to 'that dangerous figure'. From a candid list of uncool influences (Sitwells, 'very bad Flecker'), in a letter to Henry Treece of 1938, the other nap Thomas picks out is the author of 'the verse extracts from *The Plumed Serpent*'.[73] Another of Thomas's confluences of influence, like 'throats where many rivers meet', 'The force that through the green fuse' abridges one of Quetzalcoatl's chants: 'a fuse to ignite / The substance of shadow, that [. . .] explodes into sight [. . .] [and] flowers on the burning bush'.[74] Compare 'Altarwise by owl-light' with a cento from *The Plumed Serpent* (1926):

Child of the short spark in a shapeless country
Soon sets alight a long stick from the cradle;
The horizontal cross-bones of Abaddon,
You by the cavern over the black stairs,
Rung bone and blade, the verticals of Adam,
And, manned by midnight, Jacob to the stars [. . .]

Child of the living dead, the dead that live [. . .]
Man is a column of blood, with a voice in it [. . .]
The hair of night is dark over our faces [. . .]
Follow me now up the ladder of sparks [. . .]
[T]he Son on the Cross cried out to the dark sun [. . .]
Am I always and only dead, but bone on a Cross of bone?[75]

Thomas might have truncated Lawrence's lines (the first three, perhaps, at the caesura), but the synaesthetic claustrophobia ('hair of night'), the biblical oxymoron ('ladder of sparks') and the phallic synecdoche ('column of blood') are all recognisable tropes in Thomas's vein.

The 'verticals of Adam' transmit an avant-garde signal, as received by Thomas from Eugène Jolas, who relaunched *transition*, in 1932, with a manifesto, 'Poetry is Vertical', proclaiming his faith in 'a vitalistic world' of 'orphic forces', 'leading [. . .] upward toward the illumination' of 'ecstatic revelation'.[76] In 1935 *transition* Number 23 is subtitled *An Intercontinental Workshop for Vertigralist Transmutation*, eliding 'vertical' with 'grail'; and in Number 26 (Fall 1936), Thomas's 'Then was my neophyte' appears in the section headed 'Vertigral', as though commissioned on the theme: '[. . .] That the green child see like a grail / Through veil and fin and fire and coil [. . .]'.[77] In 1936, having completed 'Altarwise by owl-light', Thomas referred to it with resilient pride as 'that Work in Progress thing', alluding to the interim title of *Finnegans Wake*, concurrently appearing in *transition*.[78] Joyce's own 'aesthetic of the dream', 'where the visions pass from the trivial to the apocalyptic, where the brain uses the roots of vocables to make others from them which will be capable of naming its phantasms', does justice to both works.[79]

Thomas's 1938 review of Samuel Beckett, a signatory to the Verticalist manifesto, but too much under 'the influence of those writers who have made *transition* their permanent resting-place', leaves no doubt that his own involvement with 'those writers' is on his own terms.[80] Such sneers are a period subgenre, from the wicked antigram, 'No, it isn' art', to Clement Greenberg's exasperation with '*transition* bunk, which a psychiatrist would return to his patients for revision'; yet 'the influence of those writers' on Thomas himself is considerable.[81] In 1924, in one of his 'Rambles Through Literary Paris' in the Paris edition of the *Chicago Tribune*, Jolas extols the 'apocalyptic splendour' of the poetry of Claire Goll; and in 1925, in the same column, occurs the first contextual reference to a notoriously fugitive term: 'The currents of thought today are in the direction of a new Romanticism.'[82] In July 1940, acclaiming the 'revolution in modern poetry [. . .] to which I gave the name of "verticalist" some years ago', Jolas is thus consistent in his alert response to the American debut of the Apocalyptic movement:

> *The Virginia Spectator* presents *Seven Poets of the New Apocalypse*. This astonishing manifestation comes from war-torn England, where poets like Henry Treece, Norman MacCaig, Dorian Cooke, Nigel Heseltine, J. F. Hendry and Keidrych Rhys express their deep metaphysical anguish in the face of the cataclysm.[83]

In the spirit of Jolas's 'ascensionist mythos', the final lines of 'Altarwise by owl-light' enact an unequivocal ascent:

Green as beginning, let the garden diving
Soar, with its two bark towers, to that Day
When the worm builds with the gold straws of venom
My nest of mercies in the rude, red tree.[84]

Out of the phallogocentrism of that grisly line, '[m]an is a column of blood with a voice in it' (crudely, a walking, talking erection, like 'rhubarb man'), Thomas creates his 'rude, red tree', a descendant of the cypress's 'rude shaft' in 'Adonaïs', and an epitome of 'apocalyptic vitalism'.[85] As in 'Altarwise by owl-light', Lawrence's 'worm' of 'cold corruption' is also 'the spangled dragon of the stars at large', 'building [its] nest of peace in your bones' and 'curdl[ing] your blood like milk with electric venom'.[86] The simultaneous soaring and 'diving' of the 'garden' is an image of the *felix culpa*, as in Elizabeth Barrett Browning's vision of 'fallen Adam [. . .] red-clay and a breath, who must [. . .] Live in a new apocalypse of sense'.[87]

The hint of socialist revolution, noted by John Goodby, recalls Empson's ironically titled 'Note on Local Flora' (= 'Proclamation on Universal Efflorescence'): 'So Semele desired her deity / As this in Kew thirsts for the Red Dawn'.[88] Frank Kermode recalls his 'astonishment' when he heard Empson deliver these lines 'in a sort of strangled apocalyptic whisper', as opposed to the euphoric Apocalyptic laughter of 'the rude, red tree'.[89] The pun profanes the Anglo-Saxon *Dream of the Rood*, but also Yeats's Rosicrucian incantation, 'To the Rose upon the Rood of Time'.[90] What, asks Yeats, could be 'purer than a tall candle before the Holy Rood'?[91] By contrast, Thomas's 'candle in the thighs' might indeed appear salacious.[92] Yet one of his most original achievements, in the face of all the complaints about his titillating obscenity, is to confer erotic dignity on the supposedly ignominious mechanics of adolescent sexuality, including masturbation. I interpret the 'verticals of Adam' according to Nietzsche's insight, worthy of Freud, that 'the degree and kind of a man's sexuality reach up into the topmost summit of his spirit'.[93]

'The bush that burned and wasn't destroyed'

In identifying Owen as 'one of the four most profound influences upon the poets who came after him; the other three being Gerard Manley Hopkins, the later W. B. Yeats, and T. S. Eliot', Thomas both epitomises the interrelations between 'palaeo-modernism' and the left-modernism of the 1940s, and highlights the Apocalyptic strand of visionary modernism which extends throughout the century.[94] In *Canaan* (1996), for example, Geoffrey Hill invokes at once the 'Son of man', whose 'hairs were white like wool' (Revelation 1:14); the 'charred' senses of Wilfred Owen, and the 'Mental Cases' who elicit his deepest compassion: 'With white seraphic hair / against the sun / who are these strangers – // or who are *these / charred spirits glaring / their vitreous eyes / towards apocalypse?*'[95]

To align Thomas Hardy alongside Eliot as influences on Auden and Larkin in a parallel tradition of ironic modernism would require a sharper caveat, since none of these poets can be confined within the limits imposed on them, and on their own poetry, by the protagonists of the Movement and its posterity. Gillian Steinberg reads Hardy's 'To an Unborn Pauper Child' as 'a re-envisioning of the Christ child', its 'apocalyptic images' straight out of Revelation.[96] The wish expressed in '[v]ain' by Hardy – '[h]ad I the ear of wombèd souls' – would seem to have been granted to Dylan Thomas.[97] For Larkin in 1948, *Moments of Vision*, a supposedly sober antidote to Yeats, meant just what it said on the tin: 'They don't come any more, those moments – / Moments of Vision, as Hardy called them. / I could see astonishing pictures, splaying lines / In all directions, like the bush / That burned and wasn't destroyed'.[98] For Lawrence, Owen, Thomas, Graham and Barker – to name five – the burning bush is the symbol of the Apocalyptic sublime. And what are those 'splaying lines' but 'the verticals of Adam'? Or 'the long perspectives, / Open at each instant of our lives', of which the Movement poets go in fear?[99] In 1948 Larkin would have endorsed a remark by Elizabeth Bowen: 'We want the naturalistic surface, but with a kind of internal burning. In Lawrence every bush burns.'[100] As it happens, Bowen represents both ironic and visionary modernism. In 'Foothold', a short story of 1929, a young dilettante is teased about his mercurial poetics:

'What became of that poem about the Apocalypse?'
'I'm rewriting it', said Thomas with dignity.
'You are the perfect mixture', said Janet, 'of Francis Thompson and H. G. Wells.'[101]

An update on this shrewd ideal would combine apocalyptic sublimity with the principled intelligence of the Movement. A 'stumblingblock' (Rev. 2:14) for sixty years, Thomas is, in this long perspective, at the heart of twentieth-century British poetry. 'The stone which the builders refused is become the head stone of the corner' (Psalms 118: 12).

Notes

1. Clara Morris, *The Life of a Star* (New York: McClure, Phillips & Co., 1906), p. 51.
2. See John Goodby, *The Poetry of Dylan Thomas: Under the Spelling Wall* (Liverpool: Liverpool University Press, 2013), pp. 1–49.
3. John Goodland, typescript draft, with manuscript revisions and additions, of a proposal to Faber, enclosed in a letter to Dorian Cooke, c. 13 November 1938; rediscovered among Cooke's papers by Peter Manson, who is editing his poetry.
4. D. H. Lawrence, *Apocalypse* (London: Penguin, 1974 [1931]); Henry Miller, *Tropic of Cancer* (London: Panther Books, 1965 [1934]), p. 187.
5. Elizabeth Bowen, 'The Short Story', in *The Faber Book of Modern Stories*, ed. Elizabeth Bowen (London: Faber, 1937), p. 16.
6. J. Alban Evans, 'An Ailing Age', *Catholic Herald* (2 October 1936), 4.
7. Andrew DuBois and Frank Lentricchia, 'Modernist Lyric in the Culture of Capital', in *The Cambridge History of American Literature, Volume 5: Poetry and Criticism, 1900–1950*, ed. Sacvan Bercovitch (Cambridge: Cambridge University Press, 2003), pp. 9–178 (p. 177).
8. Frank Kermode, 'Modernisms: Cyril Connolly and Others', *Encounter*, 26.3 (March 1966), 53–8 (pp. 53–4); Selim Sarwar, 'Robert Lowell: Scripting the Mid-Century Eschatology', *Journal of Modern Literature*, 25.2 (Winter 2001–2), 114–30 (p. 114).
9. J. C. Squire, 'The Man Who Wrote Free Verse' (1924), in *Mock Modernism: An Anthology of Parodies, Travesties, Frauds, 1910–1935*, ed. Leonard Diepeveen (Toronto: University of Toronto Press, 2014), p. 37.
10. T. S. Eliot, *The Waste Land: A Facsimile and Transcript of the Original Drafts including the Annotations of Ezra Pound*, ed. Valerie Eliot (London: Faber, 1971), p. 9.
11. Ibid. p. 148.
12. Hope Mirrlees, *Paris: A Poem* (1920), in *Collected Poems*, ed. Sandeep Parmar (Manchester: Carcanet, 2011), pp. 1–20 (p. 3).
13. See Michael North, *Novelty: A History of the New* (Chicago: Chicago University Press, 2013), p. 162.
14. H.D., *Trilogy* (Manchester: Carcanet, 1997 [1945]), p. 65.
15. Wyndham Lewis, *Paleface: The Philosophy of the 'Melting Pot'* (New York: Haskell House, 1969 [1927]), p. 100.
16. A. T. Tolley, *The Poetry of the Forties* (Manchester: Manchester University Press, 1985), p. 33.
17. F. S. Flint, 'John Gould Fletcher: *Branches of Adam*', review in *The New Criterion*, 5.1 (1927), 134–6 (p. 134).
18. Edith Sitwell to Gertrude Stein, [c. April 1926], *Selected Letters of Edith Sitwell*, ed. Richard Greene (London: Virago, 1997), p. 66.
19. David Gascoyne, entry for 8 August 1938, *Collected Journals: 1936–42* (London: Skoob Books, 1991), p. 169.
20. Tolley, *The Poetry of the Forties*, p. 33.
21. Gascoyne, entry for 29 September 1938, *Collected Journals*, p. 189.

22. Gascoyne, entry for 23 January 1939, Ibid. p. 243.
23. Ibid. p. 245; see John Goodland, Dorian Cooke, J. F. Hendry et al., 'The Apocalyptic Manifesto: *Apocalypse or The Whole Man*' (1938), introduced in Giles Goodland, 'John Goodland and the Apocalyptic Movement: Notes from the Son of a Literary Footnote', *P.N. Review*, 30.2 (November–December 2003), 22–5 (pp. 23–4).
24. Samuel Hynes, *The Auden Generation: Literature and Politics in England in the 1930s* (London: Faber, 1976), p. 370 (my italics); Valentine Cunningham, *British Writers of the Thirties* (Oxford: Oxford University Press, 1989), p. 421. Each member of the so-called MacSpaunday quartet uses the word in the 1940s, including Auden, with ironic alacrity, on the first day of the new decade, in 'New Year Letter (January 1, 1940)', *The Double Man* (New York: Random House, 1941), p. 24.
25. Compare 'The Uncreating Chaos' (*The Still Centre* (London: Faber, 1939), p. 30) with the revised and retitled text (*Collected Poems, 1928–1985* (London: Faber, 1985), p. 57), in which the word 'Apocalypse' is substituted for the phrase 'that day's doom', in the original injunction to 'respond to that day's doom / with a headache'.
26. John Lehmann, *I Am My Brother: Autobiography 2* (London: Longmans Green, 1960), p. 233.
27. Keidrych Rhys, 'How are We Doing?', *Wales*, 3.1 (July 1943), 89–94 (p. 92).
28. Geoffrey Grigson, *The Romantics: An Anthology*, ed. Geoffrey Grigson (London: Routledge, 1942), p. 341.
29. J. L. Garvin, cited by Arthur S. Maxwell, *This Mighty Hour: The Message of These Stirring Times* (Watford: Stanborough Press, 1933 [1932]), p. 90.
30. J. L. Garvin, 'Germany Now Pays the Price of Aggression', *Daily Telegraph*, 1946, cited by Horace Annesley Vachell, *Now Came Still Evening On* (London: Cassell, 1946), p. 96; J. L. Garvin, *The Bookman* (March 1897), cited by Everard Meynell, *The Life of Francis Thompson* (London: Burns and Oates, 1926 [1913]), p. 185.
31. 'Hansard 1802–2005', *Hansard: UK Parliament*: <http://www.parliament.uk/business/publications/hansard> (last accessed 20 September 2015).
32. Stephen Spender, 'Some Observations on English Poetry between Two Wars', in *Transformation Three*, ed. Henry Treece and Stefan Schimanski (London: Lindsay Drummond, n.d. [1945]), p. 176.
33. Goodby, *The Poetry of Dylan Thomas*, p. 35.
34. Wilfred Owen, 'Uriconium: An Ode', *The Complete Poems and Fragments: Volume I: The Poems*, ed. Jon Stallworthy (London: Chatto & Windus, 2013), p. 67; Isaac Rosenberg, 'The Unicorn' (1917–18), *The Collected Poems of Isaac Rosenberg*, ed. Gordon Bottomley and Denys Harding (London: Chatto & Windus, 1977), p. 99.
35. David Jones, *In Parenthesis* (London: Faber, 1963 [1937]), pp. 135, 115–16, 121; Wyndham Lewis, *Blasting & Bombardiering: Autobiography (1914–1926)* (London: Eyre and Spottiswoode, 1937).
36. Owen, 'A Terre', *The Poems*, p. 179. The second of the two cited lines sounds more like Thomas than Owen.
37. *CP14*, pp. 72, 81, 24, 53, 61.
38. Ibid. pp. 61–2, 43–4.

39. Ibid. p. 52.
40. Ibid. p. 43; Owen, 'Dulce et Decorum Est', *The Poems*, p. 140.
41. Laurence Binyon, 'For the Fallen', *Collected Poems of Laurence Binyon: Volume 1: Lyrical Poems* (London: Macmillan, 1931), p. 209; Owen, *The Poems*, p. 158.
42. Owen, *The Complete Poems and Fragments: Volume II: The Manuscripts and Fragments*, ed. Jon Stallworthy (London: Chatto & Windus, 2013), p. 319.
43. 'Before I knocked', *CP14*, pp. 38–9 (p. 39); 'If I were tickled by the rub of love', ibid. pp. 59–61 (p. 60); 'My world is pyramid', Ibid. pp. 64–6 (p. 66); Owen, 'The Show', *The Poems*, pp. 155–6 (p. 155).
44. W. B. Yeats, 'The Shadowy Waters' (1906), *The Poems*, ed. Daniel Albright (London: Everyman, 1994), pp. 115–37.
45. Owen, *The Poems*, p. 170.
46. Ibid. p. 95.
47. 'Wilfred Owen' (1946), *TB*, pp. 93–101 (p. 100); 'A Winter's Tale', *CP14*, pp. 167–71 (p. 167); Thomas's urge to imagine Owen's 'smashed head' should remind us, I think, of 'the fresh-severed head of it, my head' in Owen's 'The Show' (*The Poems*, p. 156).
48. Alan Pryce-Jones, 'A Priesthood of Poets', *The Times Literary Supplement*, 13 July 1946, pp. 325–6 (p. 325); Thomas, 'Wilfred Owen', *TB*, p. 100.
49. Ibid. p. 99; Clement Attlee, *A Prime Minister Remembers* (London: Heinemann, 1961), p. 135. Bread rationing was introduced on 21 July 1946.
50. Clement Attlee, featured in footage of 1945 Party Conference, Andrew Marr, *History of Modern Britain*, BBC2 (22 May 2007).
51. Wilfred Owen to Susan Owen, 31 December 1917, cited in Jon Stallworthy, *Wilfred Owen: A Biography* (Oxford: Oxford University Press; and London: Chatto & Windus, 1974), p. 253; Edith Sitwell to Susan Owen, 3 November 1919, *Selected Letters of Edith Sitwell*, p. 32. Despite Sitwell's best efforts, Owen's *Poems* were finally seen into print by Siegfried Sassoon. For more on this, see Richard Greene, *Edith Sitwell: Avant Garde Poet, English Genius* (London: Virago, 2011), pp. 129–30.
52. Edith Sitwell to Susan Owen, 21 June 1919, cited in Michael Cotsell, '*Wheels*: An Introduction', *The Modernist Journals Project*, Brown University and the University of Tulsa: <http://modjourn.org> (last accessed 20 September 2015).
53. Edith Sitwell (ed.), *Wheels, 1919: Fourth Cycle* (Oxford: Blackwell, 1919), pp. 52–64.
54. Cotsell, '*Wheels*: An Introduction'.
55. Sherard Vines, 'Sunrise', *Wheels, 1918: A Third Cycle*, ed. Edith Sitwell (Oxford: Blackwell, 1918), p. 70.
56. Aldous Huxley, *Point Counter Point* (London: Penguin, 1955 [1928]), pp. 34–5 (the final ellipsis is Huxley's).
57. Rebecca Beasley, 'Literature and the Visual Arts: *Art and Letters* (1917–20) and *The Apple* (1920–2)', in *The Oxford Critical and Cultural History of Modernist Magazines: Volume I: Britain and Ireland, 1880–1955*, ed. Peter Brooker and Andrew Thacker (Oxford: Oxford University Press, 2009), pp. 485–504 (p. 487).

58. H. J. C. Grierson and J. C. Smith, *A Critical History of English Poetry* (London: Chatto & Windus, 1944), p. 510.

59. Philip Hobsbaum, 'The Growth of English Modernism' (1965), in *Wisconsin Studies in Contemporary Literature*, cited in *British Poetry Since 1945*, ed. Edward Lucie-Smith (London: Penguin, 1970), pp. 384–5; David Daiches, 'Isaac Rosenberg: Poet', *Commentary*, 10 (July–December 1950), 91–3 (p. 91).

60. Isaac Rosenberg, 'Significance' (1915), *The Collected Poems of Isaac Rosenberg*, p. 116.

61. Edith Sitwell, *The Collected Poems of Edith Sitwell* (London: Duckworth, 1930 [1920]), p. 80.

62. Ibid. p. 126

63. 'A Refusal to Mourn the Death, by Fire, of a Child in London', *CP14*, p. 172.

64. George Crabbe, 'The Natural Death of Love', *Tales of the Hall* (London: John Murray, 1819), p. 108.

65. Edith Sitwell, 'The Coat of Fire', *Horizon*, 17.100 (April 1948), p. 237.

66. Harold Bloom, *Yeats* (Oxford: Oxford University Press, 1972), p. 33.

67. P. B. Shelley, 'Adonaïs: An Elegy on the Death of John Keats, Author of Endymion, Hyperion, Etc.', *The Poetical Works of Shelley*, ed. Thomas Hutchinson (Oxford: Oxford University Press, 1923 [1821]), p. 436.

68. Ibid. pp. 436, 431.

69. Hugh Kenner, *The Pound Era* (Berkeley: University of California Press, 1971), p. 126; Ernest Fenollosa and Ezra Pound, *The Chinese Written Character as a Medium for Poetry: A Critical Edition*, ed. Haun Saussy (New York: Fordham University Press, 2010 [1920]), p. 54; Ezra Pound, 'Psychology and Troubadours', *The Quest: A Quarterly Review* 4.1 (October 1912), 37–53 (p. 44).

70. Charles Wrey Gardiner (ed.), *This Living Stone: The Grey Walls Anthology of New Poems* (Billericay: Grey Walls Press, 1941).

71. Harold Bloom, *The Anatomy of Influence: Literature as a Way of Life* (New Haven: Yale University Press, 2011), p. 268.

72. W. H. Auden, 'Foreword', *The Orators*, 3rd edn (London: Faber, 1966), p. 7; Hynes, *The Auden Generation*, pp. 126–7.

73. Thomas to Henry Treece, 16 May 1938, *CL*, p. 343.

74. 'In the White Giant's Thigh', *CP14*, p. 195; D. H. Lawrence, *The Plumed Serpent* (London: Penguin, 1950 [1926]), pp. 190–1.

75. 'Altarwise by owl-light', *CP14*, p. 82, ll. 5–10; Lawrence, *The Plumed Serpent*, pp. 271 [line 1], 423 [l. 2], 394 [l. 3], 293 [l. 4], 134 [l. 6], 134 [l. 7].

76. Eugène Jolas, Samuel Beckett, Hans Arp et al., 'Poetry is Vertical', *transition: International Workshop for Orphic Creation*, 21 (March 1932), 148–9; repr. in *Manifesto: A Century of Isms*, ed. Mary Ann Caws (Lincoln: Nebraska University Press, 2001), p. 529.

77. Eugène Jolas (ed.), *transition: A Quarterly Review*, 25 (Fall 1936), pp. 20–1; Thomas, 'Then was my neophyte', *CP14*, p. 90.

78. Thomas to Glyn Jones, [December 1936], *CL*, p. 272.

79. James Joyce to Edmond Jaloux, cited in Richard Ellmann, *James Joyce* (Oxford: Oxford University Press, 1959), p. 559.

80. Dylan Thomas, 'Samuel Beckett, *Murphy*; William Carlos Williams, *Life along the Passaic River*' (1938), *EPW*, pp. 186–8 (p. 186).

81. Edward W. Titus, *This Quarter*, 3 (1930), p. 130; Clement Greenberg, 'The Renaissance of the Little Mag' (1941), in *The Collected Essays and Criticism, Volume I: Perceptions and Judgments, 1939–1944*, ed. John O'Brian (Chicago: University of Chicago Press, 1986), p. 44.

82. Eugène Jolas, 'Rambles through Literary Paris: Number 2805 (22 March 1925)', in *Critical Writings, 1924–1951*, ed. Klaus H. Kiefer and Rainer Rumold (Evanston: Northwestern University Press, 2009), pp. 88–94 (p. 88); Jolas, 'Rambles through Literary Paris: Number 2714 (21 December 1924)', Ibid. pp. 71–6 (p. 75).

83. Eugène Jolas, 'Verticalist Revolution', *The Living Age: The World in Review*, 358.4486 (July 1940), 493–4.

84. Eugène Jolas, 'Prolegomenon, or White Romanticism and the Mythos of Ascension' (undated), *Critical Writings, 1924–1951*, pp. 222–6 (p. 226); 'Altarwise by owl-light', *CP14*, p. 86.

85. Ibid. p. 86; Shelley, 'Adonaïs', *The Poetical Works*, p. 434.

86. Lawrence, *The Plumed Serpent*, pp. 272, 360.

87. Elizabeth Barrett Browning, 'A Drama of Exile', *Poems* (London: Edward Moxon, 1844), p. 10.

88. Goodby, *The Poetry of Dylan Thomas*, p. 271; William Empson, 'Notes on Local Flora' (1935), *The Complete Poems of William Empson*, ed. John Haffenden (London: Allen Lane, 2000), p. 56.

89. Frank Kermode, 'William Empson: A Most Noteworthy Poet', in *London Review of Books*, 15 June 2000: <http://www.theguardian.com/books/2000/jun/15/londonreviewofbooks> (last accessed 20 September 2015).

90. Yeats, 'To the Rose upon the Rood of Time', *The Poems*, p. 35.

91. Yeats, 'Red Hanrahan's Song about Ireland', Ibid. p. 90.

92. 'Light breaks where no sun shines', *CP14*, p. 46.

93. Friedrich Nietzsche, *Beyond Good and Evil: Prelude to a Philosophy of the Future*, ed. and trans. R. J. Hollingdale (London: Penguin, 1973 [1886]), p. 73.

94. 'Wilfred Owen', *TB*, p. 100.

95. Geoffrey Hill, 'Scenes with Harlequins: In Memoriam Aleksandr Blok', *Canaan* (London: Penguin, 1996), pp. 15–22 (p. 17).

96. Thomas Hardy, 'To an Unborn Pauper Child' (1901), *The Complete Poems*, ed. James Gibson (Basingstoke: Palgrave, 2001 [1976]), pp. 127–8.

97. Ibid. p. 128.

98. Thomas Hardy, *Moments of Vision and Miscellaneous Verses* (London: Macmillan, 1917); Philip Larkin, cited in Andrew Motion, *Larkin: A Writer's Life* (London: Faber, 1993), p. 182.

99. Philip Larkin, 'Reference Back' (1955), in *Collected Poems*, ed. Anthony Thwaite (London: Faber, 2003), p. 111.

100. Elizabeth Bowen, 'D. H. Lawrence: Reappraising his Literary Influence: Review of *The Portable D. H. Lawrence*', *The New York Times Book Review*, 52 (9 February 1947), 4.

101. Elizabeth Bowen, 'Foothold' (1929), in *Collected Stories* (London: Penguin, 1983), pp. 326–44 (p. 337).

Chapter 10

Dylan Thomas and American Poetry: 'a kind of secret, but powerful, leaven'

Philip Coleman

'English disputes' and American readings

'Nothing could be more wrongheaded than the English disputes about Dylan Thomas's greatness,' Robert Lowell wrote in 1947, before going on to dismiss the 'inarticulate extravagance of Edith Sitwell and Herbert Read' and the 'methodical, controversial blindness of [Arthur] Symons, [Geoffrey] Grigson' and others.[1] In the decades since Thomas's death, however, the critical response to Thomas's work in the United States has been no less puzzling. Critics and literary historians tend to underestimate Thomas's influence, and his importance to many American poets, despite the fact that several major figures – including John Berryman, Elizabeth Bishop and John Ashbery – have expressed a sense of affinity with Thomas's work. John Goodby's view that '[t]he scope of Thomas's impact on US poetry is remarkable' is not shared by many US American poetry scholars and commentators.[2] Nick Halpern briefly acknowledges the influence of Thomas and 'the New Romantics' on Denise Levertov's early poetry in his essay in *The Cambridge History of American Poetry* (2015), but Edward Brunner, writing in the same volume, is quick to group Thomas among the '"Bohemian" poets of rhetorical excess', whose example was rejected by American poets who started to gain prominence in the 1970s, including Robert Pinsky and Mark Strand.[3] Apart from these brief references, Thomas is not mentioned in Bendixen and Burt's history – not even in discussions of those poets for whom he has been generally acknowledged as a hugely important figure, such as Berryman and others of the so-called Middle Generation.

A similar tendency to undervalue Thomas's importance in US American poetic culture is expressed by Robert von Hallberg in his essay on American poetry between 1945 and 1950 in the eighth volume of Sacvan Bercovitch's *Cambridge History of American Literature* (1996).[4]

Von Hallberg suggests, on the one hand, that 'Thomas's career was a stunning spectacle of a poet who openly refused to be minor': for 'the generation of Lowell, Berryman, and [Randall] Jarrell [. . .] [h]e was spoken of as another Shakespeare, or as a fake, but not as a minor or academic poet.'[5] Von Hallberg presents Thomas's public persona as something poets such as Lowell and Berryman sought to imitate, quite apart from any engagement with his approach to language or form. On the other hand, von Hallberg notes with approval Charles Olson's desire to write 'a very dry poetry derived not from the sympathetic emotions commonly addressed in love lyrics and energies', which he reads in turn as a reaction against the 'emotional neo-Romanticism of Dylan Thomas, who from 1950 to 1953 enjoyed enormous popularity in America as a performer of his own verse'.[6] In this reading, von Hallberg uses the example of Thomas to reinforce an orthodox literary historical designation that positions Berryman, Lowell and the Confessionals in one camp, with Olson and his Black Mountain acolytes in another. However, this categorising oversimplifies the extent to which any individual poet from either side of this divide engaged with Thomas in the post-war period, either in terms of the impact of his persona or, more importantly, through close engagements with his poetic practice. One of the problems with von Hallberg's analysis, indeed, is that his focus on the issue of Thomas's persona says nothing at all about how these and other poets actually engaged with Thomas's work.

Olson's reading of Thomas, for example, is much more complex than von Hallberg's literary historical positioning of both poets suggests. In a long letter written to the English critic Ronald Mason in 1953, Olson refers to Thomas in ways that demonstrate an important sense of connection that is elided by conventional critical categorisations. Olson writes:

> In fact, to us who are in the thicket, these happy ones (Shelley, Chaucer, Thomas – up to age 30!) are like in Paradise. And we wave to them, over the dearth, with wonderful brotherhood – as [Esteban] Vicente did put it – portrait, landscape, & narrative! / We who paint space, write dream, or compose magnetic tape![7]

Olson's insistence on a sense of 'wonderful brotherhood' tempers the suggestion that he rejected Thomas outright as irrelevant to his own poetic project. On the contrary, while he goes on to criticise Thomas (along with Stefan Wolpe, the composer) for failing to 'get away from subject-matter', Olson needs the example of Thomas's work before him as he seeks to describe the central components of his own method.[8] For Olson, the poet should seek to engage the world by what he calls '*attention* rather than analogy' – 'by the obedience of the writer to their particulars, not to his appropriation of them' – but in the end his analysis comes down to an acknowledgement of two essential elements within a single 'Law': '(1) verse is my business, but (2) [...] language, including prose, is where one does try to find how to make form out of it!'[9] In other words, while Olson recognises differences between his approach and that of Thomas, as one poet reading another he affirms the idea that they are both engaged in a larger artistic project of trying to find new ways to 'paint space, write dream, or compose magnetic tape!' Given Thomas's particular influence on the phonographic recording of the spoken word in the second half of the twentieth century, the reference to artists working in the medium of 'magnetic tape' here is significant.

Leaving aside established critical and literary historical designations, then, Olson and Thomas can in fact be read as two poets at mid-century who were equally concerned with the problem of how to give voice to the experience of twentieth-century modernity in language, often with surprisingly similar objectives and results. In his letter to Ronald Mason, Olson writes:

> The quarrel is with discourse – and thus, up to a certain, but extreme, point, with traditional syntax. Because it is not possible to say everything at once is no reason, to my mind, to lose the advantage of this pressure (or compression) which speech is when it wants to be: that it rushes into the mouth to crowd out to someone else what it is pressing in the heart & mind to be said.[10]

Thomas can also be read as a poet who took 'advantage of this pressure (or compression) which speech is when it wants to be'. Many of his poems, from 'To-day, this hour I breathe' (later revised as 'To-day, this insect') to 'The force that through the green fuse', explore the same process highlighted here by Olson – what happens when 'speech [...] rushes into the mouth to crowd out to someone else what it is pressing in the heart & mind to be said'. Thomas's sense of a 'space / And time that is already half / More than that I tell you in' resonates with Olson's description of 'both syntax and narrative [...] refounded in an order of space-time which shows up the old ordering of discourse as necessarily thin – thin of time and of logic'.[11] In his letter to Mason, Olson critiques the 'arbitrary system of presentation which [has] forced a great deal of reality into statement, where it dies, simply, that life is not the statement of itself but – itself'.[12] There is a strong affinity between this and Thomas's affirmation, in 1951, that in poetry '[a]ll that matters is the eternal movement behind it, the vast undercurrent of human grief, folly, pretension, exhalation, or ignorance, however unlofty the intention of the poem.'[13] In an essay on Thomas written in 1940, John Berryman insisted that '[a] poem is an accretion of knowledge, of which only the flimsiest portion can be translated into bromide'.[14] In this statement, Berryman articulated an understanding of the agency of poetry – which he shared with Thomas and Olson – that is easily overlooked in the rush to separate these poets from each other through certain kinds of literary critical and historical categorising of their work. It is possible, moreover, to read Olson, Berryman and others in conversation with Thomas in a way that challenges those categorisations and, in the process, affirms the correctness of John Goodby's claim regarding the 'scope' and 'impact' of his poetic presence.

'In the thicket': Thomas and American poetry at mid-century

Olson's phrase 'in the thicket' in his letter to Ronald Mason of 1953 brings to mind his poem 'In Cold Hell, in Thicket', first published in the same year.[15] Olson's distinction between the 'cold hell' of his (Cold War) experience and the 'Paradise' into which Shelley, Chaucer and Thomas have journeyed before him, suggests a radical separation, in one sense, but it is a breach across which he nonetheless feels strong accord – 'wonderful brotherhood' – with these earlier and contemporary figures. This needs to be taken seriously in terms of how Olson's relationship with Thomas, not to mention Shelley and Chaucer, is read, and especially in a poem like 'In Cold Hell, in Thicket', where Olson also strives to 'extend the language', to use Berryman's phrase in relation to Thomas's poetic achievement.[16] The 'extension' of the language has a literal dimension, for Olson, in the way that he piles parenthetical phrasal alternatives on top of each other in certain parts of his poem, as here in its opening lines:

> In cold hell, in thicket, how
> abstract (as high mind, as not lust, as love is) how
> strong (as strut or wing, as polytope, as things are
> constellated) how
> strung, how cold
> can a man stay (can men) confronted
> thus?[17]

The urgency of these lines is determined, in part, by the rush of clauses in parentheses; they suggest a vigorous determination on the part of the speaker to be clearer in his articulation of what it is he means to say, prompting the reader to hear his words in multiple ways at the same time – to hear ideas 'constellated' in several dimensions simultaneously.

The forceful sonic play of key phrases in the opening of Olson's poem – 'how / abstract', 'how / strong', 'how / strung' – turns them into questions that lead into a larger ontological question concerning the poet's sense of self: 'The question, the fear he raises himself against // is: / Who / am I?'[18] The year after he wrote 'In Cold Hell, in Thicket', in a piece called 'Notes on Language and Theater', Olson put the question another way, again invoking Thomas in his deliberations.[19] He begins by suggesting that the origins of theatre 'before the classic Greek theatre' can be explained in relation to the connections between two separate developments. These were to do with '(1) *the rhabdians*, or single actors with a stick beating out verse and acting out narrative situations in said verse, 500 hexameters at a performance', and '(2) the comedians, the gag men, no text, who survive today in Greece and elsewhere [. . .] as those traveling kerekters (the borscht circuit) who are anywhere doing the steady business of phallic jokes and situations [. . .]'.[20] As Olson develops his argument, however, it is to the example of Thomas's readings in the United States in the early 1950s that he turns. 'Let me try it this way,' he writes:

> the theater, as we call theater, will soon once more be *rhabdian*, plots gone, gab gone, all the rest of the baggage of means, stripped down, these 'recitations' now going on in public hall a sign, but Dylan Thomas more, the hunger of people merely to hang their ears out and hear, not any longer the jigging of their eyes, all that 'luxury,' Schubert seats etc.[21]

The apparent critique of the commercialisation of art in performance here might be related to Louis Zukofsky's questioning of the relationship between culture and economics in his long work '*A*' – particularly in that poem's first movement, which derides 'business devotees of arts and letters'– but this is not the aim of Olson's argument.[22] Rather, he uses the example of Thomas to point to a transformation in both the cultural role of the poet and the extent to which audiences impact upon the production of art through the physical, public expression of their own 'hunger' for different kinds of representation. The popularity of Thomas's performance of his poems in public in the years before his death, in other words, suggests to Olson a radical shift in the way that audiences engage with poetry, but this has repercussions, too, for how he thinks about the nature and production of his own work.

Olson does not dismiss Thomas, then, but reads him as a figure of central contemporary cultural and poetic importance whose example goads and guides him towards a clearer articulation of his own position. Having positioned Thomas at the heart of a new '*rhabdian*' movement in twentieth-century theatre, he asks: 'In himself, inside, it turns out a man is how?'[23] As with Thomas, who insisted that '[t]he joy and function of poetry is, and was, the celebration of man' – and notwithstanding the fact that he added 'the celebration of man [. . .] is also the celebration of God' to this claim – Olson's view of the function and form of poetry falls back on a similar avowal of the self's persistence through what he calls 'the several guises of identity [...] the single thing in the end, perhaps, we turn out to be, or settle for'.[24] As Thomas put it, 'you're back again where you began': 'You're back with the mystery of having been moved by words.'[25] Another important mid-century American poet, Delmore Schwartz, affirmed this view in his reading of Thomas's significance as a public poet in the post-war era. In 'The Present State of Poetry' (1958), he suggests that 'what Thomas accomplished by his public readings [was] meaningful in ways which extend far beyond the unquestionable importance of his work.'[26] In short, he insists that Thomas

> demonstrated by direct, eloquent, and vivid example of a truth about the nature of poetry which no amount of critical elucidation could have communicated – the truth that the actuality of a poem is not merely a matter of the explicit meanings contained in each successive line.[27]

Schwartz's insight that Thomas's public readings 'communicated to his listeners an experience of the truth that the whole being of a poem is far more than its explicit meanings' is part of what Olson, writing in 1950, called the 'revolution of the ear' in twentieth-century poetic practice.[28] This is not to say that Thomas can be labelled a 'projectivist', but both Olson and Schwartz, from quite dissimilar cultural and institutional backgrounds and perspectives, recognised something in Thomas's affirmation of the sonic character of poetry that spoke to their mutual sense of the state of the art in 1950s America.

This was, in a sense, the era of the ear in American poetry, and Thomas was central to its development for mid-century poets as different in their approach to poetic practice as Olson and Schwartz.[29] As the poet Donald Hall has put it, Thomas was 'the starting point and emblem' of the American performance poetry circuit.[30] Schwartz recognised the deep significance of Thomas's readings and claimed that '[t]he living voice communicated to Thomas'[s] readers the intensely felt attitudes and emotions which were the actual poem in its complete and concrete reality.'[31] His acknowledgement of the relationship between a 'living voice' and the 'concrete reality' of the 'actual poem' is connected to Olson's belief that 'speech is the "solid" of verse' and, furthermore, 'the secret of a poem's energy'.[32] No matter what their cultural or ideological differences, in other words, and regardless of the ways in which they have often been kept apart in literary historical representations, Olson and Schwartz read Thomas in ways that had nothing at all to do with what Robert von Hallberg has dismissed as Thomas's 'emotional neo-Romanticism'.[33] It may be true to say that there is a general turn away from lyric expression in Olson's poetry as he focuses on the composition of *The Maximus Poems* throughout the later decades of his career, but he engages with Thomas (and other lyric poets) at key moments in his development. While his critical engagement with Thomas in 'The Present State of Poetry' is an important moment in Thomas's reception in the United States, on the other hand, Schwartz's poems are more clearly informed by a 'neo-Romantic' lyric perspective. From the practice of using first lines as titles, which is a common strategy in Thomas's oeuvre, to the lush diction and free-wheeling syntax of poems such as 'May's Truth and May's Falsehood', Schwartz can be read as an American poet at mid-century whose work in the lyric mode shares many of the technical and formal features that Thomas mastered. 'May's Truth and May's Falsehood', in particular, echoes Thomas's work in several ways, as its opening lines illustrate:

All through the brilliant blue and gold afternoon
All space was blossoming: immense and stately against the blue heights
The sailing, summer-swollen milky and mounting clouds: colossal blossoms,
And the dark statues of the trees on the blue and green ground, flowing.[34]

These lines owe more to Thomas's sense of colour and temporal *ekstasis* – of speaking from the moment to a point out of time – than they do to any American precursor, no matter how much their looping enjambements recollect those of Walt Whitman. Moreover, they speak to Schwartz's sense of the importance of the dialectic between 'living voice' and 'concrete reality' in the art of poetry. As he puts it further on in the same poem: 'And every solid thing / Moved as in bloom, leafing, opening wing upon wing to the sun's overwhelmed lightning!'[35]

Towards the end of 'May's Truth and May's Falsehood', Schwartz's speaker asks '[t]o be reborn, again and again and again, to be transformed all over again'.[36] This is the spirit of 'enhanced expectation' that also informs Thomas's work, as Derek Mahon has suggested, and it is brought into being through remarkable arrangements of language.[37] As suggested already, John Berryman also recognised this, and the example of Thomas's work – which Berryman knew from the 1930s, when the two poets first met in England – challenged him to explore possibilities for his own poetry as he sought to advance away from the influence of W. B. Yeats, in particular, in the early stages of his career.[38] Berryman's essay on Thomas from 1940, indeed, can be read as a statement of what the American poet learned about the art of poetry by reading his friend across the Atlantic, and especially with regard to his suggestion that '[a] poem that works well demonstrates an insight, and the insight may consist, not in the theme, but in the image relations or the structure relations.'[39] This idea is crucial to an understanding of the relationship between image, structure and meaning in Berryman's long poem *The Dream Songs*, which cannot be summarised in terms of a single theme but is, rather, a text that develops several overlapping concerns in the course of its 385 separate sections. 'Much of Thomas's inventive energy', Berryman argues, 'goes into technique', and again the same claim could be made in relation to his work, which evolved through a stunning series of formal reinventions, from *The Dispossessed* (1948) through *Homage to Mistress Bradstreet* (1953, 1956) and *The Dream Songs* (1969) to *Love & Fame* (1970) and *Delusions, etc.* (1972).[40] Through all of these works, Berryman's attention to technical accomplishment was as, if not more, important than the problem of subject matter or thematic amplification. In a sense, Berryman learned this from Thomas, and it highlights just how little, when it came to the actual practice of writing poetry, he cared about Thomas's 'public' profile in the United States in the 1950s. Berryman may have been present in St Vincent's Hospital in New York when Thomas died in 1953, but his critical response to Thomas in 1940, in which he focused on key questions about poetic craft and language, helped him to make important advances in the development of his own work in subsequent decades.[41]

Given Thomas's importance to Berryman and Schwartz, as well as the instances of significant reference and provocation in Olson's prose writings, it is interesting to consider the ways in which these and other American poets at mid-century might have used the example of Thomas in their work as teachers of literature, from Harvard and the University of Minnesota to Black Mountain College. This aspect of Thomas's reception in the United States – his place in high school and university curricula – may help to explain the poet's popularity, also, for later generations of American readers. Elizabeth Bishop, as Consultant in Poetry at the Library of Congress in Washington, DC, also played an important role in this regard. Bishop spent a great deal of time trying to organise a reading by Thomas at the Library, and she was instrumental in getting him to record his work, as her letters from the period reveal. When she was preparing for his reading in 1950, Bishop made a special request that Thomas read 'Fern Hill', which is the poem that begins his Library of Congress recording.[42] 'I'm looking forward to seeing you & hearing Mr. Thomas', she wrote to John Malcolm Brinnin in February of that year, adding: 'do you suppose he'd record "Fern Hill" for us? I'd like extremely to have it.'[43] Bishop had 'Fern Hill' in mind since she first read it, in the 1940s, and her first letter to Robert Lowell, written in 1947, includes a reference to a specific image from the poem's final stanza ('the shadow of his hand').[44] Bishop tells Lowell that some of Thomas's poems are 'almost spoiled for [her] by two or three lines that sound like padding or remain completely unintelligible', but she says that 'Fern Hill' is 'wonderful', and she later described his visit to the Library of Congress as 'the high point' of her time there, and especially the fact that he'd made 'absolutely beautiful records' that she, effectively, had arranged.[45]

Reading Bishop's poetry, one does not detect any immediate signs of 'influence' – no more than one can when reading Olson or Berryman – but Bishop's particular fondness for 'Fern Hill', together with her sense of the importance of having Thomas read and record his work at the Library of Congress, are important elements in the history of Thomas's impact on American poetic culture at mid-century. John Malcolm Brinnin played a very significant role in the promotion of Thomas and his work in the United States, of course, and this is reflected, to a certain extent, in Bishop's engagement with him as she sought to arrange a recording by Thomas for the Library of Congress. Beyond the biographical myths and anecdotes propagated by Brinnin and others in the years after Thomas's death, however, especially in the United States, the issue of how Thomas was actually read and received in the daily reading and writing practices of a wide range of poets, from Olson and Berryman to Schwartz and Bishop, is more complex than has often been acknowledged. While books such as Brinnin's *Dylan Thomas in America: An Intimate Journal* (1955) gave many readers a deeper acquaintance with the poet in his private and public personae, the extent to which individual poets from the post-war era actually engaged with Thomas's poetry and poetics is a more complex problem, which can be understood only by considering each poet's work slowly and attentively, on a case by case basis.

Later engagements: beyond 'fraternal sympathy'

In a letter written in 1960, influential American critic Malcolm Cowley complimented James E. Miller on his contribution to *Start with the Sun: Studies in the Whitman Tradition*. 'Certainly Dylan Thomas is in the tradition too,' Cowley remarked, 'but here it isn't so much a question of literary debt as of a sort of fraternal sympathy.'[46] American critics of the 1960s had no trouble reading Thomas within a transatlantic framework. Allen Tate, in an important lecture on Edgar Allan Poe delivered at Boston College in 1951, includes Thomas with Hart Crane and Wallace Stevens as examples of poets writing 'in English' who may be compared with French writers 'from Lautréamont, Rimbaud, and Mallarmé to the Surrealists'.[47] These readings of Thomas as a poet whose work should be read either in relation to 'the Whitman tradition', as Cowley sees it, or among twentieth-century American 'homemade' modernists, as Tate suggests, are worth keeping in mind in relation to the later critical insistence on Thomas's somewhat unwelcome presence in post-war literary culture in the United States.[48] Even in the example of Olson, but certainly in the cases of Schwartz, Berryman, Bishop and Lowell, it can be seen that Thomas was widely acknowledged as a positive source of poetic enablement by American poets at mid-century.

Bishop's positive engagement with Thomas complicates Cowley's idea of a 'fraternal' company of male poets, however, as does the example of Denise Levertov, for whom Thomas was an important early influence, as Nick Halpern acknowledges.[49] Halpern's focus, however, on the 'neo-Romantic' aspect of Thomas's influence glosses over Levertov's multifarious interest in language, form and voice as essential elements in her evolving poetic practice from the 1940s onwards. It is certainly the case that Levertov's exposure to the work of William Carlos Williams, initially, and then some of the so-called Black Mountain Poets in the 1950s, helped to move her work in new directions, but her poetry returns to central questions of self that can be observed, also, in the work of Thomas. In the same way that positive affinities may be discerned in relation to Olson's reading of Thomas, Levertov's work also shares concerns with the relationship between self and world as it was being reconfigured in the middle decades of the twentieth century, and especially after the Second World War. As she puts it in the piece entitled 'Poem' from *The Double Image* (1946):

> The undertone of all their solitude
> is the unceasing question, 'Who am I?
> A shadow's image on the rainy pavement,
> walking in wonder past the vivid windows,
> a half-contented guest among my ghosts?
> Or one who, imagining light, air, sun,
> can now take root in life, inherit love?'[50]

Levertov insists here on the right of the female speaker – and poet – to engage in the discourses of artistic self-enunciation that were being so powerfully reformulated in the post-war era by writers on both sides of the Atlantic. In *her* work, however, what she calls the difficulty of writing 'the real image, real hand, the heart / of day or autumn beating steadily' is not subsumed into or by a single poetic programme.[51] Openly drawing on and expanding the possibilities of a wide range of contemporary poetic models, from Thomas to Olson, she unsettles the idea of a 'fraternal' community and shows how much can be gained by refusing to conform to any single tradition or cultural programme. As Paul A. Lacey has written, Levertov was a 'voracious reader and autodidact [who] learned from many sources'.[52] It is a mark of her cultural and artistic open-mindedness that she could engage positively with Thomas as much as she did, later on, with the American poets she encountered, and this also complicates Olson's idea of poetic history conceived in terms of a kind of sacred, male-centred 'brotherhood'.

The examples of Bishop and Levertov, then, show that Thomas appealed to women poets of the post-war era as much as he did to their male counterparts, and a wide range of poets from the next and later generations – from John Ashbery, James Wright and Richard Hugo to Joseph Massey, Lynn Melnick and Geoffrey O'Brien – have also declared affinities with Thomas's work. In an interview published in *The New York Times* in 2015, Ashbery recalls the importance of reading Thomas's work in an anthology edited by Louis Untermeyer in high school.[53] More importantly, he said that he 'continue[s] to be inspired' by Thomas, and others, even if he doesn't 'often read them'.[54] Having read them once was sufficient for the poems to have a lifelong influence, he suggests, but the way in which he left Thomas behind as his poetry took its own course is nicely suggested in the image he offers to describe this process:

> Somebody (maybe me) once described the situation as like standing on the deck of a ship that's pulling away from shore, smiling and waving at friends waving back at you. They still love you and vice versa, but they can't come along.[55]

The image evokes the experience of a transatlantic voyage for the New York poet writing in the 1960s, but it also serves as a metaphor for positive intercultural exchange between poets that counters the idea of 'influence' as a kind of genealogical quarrelling, as it is often characterised in applications of Harold Bloom's theory of influence.[56] Bloom's idea of strong poets actively swerving away from the example of their precursors may help to explain the radical distancing strategies that allowed Ashbery to remove practically all traces of Thomas's influence from his early published work, but Ashbery's repeated acknowledgement of Thomas's importance in his early development also needs to be taken seriously as an assertion of his centrality in late twentieth-century American poetry and poetic culture. Just because Ashbery's work does not display the same kind of 'rhetorical excess' that Edward Brunner associates with Thomas – which was, he suggests, rejected by American poets of Ashbery's generation – does not mean they ignored his work altogether.[57]

Another case that demonstrates the importance of poets *reading* Thomas without being actively influenced by him in any obvious (formal) way is the example of James Wright, whose sense of Thomas's achievement as a poet has an important ethical dimension. In a letter to James Dickey written in 1958, Wright made the somewhat unusual claim that 'men like Baudelaire, Villon, Dylan Thomas simply by the act of writing good poems become good men'.[58] The claim is strange, until Wright explains that he is not talking about merely 'mechanical' matters:

> I am sure, for example, that my own life is a good deal more regularly ordered, law-abiding, and even sanitary than Villon's life was; and yet, as a great artist he demonstrated something of genuine human goodness and greatness; whereas, as a counterfeit, I demonstrate nothing except the too obvious fact that I have learned, through imitating real artists, how to ape mechanically some of the devices, like meter and rhyme, which they subdued to their own creative, imaginative purposes – a purpose which involves not merely imitating somebody else, but rather illuminating some of the meanings of human life.[59]

This is a profound admission, not least because it suggests that whatever might be understood by the term 'influence' has a deeper, human dimension beyond the surfaces of textual appearance. In this regard, then, Wright sees in Thomas an example of a twentieth-century poet whose accomplishment should be gauged both in terms of its ethical and its aesthetic impact.

For Wright, Thomas was a poet whose work 'demonstrated [. . .] goodness and greatness' through its illumination of human reality beyond its formal achievement. Wright's reading of Thomas in this light also reclaims him from the negative mythologies of Bohemian self-destruction that overshadowed readings of Baudelaire and Villon before him. Wright's reading is instructive, also, in relation to the ways that later American poets have engaged with Thomas. In another letter from the 1950s, to Robert Bly, he praises a poem by Richard Hugo ('A Troubadour Removed') for the way that it engages with figures 'like Lorca and Thomas', without naming them directly, 'who [both] came to America and discovered the jungle'.[60] In Wright's reading of the poem, Thomas and Lorca are oblique sources for Hugo's poetic critique of the self's confrontation with modernity as it is experienced in the United States.[61] Thomas, then, becomes part of a composite figure for the rediscovery of America in the twentieth century, a poet who invited readers – many of whom were also poets – to see the world and themselves anew. This is relevant to Wright's sense of the need to escape the habit of 'merely imitating somebody else' as a poet – of the need, instead, to live poetically, to be inspired by poetry into a new way of being in the world.

Ashbery's early reading of Thomas was responsible, in part, for his poetic awakening, and several more recent American poets – many of whom have also acknowledged Ashbery as an important influence – have pointed to early encounters with Thomas's work as a formative experience. Reading Thomas made them want to be poets even if their work bears no discernible traces of his formal influence. In the anthology *Please Excuse this Poem: 100 New Poets for the Next Generation* (2015), for example, Joseph Massey lists 'everything by Dylan Thomas' among the 'first poems [he] read or loved', while Lynn Melnick and Geoffrey O'Brien name 'Fern Hill' as the first poem they both 'read or loved'.[62] These declarations of affection for Thomas, and for 'Fern Hill' in particular, may be related back to Elizabeth Bishop's work in popularising Thomas and that poem through her work in the Library of Congress in the 1940s. The question of Thomas's influence on these poets' work, in mechanical terms, is not important. A more complex and important question concerns the extent to which these sometimes interconnected networks of readers have, over the course of several decades, acknowledged Thomas as a source of positive enablement in vastly different ways, no matter what differences may separate them in terms of their disparate formal procedures and thematic preoccupations. In short, Thomas remains present to contemporary American poetic practice in ways that cannot be explained by paying attention to textual surfaces alone. More importantly, the acknowledgements of Ashbery, Wright, Melnick, Massey, O'Brien and others serve to problematise critical and literary historical classifications that suggest Thomas has been ignored by American poets in the last half-century altogether.

'With more to say': rereading Thomas and American poetry

In a letter to James Laughlin in 1962, written in response to a manuscript of poems by the Objectivist poet Charles Reznikoff she had been sent for comment, Marianne Moore dismissed the work but admitted that her view might change with time. 'I grew to like Dylan Thomas,' she said, 'but this is not work that suffers from momentum or defiance.'[63] Precisely how Thomas's work – or Reznikoff's, for that matter – might be said to 'suffer' from 'momentum' or 'defiance' is unclear, but Moore's terms can be used to describe the ways in which Thomas's work served as an example – for some an enabling presence, a positive spur, but for others a hindrance – to poets on both sides of the Atlantic from the 1940s to the present day. Moreover, Thomas's work itself may be read in terms of these modalities – 'momentum' and 'defiance' – by virtue of its radical energy in language, coupled with the challenge it continues to present in terms of how we understand poetic culture, process and form. John Goodby has suggested that 'Thomas's poetry has been a kind of secret, but powerful leaven in US and British poetry over the last fifty years', and that his 'contribution to the US poetry scene' may be discerned in a wide range of cultural movements, from performance poetry to L=A=N=G=U=A=G=E poetics.[64] The examples explored in this chapter provide further evidence of the many ways in which American poets engaged with his work from within very different 'schools' and 'movements' – Black Mountain/Projectivist (Olson), Confessional (Schwartz, Berryman, Bishop), New York School (Ashbery), Deep Image (Wright). By exploring each of these poets in relation to Thomas, however, these literary historical and critical designations in themselves are placed under pressure. Reading Olson and Schwartz in relation to Thomas, for example, allows a common interest in poetry in performance to come into focus, while James Wright's insistence on the ethical agency of Thomas's poetry presents a radical challenge to the idea of influence conceived solely in terms of form. The wide range of contemporary poets who have identified Thomas as a formative presence, moreover, suggests that his example continues to provoke and inspire responses that reaffirm the lasting relevance of his work in the process.

In 'Dream Song 88', John Berryman imagines Thomas in the afterlife 'with more to say / now there's no hurry, and we're all a clan'.[65] Berryman's image recalls Olson's 'wonderful brotherhood', in a sense, but the complex diversity of Thomas's positive reception by American poets over the last half-century demands more comprehensive treatment. Such a study would detail the deep ways in which Thomas's work has served as an important touchstone in the history of American poetry from the 1940s to the present moment, and it would also complicate and correct the mistaken suggestion that Thomas has been either ignored or subsumed by myth in the decades since his death.[66] In his eco-critical study *Can Poetry Save the Earth? A Field Guide to Nature Poems* (2009), John Felstiner refers to the way that 'Dylan Thomas calls up his "green and golden" Welsh boyhood at Fern Hill'.[67] By doing this, Felstiner suggests, Thomas wrote poems 'that keep exploring the universe bearing "nature" and our selves'.[68] Notwithstanding the environmental imperative in Felstiner's reading, however, this is also the central lesson that American poets have learned and continue to learn from Thomas: his work reinforces a fundamental belief in the value of language both in relation to the way we think about the world and how we conduct ourselves in it. There is, to use Berryman's phrase, a lot 'more to say' on the subject of Thomas and his impact, over several decades, on the development of American poetry. By reconsidering Thomas and American poetry, and recognising the roles he has played in relation to a multitude of individual talents, the contours of American poetic history and culture in themselves are opened up in ways that challenge conventional histories and refocus critical attention back where they begin – with the poems, and in the acts of individual readers reading them.

Notes

1. Robert Lowell, 'Dylan Thomas', in *Collected Prose*, ed. Robert Giroux (New York: Farrar, Straus and Giroux, 1987), pp. 99–103 (p. 99).
2. See John Goodby, *The Poetry of Dylan Thomas: Under the Spelling Wall* (Liverpool: Liverpool University Press, 2013), p. 439. Together with the present chapter, Goodby's survey of American poetic engagements with Thomas's work can be considered an attempt to reassess and affirm the Welsh poet's importance in the poetic cultures of the United States from the 1940s to the present.
3. Nick Halpern, 'The Uses of Authenticity: Four Sixties Poets', in *The Cambridge History of American Poetry*, ed. Alfred Bendixen and Stephen Burt (Cambridge: Cambridge University Press, 2015), pp. 869–93 (p. 879); Edward Brunner, 'The 1970s and the "Poetry of the Center"', in *The Cambridge History of American Poetry*, pp. 937–58.
4. Robert von Hallberg, 'Poetry, Politics, and Intellectuals', in *The Cambridge History of American Literature, Volume 8: Poetry and Criticism, 1940–1995*, ed. Sacvan Bercovitch (Cambridge: Cambridge University Press, 1996), pp. 9–259.
5. Ibid. p. 19.
6. Ibid. p. 84.
7. Charles Olson to Ronald Mason, 13 July 1953, *Selected Letters*, ed. Ralph Maud (Berkeley and Oxford: University of California Press, 2000), pp. 197–202 (p. 201).
8. Ibid. p. 201.
9. Ibid. p. 201.
10. Ibid. p. 198.
11. Thomas, 'To-day, this hour I breathe', *CP14*, p. 7.
12. Olson to Mason, *Selected Letters*, p. 199.
13. The poet's replies to five questions put to him by a research student in 1951 were published in the form of 'Poetic Manifesto', *Texas Quarterly*, 4.4 (Winter 1961), 45–53, repr. *EPW*, pp. 154–60 (p. 160).
14. John Berryman, 'Dylan Thomas: The Loud Hill of Wales', in *The Freedom*

of the Poet (New York: Farrar, Straus and Giroux, 1976), pp. 282–5 (p. 283).

15. See Olson, 'In Cold Hell, in Thicket', *Selected Poems*, ed. Robert Creeley (Berkeley and Oxford: University of California Press, 1993), pp. 15–21.
16. Berryman, 'Dylan Thomas: The Loud Hill of Wales', p. 285.
17. Olson, *Selected Poems*, p. 15.
18. Ibid. p. 17.
19. Olson, 'Notes on Language and Theater', in *Collected Prose*, ed. Donald Allen and Benjamin Friedlander (Berkeley and London, University of California Press, 1997), pp. 256–9.
20. Ibid. pp. 256–7.
21. Ibid. p. 258.
22. Louis Zukofsky, from '*A*' 1, in *Selected Poems*, ed. Charles Bernstein (New York: Library of America, 2006), p. 83.
23. Olson, 'Notes on Language and Theater', p. 258.
24. Thomas, 'Poetic Manifesto', p. 160; Olson, 'Notes on Language and Theater', p. 259.
25. Thomas, 'Poetic Manifesto', p. 160.
26. Delmore Schwartz, 'The Present State of Poetry', in *Selected Essays*, ed. Donald A. Dike and David H. Zucker (Chicago and London: University of Chicago Press, 1970), pp. 30–50 (p. 33).
27. Ibid. p. 33.
28. Olson, 'Projective Verse' (1950), in *Collected Prose*, pp. 239–49 (p. 239).
29. Constantine Fitzgibbon provides a detailed account of Thomas's readings and lectures in the United States in his biography of the poet: *The Life of Dylan Thomas* (London: Dent, 1965), pp. 307; 350 ff; 379–80; 384 ff; 391.
30. Donald Hall, 'The Poetry Reading: Public Performance/Private Art', *The American Scholar*, 54.1 (1985), 63–77 (p. 65).
31. Schwartz, 'The Present State of Poetry', p. 33.
32. Olson, 'Projective Verse', p. 244.
33. Von Hallberg, 'Poetry, Politics, and Intellectuals', p. 84.
34. Delmore Schwartz, 'May's Truth and May's Falsehood', in *Selected Poems: Summer Knowledge* (New York: New Directions, 1967), pp. 213–14 (p. 213).
35. Ibid. p. 213.
36. Ibid. p. 214.
37. Derek Mahon, 'Introduction', in *Dylan Thomas: Poems Selected by Derek Mahon* (London: Faber, 2004), pp. vii–xviii (p. xviii).
38. For a detailed account of Berryman's engagements with Thomas, see Philip Coleman, '"An Unclassified Strange Flower": Towards an Analysis of John Berryman's Contact with Dylan Thomas', in Glyn Pursglove, John Goodby and Chris Wigginton (eds), *The Swansea Review: Under the Spelling Wall*, 20 (2000), pp. 22–33.
39. Berryman, 'Dylan Thomas: The Loud Hill of Wales', p. 283.
40. Ibid. p. 283.
41. John Haffenden provides a good account of Berryman's recollections of Thomas's death in *The Life of John Berryman* (London: Ark Paperbacks, 1983), pp. 233–4.
42. Dylan Thomas, *Dylan Thomas Reading His Poems in the Recording*

Laboratory, 9 March 1950. 2 sound discs: analog, 33 1/3 rpm, 16 in. Archive of Recorded Poetry and Literature, Library of Congress, Washington, DC.

43. Elizabeth Bishop to John Malcolm Brinnin, 27 February 1950, in *One Art: The Selected Letters*, ed. Robert Giroux (New York: Farrar, Straus and Giroux, 1994), p. 200.
44. Bishop to Robert Lowell, 14 August 1947, *One Art*, p. 146.
45. Ibid. p. 146; Bishop to Lowell, 8 May 1950, *One Art*, p. 203.
46. Malcolm Cowley to James E. Miller, 2 May 1960, in *The Long Voyage: Selected Letters of Malcolm Cowley, 1915–1987*, ed. Hans Bak (Cambridge: Cambridge University Press, 2015), p. 537.
47. Allen Tate, 'The Angelic Imagination', in *Essays of Four Decades* (Chicago: Swallow Press, 1968), pp. 401–23 (p. 406).
48. The term 'homemade', here, is of course that used by Hugh Kenner in his study *A Homemade World: The American Modernist Writers* (London: Marion Boyars, 1975).
49. Halpern, 'The Uses of Authenticity: Four Sixties Poets', p. 879.
50. Denise Levertov, 'Poem', in *New Selected Poems*, ed. Paul A. Lacey, with a preface Robert Creeley (Tarset: Bloodaxe Books, 2003), p. 2. The poem is dated 'London, 1946'.
51. Levertov, 'Too Easy: To Write of Miracles', *New Selected Poems*, p. 3.
52. Lacey 'Afterword', *New Selected Poems*, pp. 203–11 (p. 206).
53. John Ashbery, 'John Ashbery: By the Book', *The New York Times* (7 May 2015), BR8.
54. Ibid. BR8.
55. Ibid. BR8.
56. Peter de Bolla problematises this common (mis)reading of Bloom's theory of influence in *Harold Bloom: Towards Historical Rhetorics* (London: Routledge, 1988).
57. A number of commentators have referred to James Schuyler's poem 'The Morning of the Poem', in which Schuyler's speaker claims that 'Frank O'Hara said about Dylan Thomas, "I can't stand all that Welsh spit"' (Schuyler, *Collected Poems* (New York: Farrar, Straus and Giroux, 1993), p. 286). What the figure of 'O'Hara' states in Schuyler's poem cannot be read as fact, however, and even if O'Hara *did* decline to attend a performance by Thomas, this does not mean that he did not read him.
58. James Wright to James Dickey, 20 July 1958, in *A Wild Perfection: The Selected Letters of James Wright*, ed. Anne Wright and Saundra Rose Maley, with Jonathan Blunk (New York: Farrar, Straus and Giroux, 2005), pp. 107–10 (p. 108).
59. Ibid. p. 108.
60. Wright to Robert Bly, 22 July 1958, in *A Wild Perfection*, pp. 111–20 (p. 118).
61. Richard Hugo, 'A Troubadour Removed', in *Making Certain It Goes On: The Collected Poems of Richard Hugo* (New York and London: W.W. Norton & Company, 1984), pp. 18–20.
62. See Lynn Melnick and Geoffrey G. O'Brien's responses to the prompt 'First Poems You Read or Loved', in *Please Excuse This Poem: 100 New Poets for the Next Generation*, ed. Brett Fletcher Lauer and Lynn Melnick (New York: Viking Penguin, 2015), pp. 252 and 278.

63. Marianne Moore to James Laughlin, 20 March 1962, in *The Selected Letters of Marianne Moore*, ed. Bonnie Costello, Celeste Goodridge and Cristanne Miller, (London: Faber, 1998), pp. 548–9 (p. 548). It should also be mentioned here that James Laughlin played a major role in promoting Thomas's work in the United States over several decades. Many readers, including several of the poets discussed in this chapter, may well have first encountered Thomas's work through Laughlin's New Directions selection *The World I Breathe* (Norfolk, CT: New Directions, 1939).

64. Goodby's discussion of Thomas's 'contribution' includes several other figures not mentioned in this chapter, including Richard Wilbur, Theodore Roethke, Kenneth Rexroth, Steve McCaffery, Lyn Hejinian and others. See Goodby, *The Poetry of Dylan Thomas*, pp. 433–41 (pp. 437 and 438).

65. Berryman, 'Dream Song 88', in *The Dream Songs* (New York: Farrar, Straus and Giroux, 1969), p. 103.

66. What is needed, in short, is something like like Terence Diggory's study of W. B. Yeats's influence and impact on American poetry, *Yeats and American Poetry: The Tradition of the Self* (Princeton, NJ: Princeton University Press, 1983).

67. John Felstiner, *Can Poetry Save the Earth? A Field Guide to Nature Poems* (New Haven and London: Yale University Press, 2009), p. 6.

68. Ibid. p. 6.

Chapter 11

'Fine contrary excess': Seamus Heaney, Derek Mahon and Thomas's Northern Irish Afterlives

Tom Walker

Dylan Thomas's debts to the two Irish giants of early twentieth-century anglophone literature, W. B. Yeats and James Joyce, are considerable. Writing to Pamela Hansford Johnson in 1933, Thomas listed Yeats among a roll call of the poetic greats, 'Shakespeare, Dante, Goethe, Blake, John Donne, Verlaine', against whose work Wordsworth's 'Immortality Ode' should be judged 'no more than moderately good'; the tribute of imitation and parody had already been paid in the 1930 uncollected schoolboy poems 'In Borrowed Plumes' and 'Osiris, Come to Isis'.[1] The interim title of 'Altarwise by owl-light' – 'Work in Progress' – and the published title of *Portrait of the Artist as a Young Dog* (1940) similarly signal the Joycean terrain (linguistic, autobiographical, urban) on which Thomas built. Among some Irish contemporaries, Thomas's work was in turn greeted with enthusiasm. Louis MacNeice became friendly with the Welsh poet in the early 1940s in London, where both were engaged in writing propaganda, and there are clear parallels in their poetic responses to the Second World War. When Thomas's death came, it also represented more than just a personal loss to MacNeice. As Terence Brown describes, in MacNeice's *Autumn Sequel* (1954) Thomas's passing 'is treated as if it represented the death of all poetry, the obsequies appropriately being conducted in that half-Ireland, Wales'.[2] In the work where MacNeice most closely tends towards playing the role of a British national poet (written, it should be remembered, to be broadcast on the BBC), he tries in quasi-Arnoldian fashion to pit Celtic character against London's deadening despotism of fact partly through elegising Thomas as somewhat Irish. By contrast, Patrick Kavanagh in 1950, in one of his iconoclastic columns in the Dublin magazine *Envoy*, claimed that 'Auden and Dylan Thomas, Moravia, Sartre, Pound are all Irish poets. They have all said the thing that delighted me, a man born in Ireland, so they must have a great deal of Irish in them.'[3] Thomas is so cast as a figure of international artistic reach who cuts across the diktats of cultural nationalism.

That Thomas might be presented both as a visionary regional voice and a cosmopolitan among cosmopolitans (by two poets whose own critical stereotyping has often run the other way) points not only to the complexity of Thomas's work and its critical fortunes, but also to the nature of the reception afforded to Thomas and his work by Irish writers then and since. Intersecting questions of identity, aesthetic and linguistic innovation, and literary value, in the face of a globalised and mediated modernity, have attended upon the ways in which Thomas has been critically and imaginatively processed. Such questions have perhaps been particularly acute among those poets from Northern Ireland who not only were first exposed in the 1950s and 1960s to the Welsh poet as 'the hero of a million solitary teenage bedrooms [. . .] a subversive folk-rock Dionysian celebrity before the concept was co-opted and institutionalised', as Derek Mahon has memorably described, but also then had to contend with the emerging nightmare of the Troubles that, with increasing violence, enveloped the province after 1968.[4]

Speculating that Kavanagh's appraisal of Thomas would have been more hostile after an ill-fated meeting in 1951 (while the Irish poet was visiting London and trying, unsuccessfully, to get a foothold in the BBC), Brown suggests that Thomas could have been a likely target for Kavanagh's polemic against what he termed the 'bucklep'.[5] The term is glossed by Seamus Heaney as 'one who leaps like a young buck [. . .] with a stereotypical sprightliness and gallivanting roguery [. . .] offering himself or herself too readily as a form of spectator sport'. Heaney identifies Thomas as 'a fully developed specimen of the bucklepping tribe' in his somewhat censorious Oxford Professor of Poetry lecture 'Dylan the Durable? On Dylan Thomas', given in 1991.[6] An earlier lecture, 'The Regional Forecast', draws on Kavanagh's distinction between the provincial writer (who goes 'false' and plays 'up to the larger parish on the other side of the Irish Sea') and the parochial writer (who 'is never in an artistic doubt about the social and artistic validity of his parish') in criticising Thomas's 'collusion' in his BBC broadcasts 'with the stereotype of the voluble Taffy'.[7] Given in 1986 at the University of Aberdeen, this lecture opens with a recollection of the curious authority that was granted during Heaney's childhood to the BBC's 'puzzling and askew' regional weather forecast, before drawing a literary analogy. Praised are those writers who, like Joyce, have managed to raise 'subcultural status to cultural power' by reversing the 'demonstrably [. . .] Copernican' revolving of the literary provinces around the cultural centre towards a more 'Ptolemaic condition'.[8]

As Barbara Hardy suggests, Thomas's occasional deployment of stereotypes is generally self-aware and qualified by humour and irony;

there is also scant evidence of any provincial 'anxiety about metropolitan approval' in his prose or drama.[9] Yet in trying to account for such
a misleading occlusion of the subtleties of the actual work, one might
look beyond the influence of Kavanagh's critical ideas or John Goodby's
focus on the inadequacies of Heaney's criticism as criticism – with its
adherence to a binary 'centre–periphery paradigm which has recently
been the bugbear of criticism of regional or postcolonial writing'.[10]
Heaney's reading of the Welsh poet is forcefully framed, as Brown
notes, by a wariness of the hazards of being an Irish writer working
in the English language.[11] Moreover, as a poet from Northern Ireland
operating in the context of the Troubles, any aspiration to Joycean
self-realisation has to contend too with 'the web of morality and loyalty'
through which Heaney's critical and creative work demonstrably tries
to pick a path.[12]

The closing Oxford lecture, 'Frontiers of Writing', discloses that 'the
unspoken background' to the whole series 'has been a Northern Irish
one'.[13] This subtext can be felt in how the lecture on Thomas pits innocence against experience in its account both of the Welsh poet's work
and of Heaney's reading of that work. Thomas is initially presented
as a key 'part of the initiation' of Heaney's own 'first "eleven-plus"
generation into literary culture'.[14] Heaney also praises how, in Thomas's
early poetry, adolescent 'affections and impulses have been stabilised
not into dogma but into musical form'.[15] Such youthful work not only
constitutes a remembered 'poetic Eden' for the older Heaney, but also
an 'afflatus' that is a constant poetic possibility. Thomas's 'largeness' of
voice, a 'fine contrary excess' that can be found as well in the work of
Hart Crane, Geoffrey Hill and Sylvia Plath, 'might be worth emulating
for its inclusiveness and robustness'. In turning to the later poems as a
mature reader, however, Heaney finds them wanting. They fall short of
Eavan Boland's notion of a 'tonal rectitude' whose 'origins must always
be in a suffered world rather than a conscious craft', in contrast to a
host of other poets whose utterances stem from 'veteran knowledge'.[16]
Only one late Thomas poem, 'Do not go gentle into that good night',
meets with unqualified praise. Heaney's critique is primarily carried
out as regards questions of linguistic and intellectual maturity, yet an
underlying ethical imperative comes back into focus as the lecture closes:
'Fern Hill' is unflatteringly compared to (of all poems) Wordsworth's
'Immortality Ode' as a poem that faces up to loss; Thomas is cast in the
role of Orpheus within Plato's accounts of poetry's inability 'to know
reality' in the *Ion* and the *Symposium*; and a 'too unenlightened trust in
the plasticity of language' is equated to an aversion of Thomas's 'eyes
from the prospect of necessity'.[17]

Jeffery Side cites this lecture as offering evidence of Heaney's Wordsworthian empiricism and Movement-via-Philip-Hobsbaum-derived sense of 'language as unequivocal communication'.[18] Drawing on this discussion, Goodby awkwardly describes Heaney as 'the most influential British mainstream poet since Larkin' and emphasises Heaney's critical distrust of linguistic 'ingenuity, artifice, and play'.[19] However, more is at stake in this lecture than such readings allow. Heaney's stress on the need for language to be born of the knowledge of experience sits within his broader development through the 1980s and 1990s of an ethical poetics, partly in response to the pressures of the Troubles.[20] The paralleling of Thomas's writing to Heaney's reading in terms of innocence and experience in 'Dylan the Durable?' also reflects back on the intertwined trajectories of language, ethics and identity in the Irish poet's own work.

Henry Hart describes how Heaney's juvenilia includes 'uncollected pastiches of Keats, Gerard Manley Hopkins, and Dylan Thomas' that offer a 'pastoral myth of a childhood Eden threatened by sundry afflictions'.[21] Goodby suggestively claims that Heaney's debut collection, *Death of a Naturalist* (1966), might be read as 'an extended reaction against "Fern Hill" (this is how *real* farms work) and a grudging tribute to the mimetic power and pastoral vision of Thomas's late poetry more generally'.[22] The presence of what Heaney describes as the 'apprehension of language as a physical sensation, as a receiving station for creaturely intimations, cosmic process and sexual impulses' in Thomas's early work can also be felt in this first collection.[23] In its opening poem, 'Digging', the mental impress of childhood smells and sounds is carried into the poet's language:

> The cold smell of potato mould, the squelch and slap
> Of soggy peat, the curt cuts of an edge
> Through living roots awaken in my head.[24]

Clustered rhythmic stress, fricatives, plosives, alliteration, consonance and assonance evoke but also exceed onomatopoeia. Sensations that lie beyond sound and sight are associatively suggested in part through aural effects, such as with the damp evoked by the overlapping of sense and sound in 'cold', 'mould' and 'soggy'. As Bernard O'Donoghue notes of Heaney's early work in general, '[w]ords are found for what things feel like rather than what they look or sound like.'[25] The title poem that follows, 'Death of a Naturalist', dramatises this difference between language as representation and language as feeling.[26] The schoolteacher's benign report of the procreation of frogs is filtered through what Helen Vendler describes as 'the naïve voice of the child retelling his school day':

'Miss Walls would tell us how / The daddy frog was called a bullfrog, / And how he croaked'. Such words fail to prepare the child for the shock of the more 'coarse croaking' of the real frogs' mating calls, and their aural placidity also stands in contrast to Heaney's turning loose of what Vendler describes as 'his thickest and most resonant orchestration':[27]

> Right down the dam, gross-bellied frogs were cocked
> On sods; their loose necks pulsed like snails. Some hopped:
> The slap and plop were obscene threats. Some sat
> Poised like mud grenades, their blunt heads farting.[28]

The density of sound, like the menacing figurative language, again exceeds any straightforwardly mimetic representation of the scene. Suggested, rather, is something of the child's complex psychological projections in the face of dawning sexuality and the terror of intimations of cosmic process in which rankness, violence and creativity are intertwined.

That the origins of creation are being latently explored in psycho-sexual terms in these poems is further suggested by 'Personal Helicon', the poem which closes Heaney's first volume.[29] Its account of a childhood interest in wells offers a myth of the self-reflexive mysteries of the creative ego. The title's reference to the muses' mountain acts in tension with the final stanza's reference to Narcissus, a guilt-tinged sense of self-pleasure and auto-eroticism shadowing art and self-knowledge. Neil Corcoran suggests that the poem 'owes something' to Theodore Roethke's 'greenhouse' poems 'which similarly elaborate a psychology from a symbolically suggestive childhood world of vegetal process'.[30] It is also a 'tumescent fantasia' that moves 'a load of inchoate obsession into expressed language', to again quote Heaney on Thomas's early poetry.[31] The final lines – 'I rhyme / To see myself, to set the darkness echoing' – signal a programme for the volume that follows, *A Door into the Dark* (1969). In considerable part, this darkness turns out to be erotic. Several poems – 'Rite of Spring', 'The Wife's Tale', 'Undine', 'Victorian Guitar', 'Night Drive' – imagine female sexual liberation with a male presumption that is very much of its 1960s moment. But in 'A Lough Neagh Sequence', more Thomas-like creaturely intimations are expressed:

> To stand
> In one place as the field flowed
> Past, a jellied road,
> To watch the eels crossing land
>
> Re-wound his world's live girdle.
> Phosphorescent, sinewed slime
> Continued at his feet. Time
> Confirmed the horrid cable.[32]

As Corcoran describes, the sequence acts as 'a kind of objective cor-
relative for the compulsion of human sexuality' more directly addressed
elsewhere.[33] Henry Hart also reads the collection's recurring images
of femininity, procreation and water in terms of a thorough-going
mysticism.[34] There is clearly considerable distance between Heaney's
and Thomas's work. Straightforward mimesis might be exceeded by
Heaney's language, as it offers psychological subtlety and an apprehension of the world as process, but linguistic reference to a tangible world
and a specific context of address is still in play. This stands in contrast to
Thomas's abstract and impersonal early poetic voice. A line such as 'My
veins flowed with the Eastern weather' from 'Before I knocked' baldly
asserts the actuality of weather flowing through the speaker's veins.[35]
One feels Heaney would have given the reader a sense of whom this
lyric 'I' is and set up a real-world situation in which to link symbolically
the weather and the body. Nevertheless, the possible points of influence
and continuity between Heaney's early work and Thomas's suggest that
Heaney in the later lectures might be identifying the Welsh poet with
what he perceives by then to be his own poetic immaturity.

Part of Heaney's coming to experience can be seen in the manner
in which his use of language subsequently evolves. 'Unashamed and
inexhaustible word-play' may not be a primary 'generative method',
as David Aivaz observes of Thomas.[36] But Heaney sometimes works
'from words' and their 'substance' and not just 'towards words', as
Thomas once prescribed.[37] In a 1972 interview in *The Irish Times*,
Heaney describes how he has been 'writing poems lately that grow
out of words', as well as citing T. S. Eliot's notion of 'the auditory
imagination' – described by Eliot as

> the feeling for syllable and rhythm, penetrating far below the conscious levels
> of thought and feeling, invigorating every word; sinking to the most primitive
> and forgotten, returning to the origin and bringing something back, seeking
> the beginning and the end.[38]

Heaney makes it clear, though, that his attempt to work from words
and to pursue their depths is a question of specifically grasping 'the
auditory imagination of people in the north of Ireland'; he explains that
the word 'Broagh' is scrutinised in the poem of the same name in an
effort to touch 'the nerve of history and cultures'.[39] Goodby contrasts
Eliot's attempt to align language's unconscious aspects to a more stable
sense of reference with Thomas's more Joycean treatment of 'words as
fissile bundles of signification' whose rich instability is to be harnessed
by the writer.[40] In contrast to his (Thomas-like) earlier work's at once
more personal and universal engagements with the materiality of words

and their psychological suggestiveness, Heaney is explicitly engaging by the early 1970s with a socio-linguistic situation in Northern Ireland in which words might be unstable and arbitrary, yet also determinative and deadly. A further development on Heaney's scrutiny of language is a growing embrace from the late 1970s onwards of a paradox (drawing on Dante and indeed on Eliot's reading of Dante) in which faithfulness to one's origins and present urgencies is best served, as O'Donoghue observes, by 'transparency in lyric utterance'.[41] By the early 1990s, this quest for linguistic transparency explicitly incorporates the mystical too, as Heaney gestures towards in the title of his 1991 collection *Seeing Things*. Hence the eventual praise Heaney gives in the Oxford lecture to 'Do not go gentle into that good night' for moving 'towards' words and 'a destination in knowledge', rather than for following the young Thomas's (and, in part, his own) insistence that poets should 'begin with words'.[42]

A further aspect of Heaney's coming to experience and his later unease with Thomas can be seen in the manner in which his early work developed in relation to being a poet in a media-saturated age. 'Dylan the Durable' stresses the mediated nature of Thomas's impact on Heaney's generation. The Welsh poet died 'at the moment when print culture and the electronic media were perfecting their alliance in the promotion of culture heroes', and it was the records of him reading that then opened 'a thrilling line between the centre and the edges of the Anglophone world' for Heaney and others across the globe.[43] At this time, Heaney perhaps hoped that Northern Ireland might rise on a growing international wave of liberty operating on several fronts (primarily sexual and political) – a wave represented in part by the carrying of Thomas's rebellious and licentious poetic voice into so many undergraduate bedrooms. The young Heaney was certainly willing to try to further what might be considered a broadly liberalising agenda through his own embrace of the media, as can be seen in his contributions at this time to the BBC magazine *The Listener*.[44]

The issue of 11 April 1968 carried the sexually suggestive 'Night Drive' and 'Undine' on its inner pages; by the 25 October, the front page was carrying Heaney's prose reportage on recent events in Northern Ireland. Outlining the rise of the civil rights movement and the backlash it provoked that autumn, this piece optimistically asserts that '[a] real change is taking place under the thick skin of the Northern Irish electorate.'[45] Events were sadly to prove otherwise. In an Ulster special issue of *The Listener* in September 1969, Heaney contributed seven poems. In doing so, he was editorially framed as offering a romantic rural Catholic Irish response to the violence that had now started to engulf the Province, being trailed on the front page as 'the Irish nightingale' (quoting from one of the poems printed, 'Serenades'), and with his author's note explaining that he comes 'from a long line of Catholic farmers' in County Derry.[46] Three of the poems printed were never subsequently collected. They show Heaney struggling to write to the present's pressures. 'Medallion', for instance, responds to a medal struck in honour of George Walker, the governor of Derry during the siege of 1689, but offers little meaningful insight into the history it invokes. The first line crudely likens the image of Walker's head to 'a death-mask', and the close simplistically emphasises continuity between Walker and the present, which is described as still holding out, 'impervious / To argument, sit-downs and bombs'.[47]

Michael Parker describes how Heaney's work of this time is suffused by 'public concerns' and 'explicit' affiliations; the poet is also willing to print and broadcast such affiliations in relation to contemporary public events.[48] Heaney later displayed considerable distrust of the role of the media in the developing conflict and self-awareness about the dangers that entering into it posed. This is clear in the 1972 interview mentioned above, in which Heaney contrasts 'the television crews of the world' – coming to Northern Ireland 'like glossy flies to a dungheap' – with his poetry's oblique pursuit of language.[49] A wariness and weariness of journalists and journalese is also an explicit theme of 'Whatever You Say, Say Nothing' – a poem that shadows Heaney's thinking through the early 1970s – first printed in *The Listener* in 1971, excerpted for the dedication to *Wintering Out*, and then printed in a revised form in *North* (1975).[50] This shift in Heaney's attitude to entering into the media of course lies at a considerable distance from Thomas's mediation – the BBC work, the success of his recorded readings, or his posthumous transformation into 'a subversive folk-rock Dionysian celebrity'.[51] That it might offer some context for Heaney's misapprehension of Thomas as an insufficiently wary radio bard, a colluder 'with the stereotype of the voluble Taffy', is perhaps clearer, though, when placed against the Irish poet's own more general anxieties about collusion.[52] The closing Oxford lecture, 'Frontiers of Writing', recounts how in May 1981 Heaney had attended an Oxford college dinner, staying in the room of a fellow who was also 'a minister in the then Tory Cabinet'. That same evening, the wake took place of an IRA hunger striker who 'belonged to a neigh-bour's family in Co. Derry', provoking 'a classic moment of conflicting recognitions, self-division, inner quarrel, a moment of dumbness and inadequacy when it felt like a betrayal' to be enjoying such hospitality.[53] Self-division is an apt phrase to describe something of Heaney's inner quarrel with Thomas's 'fine contrary excess'.

Heaney's lecture on 'The Regional Forecast' does not only misread Thomas. The lecture closes with Heaney asserting the 'modernity' of Norman MacCaig's unwavering parochialism, before suggesting that his argument could be similarly capped by adducing 'the light in the desert which my countryman and contemporary Derek Mahon has seen without moving from the bleak cliffs of North Antrim'.[54] Heaney was often generous in drawing attention to his Northern Irish contemporaries, but he here seems to misplace Mahon. North Antrim features in his work, but this location has also been on the move in ways that undermine Heaney's earlier proscription in the lecture that '[t]he writer must reenvisage the region as the original point.'[55] The Mahon poem that Heaney implicitly refers to, 'North Wind: Portrush', ends with a deliberate glance south:

> Elsewhere the olive grove,
> *Le déjeuner sur l'herbe*,
> Poppies and parasols,
> Blue skies and mythic love.[56]

This suggests comparatively, in social, religious and more personal terms, the 'stricken' mindset and 'plaintive voice' to which the Antrim coast's climate gives rise. Such a comparison is at some distance from Heaney's advocacy of a binary power-reversal of the cultural centre and periphery. Mahon acknowledges difference without seeking to overturn any kind of hierarchical cultural gravity in his clear-eyed evocation of the conditions that in this locale undermine 'the subtler arts'. Portrush is another place, not an empowered point of origin – and, come to that, a place partaking in a form of modernity that extends beyond the provincial and parochial:

> But the shops open at nine
> As they have always done,
> The wrapped-up bourgeoisie
> Hardened by wind and sea.[57]

That Mahon sits uneasily within Heaney's critical schema is reflected in the contrasting manner in which Mahon reads Thomas's work. In the introduction to his Faber Poet to Poet selection, Mahon slightly misquotes the letter in which Thomas states that he is not 'a countryman': 'I stand for, if anything, the aspidistra, the provincial drive, the morning café, the evening pub, hotel and cinema, bookshop and tube station.'[58] There is a strong degree of self-identification in Mahon's presentation of Thomas as a provincial suburbanite, straddling the urban and the rural, who in his short stories 'takes a dim view of the industrial landscape' and dreams of escaping 'to make a career in Chelsea as a freelance journalist'.[59] Thomas's peripatetic years as a journalist, screenwriter and broadcaster mirror Mahon's own precarious freelance career, much of it spent in London, while Thomas's Swansea might be Mahon's Belfast – the 'wonders' of which, according to the poem named after the Belfast suburb of 'Glengormley', include the 'man / Who has tamed the terrier, trimmed the hedge / And grasped the principle of the watering can'.[60] This different Thomas does not just reflect a less hierarchical and more adulterated attitude to place and identity than Heaney's. It is clear from his introduction that Mahon has read Heaney's Oxford lecture on Thomas; at several points he quotes from it approvingly. However, Mahon's appraisal of the Welsh poet is a more generous and wide-ranging tribute, looking beyond the poetry to praise the fiction and radio work, and viewing the late poetry as a 'crowning achievement'. This introduction suggests too that Dionysus, rather than Heaney's Orpheus, might offer a more positive model for Thomas, as a poet of tragic ruination whose work is nonetheless empowered by 'a festive potential'.[61] Self-identification with Thomas is again in play, but Mahon is also signalling that his artistic maturity has lain in keeping faith with Thomas's poetry of 'enhanced expectation'.[62]

In his own undergraduate bedroom, Mahon might have inhaled Dylan Thomas along with his 'untipped Sweet Afton cigarettes'.[63] However, festive potential is somewhat thin on the ground in his early poetry. This can be seen in how 'An Unborn Child', a poem from his debut collection, *Night-Crossing* (1968), rewrites Thomas's 'Before I knocked'. Mahon's introduction praises this 'extraordinary, renegade-Christian poem' and quotes the fourth stanza in which procreation is violently crossed with constraint – 'The rack of dreams my lily bones / Did twist into a living cipher' – before observing more generally of Thomas's early work: 'What is at issue here is the creative principle itself'.[64] Thomas's poem offers a striking dramatisation of the suffering and determinism shadowing creation. Yet it occurs alongside what Chris Wigginton describes as the unborn child's identification with 'even as he rebels against, paternal and metaphysical authority'.[65] If Christ's fleshly death at the hands of his father is to be pitied, it at least holds out the possibility for some form of condition beyond original sin; ongoing suffering and sin also offer the assurance of ongoing creation within such a theological schema. Mahon's speaker, by contrast, may not yet be born but has already been made. As such, he is now beyond religious assurance, his 'bones [. . .] embrace / Nothing', and the life to come is envisaged as a sensual freedom shadowed not by sin but by the material world itself: 'I want to see, hear, touch and taste / These things with which I am to be encumbered.'[66] Metaphysical abandonment is a condition with which much of Mahon's work reckons. Edna Longley describes how 'Mahon's fundamentalist view of Ulster Protestants as "a lost tribe", rather than the elect, extends to the whole human race, and its lack of truly human or spiritual qualities.'[67] Thomas's mapping of the human body onto a sense of cosmic process of course links the human and spiritual. In Mahon's early work, by contrast, a more materialist sense of process dwarfs not only the body but also undermines embracing what the title poem to his 1972 collection *Lives* castigates as any sense of 'insolent ontology'.[68] Mahon's recurring stress in his early work on 'mute phenomena' leads him to contemplate but not deplore utter human negation: 'Already in a lost hub-cap is conceived / The ideal society which will replace our own'.[69]

That such a chastening worldview builds on as much as it diverges from Mahon's reading of the Welsh poet is indicated by the reference in 'Beyond Howth Head' (the verse letter to Jeremy Lewis that closes *Lives*) to 'the Spartan code of Dylan Thomas' and his association of it with directing youth 'into the knacker's yards / of humanistic self-regard'.[70] This Spartan reception recurs in 'A Refusal to Mourn', whose title signals a homage to Thomas's wartime anti-elegy 'A Refusal to Mourn the Death, by Fire, of a Child in London'.[71] Mahon's poem begins in an altogether more muted manner, though, as it recollects with unsparing clarity his grandfather's lonely and event-bereft retirement: 'if a coat-hanger / Knocked in an open wardrobe / That was a great event'. The prospect of death then causes not only his grandfather to grin but also the poem's tone and register to rise. Offering an image of the rain cleaning 'the words from his gravestone', which might owe something to Thomas's 'In the White Giant's Thigh' ('[t]hough the names on their weed grown stones are rained away'), the poem wittily reanimates personal and cosmic truths in the cliché that, in death, his grandfather's 'name' will 'be mud once again'.[72] It then looks forward to the destruction of another ice age, the earth 'gone like Neanderthal Man'. In Thomas's poem, the final stanza offers a sense of the dead child's kinship with 'the first dead' and the earth, '[r]obed in [...] the dark veins of her mother'. Mahon's imagined return to the earth, by contrast, contemplates (with some relish) the isolation of utter obliteration. A final further image asserts that some 'secret bred in the bone' will persist, which is then figured as 'a claw-print in concrete / After the bird has flown'. The bone as the site of such a surviving aesthetic impulse perhaps again reworks the imagery of 'Before I knocked' – 'The rack of dreams my lily bones / Did twist into a living cipher' – in relation to Mahon's sense of Thomas's early obsession with 'the creative principle'.[73] Mahon's poem, in recalling Thomas, may draw 'resolutely' on his 'own astringent metaphysics', as Stephen Regan suggests, but these ideas themselves seem to be partly based on an austere reading of early Thomas.[74]

The closing 'claw-print' image in 'Refusal to Mourn' offers a fragile counterweight to future destruction (the ice age to come) and present deprivation (the modernity of concrete). It suggests how Asiatic visual culture is a touchstone of delicate but present beauty for Mahon – a sense of the persistence of the aesthetic that 'Another Sunday Morning', amid religious doubt and historical destruction, affirms again in relation to Asia as the value of 'every artefact' being 'a pure, self-referential act'.[75] Mahon may have a consciousness of history as 'guilty and punitive as Beckett's', as Longley describes, and his sense of language's inadequacy and treachery can be thorough-going too, but his work paradoxically pays tribute to the persistence of the beautiful and the mental processes it gives rise to amid such conditions.[76] A sense of aesthetic breakdown and fracture, as well as self-implication, is present in several of the poems of the early 1970s, such as 'Rage for Order' (even if shaded by 'germinal ironies').[77] However, through the 1970s and into the early 1980s, this is increasingly balanced against a more insouciant use of voice and form. For instance, 'The Hunt by Night', an ekphrastic response to the Paolo Uccello painting of the same name, not only states but also performs in kind its startling revelation that violence itself might be a form of playful aesthetic arrangement:

> As if our hunt by night,
>   So very tense,
>
>   So long pursued,
> In what dark cave begun
> And not yet done, were not the great
> Adventure we suppose but some elaborate
>   Spectacle put on for fun
>   And not for food.[78]

Such a poem sings amid death and destruction in ways that seem to follow the manner of Thomas's wartime poetry. There is an embrace of rhyme, rhetoric and indeed spatial organisation that seems analogous to a poem such as 'Ceremony after a Fire Raid':

> Begin
> With singing
> Sing
> Darkness kindled back into beginning
> When the caught tongue nodded blind,

A star was broken
Into the centuries of the child
Myselves grieve, and miracles cannot atone.[79]

Mahon might be seen as persistently, albeit somewhat dialectically, embracing Thomas's 'fine contrary excess', as Heaney describes it, in poems that are of course written against the backdrop of the Troubles.

More so even than Heaney's, the engagement of Mahon's poetry with these events is characterised by indirection and obliquity. Nevertheless, Mahon's poems display considerable awareness, as Hugh Haughton describes, of the 'pressure of history upon the privileged realm of verse', including being shaped by 'a sense of horror towards his home culture'.[80] 'A Refusal to Mourn' can be read as not just bringing 'Mahon's view of modernity to bear on an intimate portrait of one retired shipyard worker', but also as a refusal to mourn the passing of Belfast's industrial heyday, and the broader confessional mindset and imperial history that underpinned it.[81] If Heaney's socio-linguistic turn towards myth and history is a response to the Troubles that also turns away from Thomas, Mahon's differing response of contemplating altogether more inhuman historical perspectives seems to draw licence from Thomas's sense of cosmic process (though read by Mahon as a 'Spartan code').[82] What Regan describes as a Yeatsian elegiac sense of the 'apocalyptic sublime' is of course in play in Mahon's work, but the particular terms of its apprehension in 'the mute phenomena', as well as certain aspects of its expression, seem more in keeping with Thomas's work.[83] This may partly illuminate the praise he later bestows in his introduction to the poems of Thomas's late unfinished *In Country Heaven* project, 'In Country Sleep', 'Over Sir John's hill' and 'In the White Giant's Thigh'. In contrast to the anthropomorphic and microcosmic focus of the earlier poems, these poems move towards perceiving and celebrating what Mahon describes as 'the unity of creation' in 'the menacing external world', including not only landscape, plants and animals but also the 'dust' of 'kettles and clocks' and 'rust' of 'kitchens' – in the lines from 'In the White Giant's Thigh' that Mahon chooses to quote in his introduction.[84] As Brown suggests, Mahon's stress here on the ecological and feminist aspects of Thomas's work may be a 'liberating force' in the Irish poet's own more benevolent and humanistic later aesthetic, as seen in poems such as 'The Cloud Ceiling' from *Harbour Lights* (2005).[85] However, amid the shock of the Troubles, Mahon also seems to have drawn on the more forbidding aspects of Thomas's historical reach, as well as his formal brio.

Mahon is another poet awkwardly described by Goodby as British. This labelling of Mahon and Heaney occurs in Goodby's 'traditionalist' versus 'alternative' account of Thomas's poetic afterlife.[86] Such a mis-placing of these poets indicates the extent to which their engagements with Thomas exceed such a narrative of post-war poetry, British or otherwise. Fran Brearton has argued that Northern Irish 'poetry's radical formalism raises questions as to whether experimentalism may become its own form of conservatism'.[87] Heaney's and Mahon's responses to Thomas raise further questions, along similar lines, as regards the occlusions effected by attempts to construct experimental and conservative lineages in relation to the afterlives of Thomas's work. As I have argued above, anxiety and guilt of various kinds shadow Heaney's critical sense of Thomas. But the poetry at times tells of another kind of ongoing reception too. In the closing poem of the sequence, 'Station Island', Heaney encounters Joyce's ghost, who counsels '[t]hat subject people stuff is a cod's game':

> ['] Keep at a tangent.
> When they make the circle wide, it's time to swim
>
> out on your own and fill the element
> with signatures on your own frequency,
> echo soundings, searches, probes, allurements,
> elver-gleams in the dark of the whole sea.'[88]

Heaney is having Joyce counsel him to return to broadcasting the self-involved freedoms of his poetic youth, in making clear references here to 'Personal Helicon' and 'A Lough Neagh Sequence'. In doing so, Heaney as Joyce is also counselling a return to a Thomas-like sense of language as 'a receiving station for creaturely intimations, cosmic process and sexual impulses'.[89] He is pointing forward too to the visionary aspirations of subsequent work. But these lines also offer a moment in which Heaney, in contrast to his Oxford lecture, seems close to Mahon's apprehension of Thomas, via an antithetical comparison with Saint-John Perse, as a student of 'the prospects of the sea'.[90] The 'fine contrary excess' of Heaney's and Mahon's poetic and critical responses to Thomas and his work are a no less humbling prospect.

Notes

1. Dylan Thomas to Pamela Hansford Johnson, [15 October 1933], *CL*, p. 42; *NP*, pp. 7–8, 17–20.
2. Terence Brown, 'The Irish Dylan Thomas: Versions and Influences', in *The Literature of Ireland: Culture and Criticism* (Cambridge: Cambridge University Press, 2010), pp. 260–72 (p. 263). For further considerations

of the connections between Thomas and MacNeice, see John Goodby, '"Bulbous Taliesin": MacNeice and Dylan Thomas', in *Incorrigibly Plural: Louis MacNeice and his Legacy*, ed. Fran Brearton and Edna Longley (Manchester: Carcanet, 2012), pp. 204–23; Tom Walker, *Louis MacNeice and the Irish Poetry of his Time* (Oxford: Oxford University Press, 2015), pp. 107–34; and Chris Wigginton, *Modernism from the Margins: The 1930s Poetry of Louis MacNeice and Dylan Thomas* (Cardiff: University of Wales Press, 2007).

3. Patrick Kavanagh, 'Diary', *Envoy: A Review of Literature and Art*, 2.7 (June 1950), 85.

4. Derek Mahon, 'Introduction', in *Dylan Thomas: Poems Selected by Derek Mahon* (London: Faber, 2004), pp. vii–xviii (p. xviii). This introduction is reprinted under the title 'Prospects of the Sea', in *Selected Prose* (Loughcrew: Gallery Press, 2012), pp. 149–59.

5. Brown, 'The Irish Dylan Thomas: Versions and Influences', p. 261; Antoinette Quinn, *Patrick Kavanagh: A Biography* (Dublin: Gill and Macmillan, 2001), p. 307.

6. Seamus Heaney, *The Redress of Poetry: The Oxford Lectures* (London: Faber, 1995), pp. 124–45 (p. 125).

7. Seamus Heaney, 'The Regional Forecast', in R. P. Draper (ed.), *The Literature of Region and Nation* (Basingstoke: Macmillan, 1989), pp. 10–23 (p. 13); Patrick Kavanagh, *A Poets' Country: Selected Prose*, ed. Antoinette Quin (Dublin: Lilliput Press, 2003), p. 237.

8. Heaney, 'The Regional Forecast', pp. 12–13.

9. Barbara Hardy, *Dylan Thomas: An Original Language* (Athens: University of Georgia Press, 2000), pp. 5–6.

10. John Goodby, '"Very profound and very box-office": The Later Poems and *Under Milk Wood*', in *Dylan Thomas: New Casebooks*, ed. John Goodby and Chris Wigginton (Basingstoke: Palgrave, 2001), pp. 192–220 (p. 198).

11. Brown, 'The Irish Dylan Thomas: Versions and Influences', pp. 268–9.

12. Rosie Lavan, 'Seamus Heaney and the Audience', *Essays in Criticism*, 66.1 (2016), 54–71 (p. 68).

13. Heaney, *The Redress of Poetry*, p. 191.

14. Ibid. p. 124.

15. Ibid. p. 130.

16. Ibid. pp. 133–5.

17. Ibid. pp. 143–4.

18. Jeffrey Side, 'The Influence of Wordsworth's Empiricist Aesthetic on Seamus Heaney's Criticism and Poetry', *English*, 59.225 (2010), 128–53 (p. 147).

19. John Goodby, *The Poetry of Dylan Thomas: Under the Spelling Wall* (Liverpool: Liverpool University Press, 2013), p. 453.

20. See David-Antoine Williams, *Defending Poetry: Art and Ethics in Joseph Brodsky, Seamus Heaney and Geoffrey Hill* (Oxford: Oxford University Press, 2010), pp. 99–158; and Piers Pennington, 'Reparation, Atonement, and Redress', in *The Oxford Handbook of Contemporary British and Irish Poetry*, ed. Peter Robinson (Oxford: Oxford University Press, 2013), pp. 676–93.

21. Henry Hart, *Seamus Heaney: Poet of Contrary Progressions* (New York: Syracuse University Press, 1992), pp. 12–13.

22. Goodby, *The Poetry of Dylan Thomas*, p. 454.
23. Heaney, *The Redress of Poetry*, p. 126.
24. Seamus Heaney, *Death of a Naturalist* (London: Faber, 1999 [1966]), pp. 3–4.
25. Bernard O'Donoghue, *Seamus Heaney and the Language of Poetry* (Hemel Hempstead: Harvester Wheatsheaf, 1994), p. 14.
26. Heaney, *Death of a Naturalist*, pp. 5–6.
27. Helen Vendler, *Seamus Heaney* (London: Fontana, 1998), pp. 29–30.
28. Heaney, *Death of a Naturalist*, p. 6.
29. Heaney, *Death of a Naturalist*, p. 46.
30. Neil Corcoran, *The Poetry of Seamus Heaney: A Critical Study* (London: Faber, 1998), p. 11.
31. Heaney, *The Redress of Poetry*, pp. 129–30.
32. Seamus Heaney, *Door into the Dark* (London: Faber, 1972 [1969]), p. 33.
33. Corcoran, *The Poetry of Seamus Heaney*, p. 16.
34. Hart, *Seamus Heaney: Poet of Contrary Progressions*, pp. 32–48.
35. *CP14*, p. 38.
36. David Aivaz, 'The Poetry of Dylan Thomas', *The Hudson Review*, 8.3 (Autumn 1950), 190–1.
37. Dylan Thomas to Charles Fisher, [early 1935], *CL*, p. 208.
38. T. S. Eliot, 'Matthew Arnold', in *The Use of Poetry and the Use of Criticism: Studies in the Relation of Criticism to Poetry in English* (Cambridge, MA: Harvard University Press, 1961 [1933]), pp. 95–112 (p. 111).
39. Elgy Gillespie (talks to Seamus Heaney), 'A Political Stance', *The Irish Times* (19 May 1972), 10.
40. Goodby, *The Poetry of Dylan Thomas*, p. 130.
41. O'Donoghue, *Seamus Heaney and the Language of Poetry*, p. 20.
42. Heaney, *The Redress of Poetry*, p. 141.
43. Ibid. p. 124.
44. For an account of Heaney's writings for the radio during this period, see Richard Rankin Russell, 'Imagining a New Province: Seamus Heaney's Creative Work for BBC Northern Ireland Radio, 1968–71', *Irish Studies Review*, 15.2 (2007), 137–62.
45. Seamus Heaney, 'Old Derry's Walls, *The Listener* (24 October 1968), 521–3.
46. *The Listener* (4 September 1969), 297, 311.
47. Seamus Heaney, 'Seven Poems', *The Listener* (4 September 1969), 311.
48. Michael Parker, *Northern Irish Literature, 1956–1975. Vol I: The Imprint of History* (Basingstoke: Palgrave, 2007), p. 82.
49. Gillespie, 'A Political Stance', 10.
50. 'Whatever You Say, Say Nothing – Seamus Heaney Gives His View on the Irish Thing', *The Listener* (14 October 1971), 496–7.
51. Mahon, 'Introduction', p. xviii.
52. Heaney, 'The Regional Forecast', p. 13.
53. Heaney, *The Redress of Poetry*, pp. 186–8.
54. Heaney, 'The Regional Forecast', p. 23. This lecture also mentions, no more convincingly, Paul Muldoon, who has since gone on to write his own introduction to Thomas: Paul Muldoon, 'Dylan and Delayment', in *The*

Collected Poems of Dylan Thomas: Original Edition (New York: New Directions: 2010), pp. xiii–xviii.

55. Heaney, 'The Regional Forecast', p. 13.
56. Derek Mahon, 'North Wind: Portrush', *The Hunt by Night* (Oxford: Oxford University Press, 1982), pp. 12–13.
57. Ibid. pp. 12–13.
58. Mahon, 'Introduction', p. viii. The original quotation has the following clause in between 'pub' and cinema': 'I'd like to believe in the wide open spaces as the wrapping around walls, the windy boredom between house and house' (Thomas to Vernon Watkins, Monday [postmarked 20 April 1936], *CL*, p. 248).
59. Mahon, 'Introduction', pp. viii–ix.
60. Derek Mahon, 'Glengormley', *Night-Crossing* (Oxford: Oxford University Press, 1968), p. 5.
61. Mahon, 'Introduction', p. xv.
62. Ibid. p. xviii.
63. Michael Longley, 'The Empty Hole of Spring: Reminiscences of Trinity', *Irish University Review*, 24.1 (Spring–Summer 1994), 51–5 (p. 53).
64. Mahon, 'Introduction', p. x; *CP14*, p. 39.
65. Chris Wigginton, '"Birth and copulation and death": Gothic Modernism and Surrealism in the Poetry of Dylan Thomas', in *Dylan Thomas: New Casebooks*, pp. 85–105 (p. 94).
66. Mahon, *Night-Crossing*, pp. 25–6.
67. Edna Longley, '"When Did You Last See your Father?': Perceptions of the Past in Northern Irish Writing, 1965–1985', in *The Living Stream: Literature and Revisionism in Ireland* (Newcastle: Bloodaxe, 1994), pp. 150–72 (p. 160).
68. Derek Mahon, *Lives* (Oxford: Oxford University Press, 1972), p. 16.
69. Derek Mahon, 'After Nerval', in *The Snow Party* (Oxford: Oxford University Press, 1975), p. 23.
70. Mahon, *Lives*, p. 35.
71. Mahon, *The Snow Party*, pp. 32–4; *CP14*, pp. 172–3.
72. 'In the White Giant's Thigh', *CP14*, p. 195.
73. *CP14*, p. 39; Mahon, 'Introduction', p. x.
74. Stephen Regan, 'Irish Elegy after Yeats', in *The Oxford Handbook of Modern Irish Poetry*, ed. Fran Brearton and Alan Gillis (Oxford: Oxford University Press, 2012), pp. 588–606 (p. 593).
75. Mahon, *The Hunt by Night*, p. 29.
76. Longley, '"When Did You Last See your Father?"', p. 161.
77. Mahon, *Lives*, pp. 22–3.
78. Mahon, *The Hunt by Night*, pp. 30–1.
79. *CP14*, pp. 142–3.
80. Hugh Haughton, *The Poetry of Derek Mahon* (Oxford: Oxford University Press, 2007), p. 60.
81. Ibid. p. 112.
82. 'Beyond Howth Head', *Lives*, p. 35.
83. Regan, 'Irish Elegy after Yeats', p. 588.
84. Mahon, 'Introduction', pp. xvi–xvii; *CP14*, p. 197.
85. Brown, 'The Irish Dylan Thomas', pp. 270–1.

86. Goodby, *The Poetry of Dylan Thomas*, pp. 453, 437.
87. Fran Brearton, 'Poetry of the 1960s: the "Northern Ireland Renaissance"', in *The Cambridge Companion to Contemporary Irish Poetry*, ed. Matthew Campbell (Cambridge: Cambridge University Press, 2003), pp. 94–112 (p. 109).
88. Seamus Heaney, 'Station Island', in *Station Island* (London: Faber, 1984), pp. 93–4.
89. Heaney, *The Redress of Poetry*, p. 126.
90. Mahon, 'Introduction', p. xviii.

About Time: A Modernist Coda for Thomas

Vincent Sherry

When Ned Allen asked me to contribute a piece to this collection of critical chapters on Dylan Thomas, my reflex to say 'yes' was checked almost immediately by the recognition that I had no critical context for doing so. I write 'almost immediately' because my first response was a surge of affirming interest at the chance. And that is the double measure I want to unpack and formulate here – as a frame not just on the thoughts I am offering in this piece, but on the use and value of the collection for which it will serve as a coda.

My 'yes' came from a history and memory, from a personal depth of connection to this verse that I take to be representative of many others'. This is a poetry we read, and reread, and sang silently or whisperingly to ourselves in those years of middle or late adolescence when we were beginning to get some understanding feel for what poetry is, or can be, and can do. Involuntarily or inadvertently, I was memorising the poems of Dylan Thomas; gradually but inevitably, I had metabolised the poems of Dylan Thomas. The reasons why this could happen involve the strengths of a poetry that turn out to be limitations – not necessarily the limitations of the poems as poems, but of ourselves as readers, that is, of our propensity to put them into certain systems of critical translation, interpretive understanding. One of those systems, unwittingly undergone but then wittily (we would say) named, was 'hormonal poetics': here was a poetry opening up like the chemical experience of puberty – the intense but confusing sensorium of rhythm and image, a music of meaning as compelling but indeterminate as the urges of the unknown we were undergoing at the cellular level, impulses now turned outward into pulses in the physical body of language and displaced ultimately into the cultural bloodstream in the lyrics of the musician who traded Zimmerman for Dylan as his surname. In this spot of time – in physical as well as political history – the tremendously affective power of Dylan Thomas seems to be concentrated and intensified. And, most importantly, limited: so that, in the instant between the automatic 'yes' and the considered 'but wait' of my responses to the editor's invitation, I moved into that constricted vision of Thomas that had been prepared for me. Again inadvertently, but irresistibly, I found myself reciting the final line of 'Fern Hill' – 'I sang in my chains like the sea' – not just as the image of the poet's own chosen pathos, but also (admitting the grandiosity of the analogy) as the ironic motto and defeated anthem of my own reflex wish to write a considered piece.[1] I had no critical context for doing so.

What, one may well ask, is a 'critical context'? There may be something in the quality of the poetry as I have invoked it that makes this phrase forbiddingly stiff, impossibly 'professional' in the wearily predictable way that 'professionals' have. Yes, good criticism is usually issue-driven, it takes up questions that comprise but exceed personal response, but there is something in that quality of terrible urgency in Thomas's poetry, though that is not its only quality, which makes most topical critical problems seem more than usually secondary, appliqué, even alien. Whether or not that is the reason why the critical tradition on Thomas is underdeveloped, it is so underdeveloped relative to his gifts (despite the singular successes of scholars like John Goodby) that questions stemming from even the most preliminary settings for the poetry acquire their own urgency and necessity.

Of these preliminary settings I'd be looking for some contextualised understanding of who Dylan Thomas was, or is, in the larger historical world. If, in our mind's ears, we tend still to hear the poet singing solo on the strand in front of the unfathomable ocean of his own gift, which is also his own affliction, we still need to find a way of reading his words on the page – and *beyond* the page – within a broader, world-cultural and world-historical frame of reference; this is the context of a pan-European and transatlantic history that conditioned him, and continued to impinge on him, from the 1910s through the 1950s. And if an historically informed reading of this verse seems a first imperative, not far second would be an understanding of this poetry in literary history – not an account that places him simply in a linear or even diffusional scheme of influence and resemblance, not a featuring of his career as the focal point of developments feeding into him or eventuating from him and whose representatives are defined but limited by what they contribute to that narrowing developmental narrative, but a story that resizes Thomas to a figure of major significance and in relation to whom the whole map of the literary twentieth century needs to be adjusted. And what, to begin with, do we make of the sensibility with which our interest begins: how do we understand the crafting of imaginative language and the ways in which, in verse, it unmakes and remakes the world around its words? If I had had a frame of critical reference that offered formulations about these fundamental questions in a concerted form, not in a random series of individual articles that could be subpoenaed through Google, I might have taken up Ned's request right at the start. And now, wrong or right at the end, I am in fact able to imagine the chapter I would have written.

For these three fundamental critical contexts – a world-cultural world-historical frame; a literary historical frame; a poetics frame – are offered in this volume, and they are offered in a fashion fully adequate to an orientation of informed critical effort. Not that Ned Allen designed it precisely along these tripartite lines; what I can see through the sequence of chapters – as they are presented in this volume – is a directed address to essential and recurring concerns, which I have organised according to my own requirements. From here, then, I'll review the contributions these chapters make towards the formation of that primary ground upon which I could have written (the tense of apology for the delinquent contributor) that piece, the more particular context and point of which I'll describe in short course.

In the world-cultural and world-historical frame of reference, I'd be looking in some detail at chapters by John Goodby, who places Thomas in the apparently – now no longer – alien land of modern and even con-temporary scientific discourse; by Ned Allen, who reattaches Thomas to the familiar aural scenes of BBC radio, but who retunes our awareness to hear something more interesting and historically thick and complex than the voice of the Welsh poetic crooner; by Zoë Skoulding, who pairs Thomas with the Welsh poet Lynnette Roberts and finds in their shared poetic circumstances of pastoral Wales the orienting force not of the sounds of church bells or cowbells but the noise of contemporary media technology; and by Leo Mellor, who also pairs Thomas with a companion talent, here the Welsh painter Ceri Richards, and who reveals the coherence of their joint response to the Second World War, the event that most significantly shaped the experiences of Thomas's historical generation. This is the generation in literary history – its most conspicuous if not most indicative figures are the slightly older Evelyn Waugh and W. H. Auden – that is usually understood as having a formatively difficult relationship to the literary modernism of the generation before them. And one of the values in the series of chapters that fill out the frame of reference in literary history here is the adequate scaling, that is, the *re*scaling, of the problem of Thomas's relation to his-torical modernism. It is taken up centrally in the piece by James Keery, who relocates the understanding of modernism to the later scene of the Second World War and the literary coterie of the New Apocalyptic

Poetry of that day. This is complemented by chapters on Thomas's presence in the history and historical understanding of poetry, first in North America and finally in Ireland, where it is not the influence of Thomas on individual styles so much as his orienting and negotiated presence, his status as a virtual landmass on the terrain of English poetry's northern hemisphere, that comes into view in Philip Coleman's and Tom Walker's chapters. And the poetic sensibility that this literary history records as a force in motion over time is engaged, not exhaustively of course but promisingly, not as the reductive summary of a poet's corpus so much as the pluripotent stem cell of its multiplying productions, in chapters by Rod Mengham and John Wilkinson, who situate this temperament equally and respectively in nature and in language, attending in turn to Thomas's animal imaginary and prosodic psychology.

From this resource, of which I've offered an ordering that is implicit if not explicit, I have the basis for a piece on Thomas and ... well, this ellipsis is not a further deferral but a sign of unclosed possibility here. The use I settle on would of course not exclude others, and necessarily leaves out of its account a number of chapters that are manifestly valuable on their own, and which fill out additional frameworks of important, even essential, reference. But because I've done a fair amount of work on literary modernism, enough at least to recognise that I've got the basis here for an inquiry that might refine and expand my understanding, I'd undertake a chapter on Thomas and modernism. I'd be working through the very time-specific quality of James Keery's placement of Thomas as a modernist sensibility, taking the crisis-time of the Second World War and the Apocalyptic poetry that consummates it as points of reference in political and literary history for a chapter that would begin by taking 'modernism' as a word, at its word.

As a word: from the Latin *modo*, a temporal adverb, from which we get 'modernus', the temporal adjective. The root of the word includes, not the adjectival sense of 'recent' or 'current', not even the adverbial meaning of 'today' or 'now', but, rather, 'just now'. A special present, a brink (as well as a blink) of time, a precipitous instant, all in all, a crisis time, and a time in crisis: the word's memory extends back to the late sixth century, when it was introduced into Latinity as a very present tense register of crisis time. These are the late later days of empire and, for Romans, the early time of dark and darkening ages. That is a redolent memory in the word when it is stirring into currency again in the early twentieth century, or, rather, over the long turn of that century, when, with the sense of endings as well as beginnings that attends such moments, the Latin radical attracts the intensive suffix 'ism', which adds the idea of a self-conscious awareness, maybe even a faith or belief, to this feeling of quicksilver existence, this sense of living in the vertiginous instant.

At its word: working from Keery's placement of Thomas as a modernist sensibility in the Second World War, I'd be emphasising the time-specific quality of this placement as an indicator not only of its historical moment but of its temporal sensibility. I'd take the 'Apocalyptic' quality of that moment and its signal poetry not as a sign of the imaginative bathos to which that poetry has been wrongly reduced but as the invocation of a special sense of 'crisis-time' that is essential to the temporal imaginary as well as the historical experience of 'modernism'. This idea of 'crisis time' of course describes one of the most powerful emotional tenses in the imaginative grammar of Thomas's poetry. More than an idiosyncratic matter or personal peculiarity, this idea of 'crisis time' is working in a world-cultural and world-historical frame of reference and experience that provides the wider context of Thomas's work as a poet and, now, of our understanding of it. That is an understanding for which this book provides a most comprehensive resource. For, if there is one thrust in the chapters I've designated, it is a pressure to move Thomas from the sea-strand of his private poetic sublime to an epicentre in the force-field of the modern century's cultural and political history.

These chapters might be taken, then, to reset the site of Thomas's poetry as a place of interface. Here the assignably 'peripheral' location of 'rural' Wales provides the staging area for a poetry that encounters and interacts with the material experience of urban 'modernity' in its twentieth-century expressions. As in these two stanzas from 'I dreamed my genesis', where, already in 1934, in Thomas's first volume, *18 Poems*, we find images of a child's nature, configured around the prime site of the biblical genesis in Wales, being juxtaposed with and confronted by these potent reminders of the technology of the First World War:

> I dreamed my genesis and died again, shrapnel
> Rammed in the marching heart, hole
> In the stitched wound and clotted wind, muzzled
> Death on the mouth that ate the gas.
>
> Sharp in my second death I marked the hills, harvest
> Of hemlock and the blades, rust
> My blood upon the tempered dead, forcing
> My second struggling from the grass.[2]

First birth as second death, nature conflated with machine as the place or origin: the coordinates of any polarised form of relation between pastoral life and political history are being reoriented pretty clearly. This interface between an end-of-the-world history and a mythic beginning of time locates an edge of critical difference, if not of critique, so that, when we combine these figures of historical modernity and mythic antiquity as a larger temporal imaginary, we find a very powerful presentiment of crisis time.

Not that all or even most of Thomas's poems exhibit so vividly and conspicuously this juxtaposition and confrontation of ways new and old, rural and urban, natural and technological. Yes, the insignia and instruments of scientific modernity appear and reappear in the poems in ways we may not have noticed so sharply before reading this book. As a crucial point of critical awareness and understanding, however, these figures are not significant in being obtrusive; they are important because the sensibility they represent has been assimilated to the living tissues of this verse. And so Ned Allen's critical narrative about the voice of Dylan Thomas on the Eastern Service of BBC radio may be taken beyond its own important point – a hearing of this poet in the theatre of political as well as literary history – to prompt thinking about the technology of voice and its work in the service of literary modernism, modernist poetry most notably.

We could be thinking in this regard about one of the most iconic devices and charged images in Eliot's *The Waste Land*. This is the 'gramophone' set going after the encounter between the 'typist home at teatime' and 'the young man carbuncular'.[3] The sense of mechanism extends beyond the ready condemnation of the appallingly mechanised sex that Eliot represents in this vignette; it goes to an understanding of the very nature of poetic voice in the age of mechanical reproduction of voice, on radio and telephone as well as gramophone. This is an understanding manifest already and first of all in that working title of Eliot's poem, 'He Do the Police in Different Voices'. Here the idea of vocal impersonation is realised in his sequence in a series of characters-in-voice, who (or which) are as disembodied and detached and secondary to natural characters as unnamed vocalisers on a randomly accessed radio band. So, how do we hear that famous voice of Dylan Thomas when it has been denaturalised and defamiliarised through the technology of a modernist reinvention, when the aura of authorial voice has been lost to the machine of its reproduction? As differently as he sounds when he is retuned and heard anew here in Zoë Skoulding's chapter. In her acuter hearing, she picks up the wavelength energies of modern sound media and their contributory noise, which provides a kind of second nature, all in all, a new native ground for this poet's voice and a dimension of his vocal character that is inseparable from the mechanisms with which modernism makes its formative negotiations.

For Thomas, who was born in the year that gave its number to one of the names of that first modernist generation, 'The Men of 1914', the long aftermath of the First World War turned out of course to be the equally long approach of the Second. In sum, then, this Next World War becomes the long watershed event of his generation (the world of *l'entre deux guerres*, as Eliot puts it in *Four Quartets*). Our sense of Thomas as poet in this frame of historical reference is immensely enriched in this collection of chapters, working in ways little and large, subtle as well as striking. Whether or not it is interaction with the actuality of history that helps to proportion the importance of poets, it is certainly the establishing circumstance of any valid understanding of Thomas as a modernist sensibility. And so the chapter I could now write would work from a new grounding of this poetic temperament, in the ways I've outlined above, to a focusing of the poet's work in the middle of the middle of the century of war.

It is the novelty of constant war, a condition initiated on or about July 1916, when the war of attrition started to show no signs of ever ending (there was an actual partisan wing of war policy called 'The Never Enders'), that needs to be entered into this reckoning. This development provides the spur, for example, for the historical fiction of Orwell's *Nineteen Eighty-four*, which witnesses a constant of international war, where the sides of rival alliances may shift without ever ending the conflict that becomes the only reason for the State's existence. First published in 1949, Orwell's novel merges into an historical narrative that remains relevant through most of the remaining years of the century, certainly through Thomas's life. And so, closer to his poetry, the chapter by Leo Mellor reinforces and augments the placement that Keery's piece provides, giving us a sense of Thomas's growth as a poet being determined by the approach of that conflict and of its contribution epitomised in that conflagration. More impressionistically, I would say, there is an agonistic quality in virtually every line of Thomas's poetry: the combat between the extraordinarily inventive musical language and the standard measures that establish but cannot maintain the cadence, which work something like the ghost of metre in the background sound of Eliot's own inventively modernist prosody (Thomas's version of this might be heard through John Wilkinson's superb chapter on Thomas's practice of caesura manqué). The words of poetry are at war with the rules of poetry, and whether or not this goes back to Surrealism or Rimbaud in literary history, it is echoed in its making and clarified in our understanding as it is amplified by the sounds history was making. And, yes, in literary history, this interaction between the words of poetry and the language of history – here, more directly, with the noise of war – is surely one of the most powerful formations and measures of importance, the importance that makes Dylan Thomas undeniable as a presence in the literary history of Ireland and America, even – or especially – for poets who neither admire nor imitate him.

The historical and critical picture I am redrawing of Thomas working at the interface of times, of the temporal imaginaries as well as tempi of nature and technology, of antiquity and modernity, may be tinted for its last note with its particularly Welsh accent. I am thinking of the political history that impinges on the etymology – cultural memory as well as linguistic root – of the word 'Wales'. From the Anglo-Saxon *wealh*, meaning 'foreigner' or 'stranger': as one of the first impertinences of an historically Greater Britain, this word was conferred on the native Britons in the plural, as the *wealas*, which becomes the 'Welsh', where the word turned readily enough from 'foreigner' into a synonym for 'serf' or even 'slave'. If the modernity relevant to Thomas turns a good deal of its augmented force through the long forming history of a Greater Britain, the edge of critical difference that I have identified as the staging area of Thomas's poetry might well be located at the edge of England and Wales. In Thomas's case, the productive struggle for the tongue of one's own people redoubles through the parallel narratives of modernism, most notably Joyce's, whose counterpart Stephen Dedalus remarks of the English spoken by the prefect of studies in his preparatory school, which is the English his author is now in the process of turning into something formerly unrecognisable: 'My soul frets in the shadow of his language.'[4] The great critic of literary modernism Hugh Kenner once quipped that literary modernism in Ireland and Britain and America occurs in an English spoken like a foreign language.

I'd put it another way, in titling the chapter I haven't written 'About Time'. It's about time that modernism is fundamentally concerned, and it's about time that we take the measure of Dylan Thomas as a poet whose importance may be scaled – but not limited – to the importance modernism owns in the literary history of its century.

Notes

1. 'Fern Hill', *CP14*, pp. 177–9 (p. 179).
2. 'I dreamed my genesis', *CP14*, pp. 61–2 (p. 61).
3. T. S. Eliot, 'The Fire Sermon', *The Waste Land*, in *The Poems of T. S. Eliot: Volume I: Collected and Uncollected Poems*, ed. Christopher Ricks and Jim McCue (London: Faber, 2015), pp. 62–6 (pp. 64, 63).
4. James Joyce, *A Portrait of the Artist as a Young Man*, ed. Jeri Johnson (Oxford: Oxford University Press, 2000), p. 159.

Index

Spinoza, Baruch, 141
Stallworthy, Jon, 185
Starling, Ernest, 101
Stein, Gertrude, 182
  Tender Buttons, 65–6
Steinach, Eugen, 101, 109n52
Steinberg, Gillian, 191
Steiner, George, 7
Stevens, Wallace, 122, 206
Stonebridge, Lyndsey, 167
Strand, Mark, 197
Strand Films, 122–3, 138, 168
Stravinsky, Igor, 175
subaltern, 8
surrealism, 16, 22, 117–18, 138,
    157–8, 164, 182, 184, 206,
    239
Surrealist Exhibitions, 158, 165
Sutherland, Graham, 172
Swansea, 27, 31, 44, 79–80, 113, 121,
    141, 158, 224; *see also* Second
    World War; Swansea Blitz
Swansea College of Art, 158
Swansea University, 12n35
Swinburne, Algernon Charles, 7
syllabics, 10, 16, 18–19, 21, 23, 26–7,
    30, 32n13, 56–8
Symons, Arthur, 197
Symons, Julian, 60–1
synaesthesia, 10, 146, 148
Synge, John Millington, 6

Tambimuttu, M. J., 172
Tate, Allen, 205–6
Taylor, Donald, 122
Telegraph, The, 92
telephone *see* media
television *see* media
Terminator, The, 92
Themerson, Stefan, 39
  Bayamus, 40–1, 43
  Critics and My Talking Dog, 39,
    41–2, 44
  *Wooff, Wooff, or Who Killed
    Richard Wagner*, 39
Thirkill, Angela, *August Folly*, 62
This Living Stone, 188
Thomas, D. J., 101–2
Thomas, Dylan
  CRITICISM
  'The Films', 153n38

'Poetic Manifesto', 65, 199, 202
'Samuel Beckett, *Murphy*; William
    Carlos Williams, *Life along the
    Passaic River*', 189
see also Deren, Maya: 'Poetry and the
    Film: A Symposium'
FICTION
A Doom on the Sun, 96–7
'The Holy Six', 97
'Just Like Little Dogs', 44–5, 65
'The Lemon', 102–3
'The Map of Love', 102
'One Warm Sunday', 44
'The Peaches', 64–7
Portrait of the Artist as a Young Dog,
    37, 43–4, 47, 65, 215
'The School for Witches', 102
'Where Tawe Flows', 107n14
FILM SCRIPTS
Balloon Site 568, 168
Battle for Freedom, 123–5
Is Your Ernie Really Necessary?, 143
Our Country, 168–9
A Soldier Comes Home, 123
These are the Men, 143
The Three Weird Sisters, 144
*Wales – Green Mountain, Black
    Mountain*, 141–2, 144, 168
PERSONAL LIFE AND CAREER
birth, 63, 185, 238
celebrity, 5, 7, 59
children, 100, 105
death, 1, 60, 84, 161, 172, 175,
    204–5, 210, 212n41, 215, 221
drinking, 4–5, 47, 56, 168
father, 100–1
travels to North America, 4, 198,
    201–2, 204–5, 212n29, 236
wife, 86n13, 105
POETRY
'A grief ago', 99–100, 185
'All all and all', 94–5, 104
'Altarwise by owl-light', 93, 102,
    188–90, 215
'Among those Killed in the Dawn
    Raid was a Man Aged a Hundred',
    78, 116–19, 164–5
'And death shall have no dominion',
    25, 93, 96, 106, 185
'A process in the weather of the
    heart', 95–8